The Campus History Series

SOUTHWESTERN COLLEGE

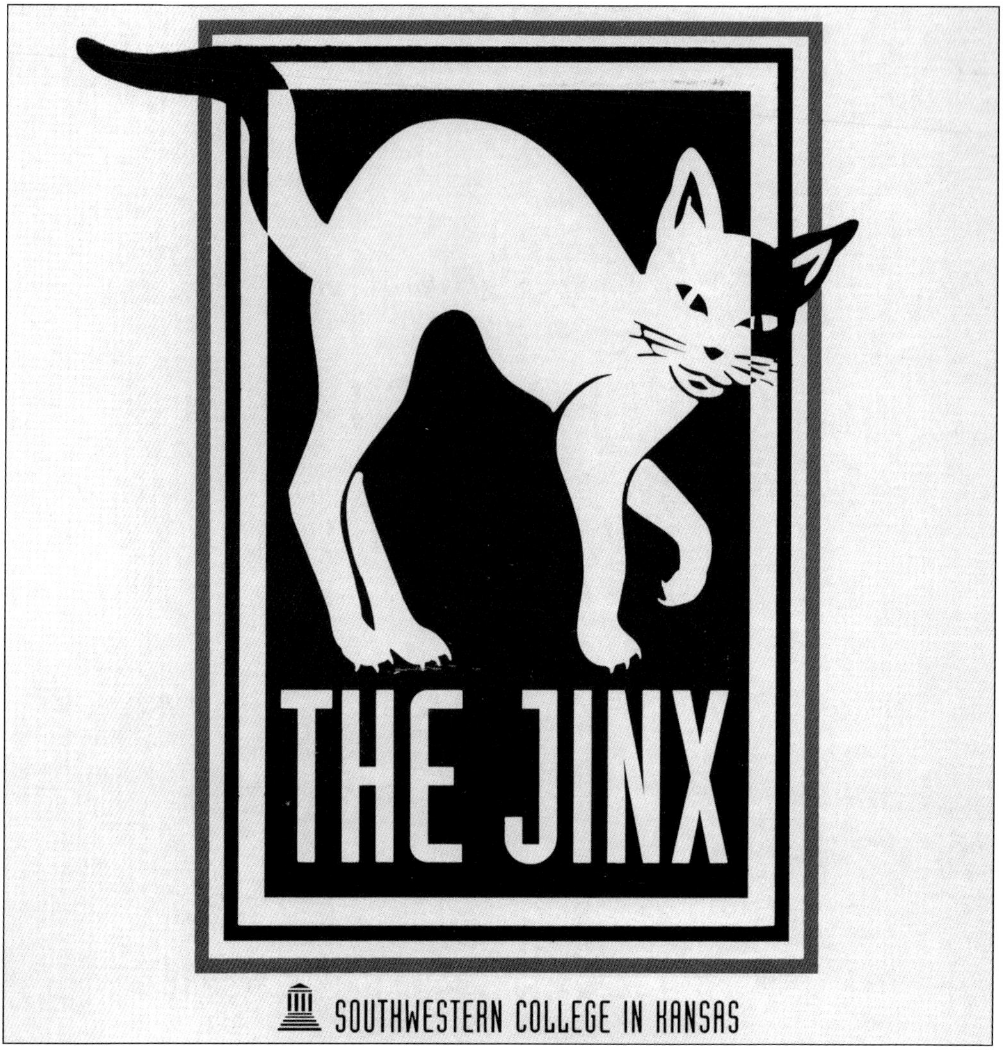

On Southwestern, on Southwestern,
Fight out for your fame,
Fight, Fellows, Fight,
And we will win this game!

—a college yell

On the Cover: Students descend Southwestern College's 77 Steps in the middle of the 20th century. These historic steps, built in 1910, unite the present with the past and the future. Pres. C. Orville Strohl observed, "Southwestern College is not a custodian of an old order, a perpetuator of the proven, or a curator of the present. This college is an open-ended venture—selective of the past—a creative critic of the present oriented toward the tomorrows."

Background: This is a 1960s aerial photograph of the Southwestern College campus. To the right is Christy, the college's principal building, housing the school's administrative offices, classrooms, and a large auditorium. Opened in 1952, Christy was the replacement for Richardson Hall, which was destroyed by fire in 1950. On the left stands Darbeth Fine Arts Center, built in 1965. The Messenger Recital Hall is part of the arts complex.

The Campus History Series

SOUTHWESTERN COLLEGE

JERRY L. WALLACE AND PAMELA S. THOMPSON

ARCADIA
PUBLISHING

ISBN 978-1-4671-1482-0

Published by Arcadia Publishing
Charleston, South Carolina

Printed in the United States of America

Library of Congress Control Number: 2015942090

For all general information, please contact Arcadia Publishing:
Telephone 843-853-2070
Fax 843-853-0044
E-mail sales@arcadiapublishing.com
For customer service and orders:
Toll-Free 1-888-313-2665

Visit us on the Internet at www.arcadiapublishing.com

Other men labored, and ye are entered into their labor.
—John 4:38

Contents

Acknowledgments 6

Introduction: A Methodist College on the Plains 7

1. Founding and Struggle: 1885–1905 9
2. Building a Modern College: 1906–1928 27
3. Depression and War Years: 1929–1949 53
4. Fire's Desolation: 1950–1953 71
5. Rebuilding and Revival: 1954–1972 87
6. Stability and Growth: 1973–1998 103
7. Moving into the 21st Century: 1999–Present 115

Acknowledgments

The reader should understand that the materials presented herein are restricted by the limitations of space and the loss of irreplaceable historical records and memorabilia in the fire of 1950. In the 130-year history of Southwestern College, an untold number of notable individuals—trustees, administrators and staff, teachers, alumni, and friends—have played significant roles. Indeed, they have made it what is. While we would like to recognize them all, that is not possible in this small volume. Readers, however, are urged to keep in mind the essential role they have played throughout the history of the college.

The authors would like to sincerely thank the following individuals for their friendly support and cooperation: W. Richard Merriman, president, Southwestern College; J. Andrew Sheppard, provost, Southwestern College; the staff of the Deets Library and Southwestern College Archives, particularly Dalene McDonald (librarian), Marjorie Snyder (technical services librarian), and Jessica Arnoldy (student library aide); Sara Weinert and the staff of the communications and publications office; students of COM 355 Academic Press class: Dalton Carver, Maecy Charleston, Brenna Truhe, Alyssa Richardson, Nicholas Kraft, Ukim Anifiok, Jonahs Jourdrey, and Gabriella Gamez; Dr. Carl Martin, former Southwestern president; Susan Lowe, Alumni Outreach; Stacy Sparks, assistant professor of journalism; Mike Kirkland, sports historian; Peter Heckman, academic dean; Beverley Olson Buller, Winfield historian; Bill and Lou Tharp, genealogists; and the many other individuals who have kindly offered their assistance to us. A special word of appreciation is due to the staff of Arcadia Publishing, specifically Sophia Mathelier, Julia Simpson, Maggie Bullwinkel, Sarah Gottlieb, and Katie Parry, for their kindly assistance, understanding, and patience. Finally, we would like to thank our spouses, Delia E. Wallace and Peter G. Heckman, for the support and encouragement they provided us during this demanding project.

Unless otherwise noted, all images appear courtesy of Southwestern College.

A Methodist College on the Plains

Southwestern College (SC) arose on the plains of Kansas in the mid-1880s, when many small colleges were being founded. Most are only memories now, but Southwestern College still stands strong.

Some argue that the school has survived because of the challenges that have come its way, forcing it to unite and persevere. True enough, but the real answer could be that, throughout its 130-year history, Southwestern has always tailored its courses to the needs of its students, while not allowing monetary concerns to restrict its natural growth and development. Southwestern has trusted that, in doing the Lord's work, as its founders put it, the Almighty would provide, and so He has done over the years. Credit and honor is also owed to those wise and capable presidents who have shepherded the college, its loyal and talented faculty, and its devoted and supportive students and alumni.

Southwestern College is a United Methodist school, but it has always welcomed members of other denominations and faiths. The college has also extended that welcoming spirit to foreign and minority students from its earliest days. Over its long history, Southwestern has sent out into the world 25,000 graduates, who, endowed with the Builder's spirit, have become fine citizens in various callings, striving to make this world a better place.

On March 23, 1885, the Southwest Conference of the Methodist Episcopal Church authorized Southwestern's creation and gave it the name Southwest Kansas Conference College, which it retained until 1908. The conference delegates were interested in making available a quality education to its parishioners, who were spread over 32 prairie counties located in the lower southwestern corner of the state. The founders were confident that they could support a college in a flourishing region in need of a faith-based institution of higher learning.

In June 1885, Winfield, a community of 5,151, won a tough competition for the college site. Winfield had much to offer. It was the fastest-growing and one of the most prosperous towns in the Methodist Conference's area. It had a good moral climate and was well served by railroads. Winfielders also made good use of their connections within the Southwest Conference and, perhaps most important, extended a generous offer of money, materials, and land. The college's charter of incorporation was filed with the secretary of state on June 19, 1885, and it thus became a legal entity. Soon, plans were under way for the construction of a college building costing $60,000, making it one of Winfield's most expensive structures.

On April 26, 1886, the board of trustees offered the presidency of Southwestern to Dr. John Evanston Earp. At 40 years old, he was an outstanding choice: an impressive, capable man with a good personality and a proven scholar, teacher, and preacher. His colleagues called Earp "a Christian gentleman," and he proved to be the ideal man for the task. With his deep interest in education that focused on students' moral and intellectual development and the need for inspirational teachers to awaken the young, his work set the tone for years to come.

When Southwestern College opened its doors on September 8, 1886, the College Building (known after 1910 as North Hall) was not yet finished, so the school met in rented rooms on the second floor of the McDougall Building, at the southeast corner of Tenth and Main Streets. Initially, the student body was small, but it grew rapidly. After the College Building opened in September 1887, Earp oversaw construction of the President's House (which would serve as a campus home for every president for over 65 years) and a women's dormitory.

The early school comprised three principal departments: literary, music, and business. The literary department consisted of a college, a normal school, and an academy, equivalent to today's high school. The "collegiate" unit was quite small relative to the other elements of the school. This basic arrangement would continue into the early 20th century, when Pres. Frank E. Mossman put the modern-day college in place.

The college acted very much in *loco parentis*, which would continue until the mid-20th century. Indeed, maintaining a proper Christian atmosphere was one of its selling points, along with the fact that it was located one and a half miles from the potential evils of downtown Winfield. From the beginning, there was a close, friendly relationship between faculty and students as they worked their way toward the "attainment of knowledge and establishment of character."

Earp resigned in June 1890 and was followed by Milton E. Phillips, who presided over a period of exceptional growth. Then came the depression of 1893, as well as a serious drought. The college's rural constituency suffered greatly. This brought the first serious threat to the school's existence. Indeed, it would have closed if not for the dedication of its faculty, the loyalty of its students, and the generosity of its supporters. When Chester A. Place stepped into the presidency in 1895, the school's condition slowly stabilized, and it continued to improve under Frederic C. Demorest and George F. Cook.

In 1905, Frank E. Mossman assumed the presidency. Under him, the college was transformed from a rural 19th-century institution into a 20th-century college. He built the majestic Richardson Hall and improved the campus in general. Academically, he integrated the work of individual departments into an overall curriculum. Beginning in 1919, Pres. Albert Emmanuel Kirk continued to upgrade and expand the college, with particular interest in the area of fine arts. This expansion in the 1920s bought with it budget and endowment difficulties. Pres. Ezra T. Franklin's efforts to address these problems proved unsuccessful. To meet this crisis as the Depression unfolded, former president Mossman was recalled. He faced a strenuous period of austerity. With difficulty, he righted the college and brought its finances into line before his retirement in May 1942.

Charles E. Schofield assumed the presidency six months into World War II. Southwestern would do its part during these difficult years. Training for naval personnel was provided during the first years of the war, but once training ended, male enrollment decreased because of the draft. In a Christian spirit and defying local opposition, Japanese American students were enrolled from their internment camps. Pres. Mearl P. Culver supervised the college's return to peacetime, welcoming into the student body a large number of veterans. New buildings were constructed on campus using former military barracks.

Alvin W. Murray (class of 1924) became president in late 1949 and faced the greatest challenge since the financial collapse of the 1890s. On April 15–16, 1950, Richardson Hall burned down. A condemned North Hall was concurrently being dismantled. Many questioned whether the college could survive, but again, the faculty, students, and alumni, along with strong support from the Winfield community, rallied to save it.

On January 1, 1954, another Southwestern graduate, C. Orville Strohl (class of 1931) began his presidency, which lasted until June 1972. With his vision and administrative and financial skills, Strohl transformed Southwestern into a modern mid-century educational institution. His long tenure was followed by shorter stints of three presidents: Donald B. Ruthenberg, Robert Paul Sessions, and Bruce P. Blake. The college's third alumni president took office in 1988. Carl E. Martin (class of 1960) made significant improvements in the school's physical plant and started innovative off-campus adult education programs. Beginning in 1998, Dr. W. Richard Merriman brought the college squarely into the 21st century by developing a comprehensive college program and reaching out to students around the world using new technologies.

Southwestern has had many great days, but one suspects that its best days are still ahead. "On Southwestern!"

One

Founding and Struggle 1885–1905

Southwestern College opened its doors in rented quarters to 43 students on September 8, 1886. Dr. John E. Earp was the institution's founder, serving as a teacher and its first president. He put the college in place, overseeing construction of the College Building, the President's House, and a women's dormitory. The school consisted of a literary department with its four-year college, a standard school for prospective teachers, a three-year academy, and specialized departments of music and business.

In June 1890, Milton E. Phillips succeeded Earp. Described as "a builder," he moved the college forward. During his administration, the Magdalena Phillips Library, named for his wife, was established. At the time, the college was said to be "the most promising college enterprise known west of the Mississippi."

As the 1890s progressed, the college faced its first crisis of survival, due to an economic depression and serious drought. The school was in debt and had little income to support its operations. In June 1894, Phillips resigned. Then, two acting presidents followed. The school fell into a deplorable state. At one point, W. C. Robinson, a Winfield banker and college trustee, bought up the institution's debt and received a deed to the college. In 1896, a "daring faculty," headed by Pres. Chester A. Place (1896–1900), leased the school and, for two years, operated it on a balanced budget, reducing old debt. President Place and the faculty worked under trying conditions, with meager and irregular pay. With William McKinley's election as president of the United States, the nation returned to prosperity. In addition, the long drought ended. Through the dedication and determination of its supporters, Southwestern had weathered its first serious crisis.

There then followed the presidencies of Fred C. Demorest (1900–1903) and George F. Cook (1903–1905). Demorest's presidency was uneventful, except for a Winfield prohibitionist uprising involving students in 1901. Cook was very popular with faculty and students, and he provided a stable administration. The school, however, was in need of an energetic, forceful leader with fundraising skills to build itself into a 20th-century educational institution. Cook, knowing himself unsuited for this role, resigned on August 8, 1905, making way for a new and exciting era in the life of the college.

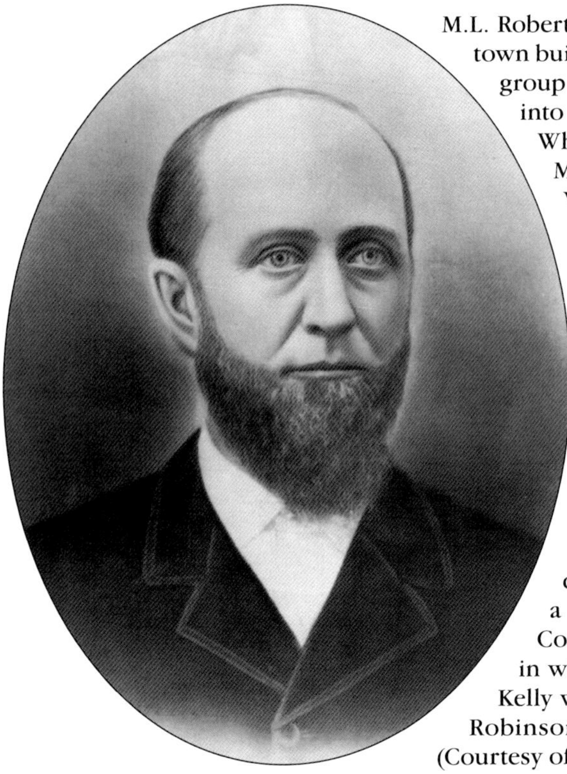

M.L. Robertson, a banker and prominent Winfield town builder, was a leader among an influential group who sought to make their hometown into "the Queen City" of southern Kansas. When the opportunity arose to secure a Methodist college, they acted, using the Winfield Enterprise Association to gain public backing. Going all-out in their offer and using all their connections, these determined Winfielders won the college. (Courtesy of the Cowley County Historical Society [CCHS].)

Winfield's First Methodist Church grew rapidly in its early days. By 1877, this imposing structure was erected to accommodate its members. The church has always had a close relationship to the college. In 1885, its pastor, Bernard Kelly, a member of the Southwest Methodist Conference, played an instrumental role in winning the college for Winfield. It was Kelly who sent the June 10 telegram to M.L. Robinson, announcing, "Winfield selected." (Courtesy of CCHS.)

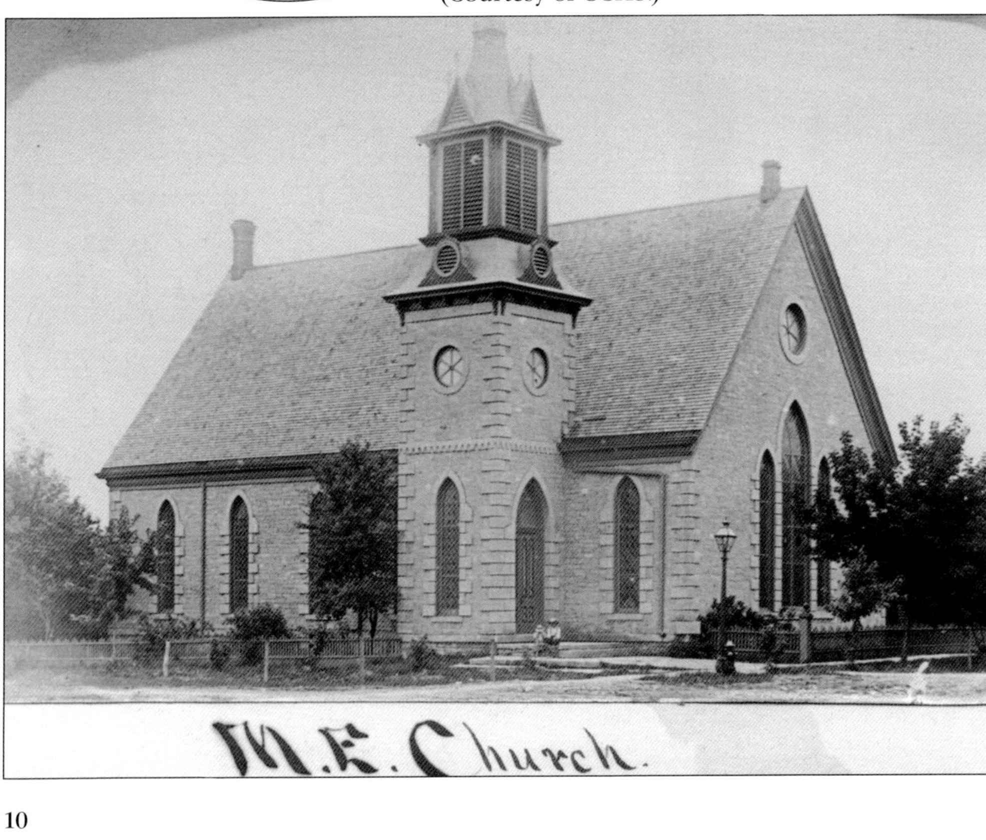

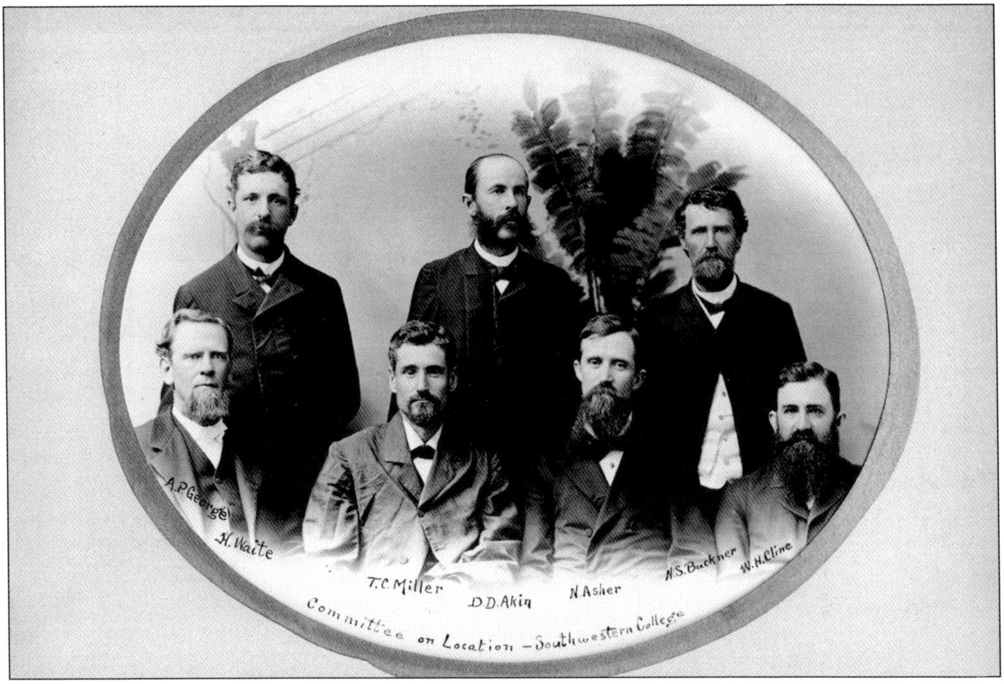

The Southwest Methodist Conference charged these men, all strong proponents of education, to locate their college. After visits and deliberation, they chose Winfield on June 10, 1885. In their zeal for the college, Winfielders had made the most generous offer of money, materials, and land. The committee knew Winfield to be an attractive and progressive community inhabited by sociable, enterprising, and upright citizens. Winfield was, moreover, in a good location and accessible by rail.

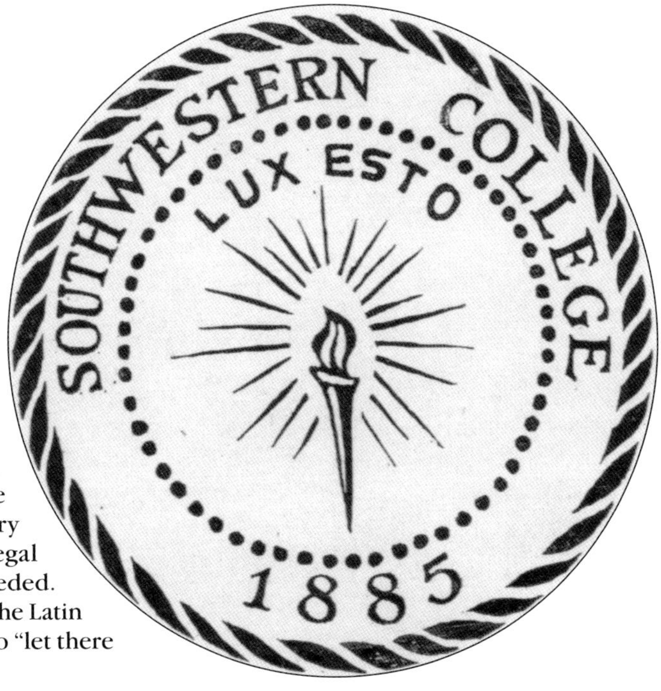

On June 19, 1885, the board of trustees filed a charter of incorporation for the South West Kansas Conference College with E. B. Allen, Kansas secretary of state, making the college a legal entity. An official seal was needed. Here is the design used today. The Latin motto "Lux Esto" translates into "let there be light."

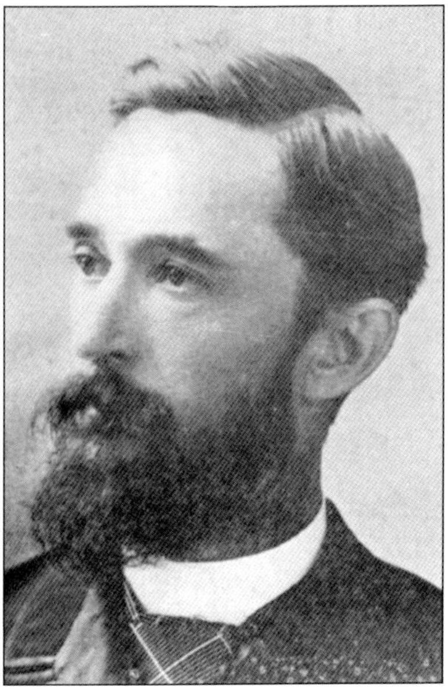

John E. Earp, the first president of the college (1886–1890), was well qualified to develop a new educational institution. Earp rejected offers from established colleges, wishing instead to experience the satisfaction of initiating a new enterprise. His challenge was to put in place a college—"a knowledge emporium," as described in 1925's *The Story of Southwestern*—on the plains of Kansas. To his credit, he succeeded in this demanding and trying task. His wife, Ella Earp, an accomplished musician, established the college's music department.

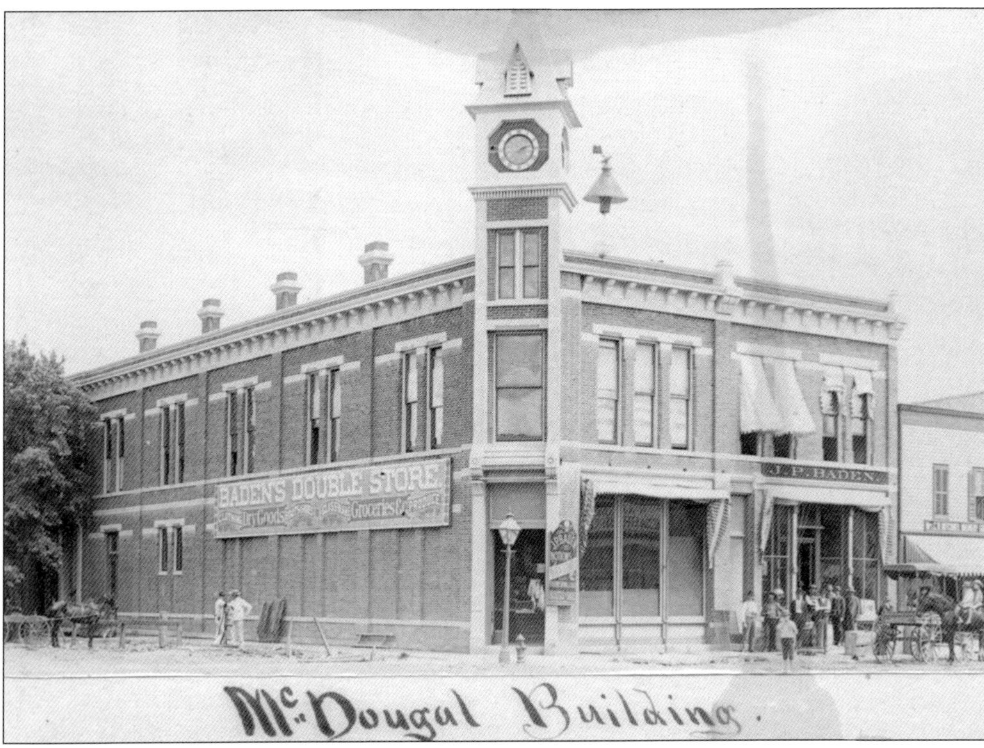

On September 8, 1886, Southwestern College opened its doors to learning. As the College Building was under construction, students and faculty gathered in the rented upper rooms of the McDougall Building (pictured), located on the southeast corner of Tenth and Main Streets in downtown Winfield. There were only 43 students, but that number would soon grow to well over 100. Behind the building was a poultry business, from which "interesting sounds and smells drifted into the classrooms," according to *The Story of Southwestern*. (Courtesy of CCHS.)

This photograph is perhaps the earliest extant of the College Building. Workers appear to be putting the final touches on the structure. The group in front is believed to be members of the Southwest Kansas Methodist Conference, which met in Winfield in March 1887. On September 6, the school convened in the new building, "then shining garishly new, sparsely furnished, [and] as yet unhumanized," as described by early historian Eleanore Hayes. (Courtesy of CCHS.)

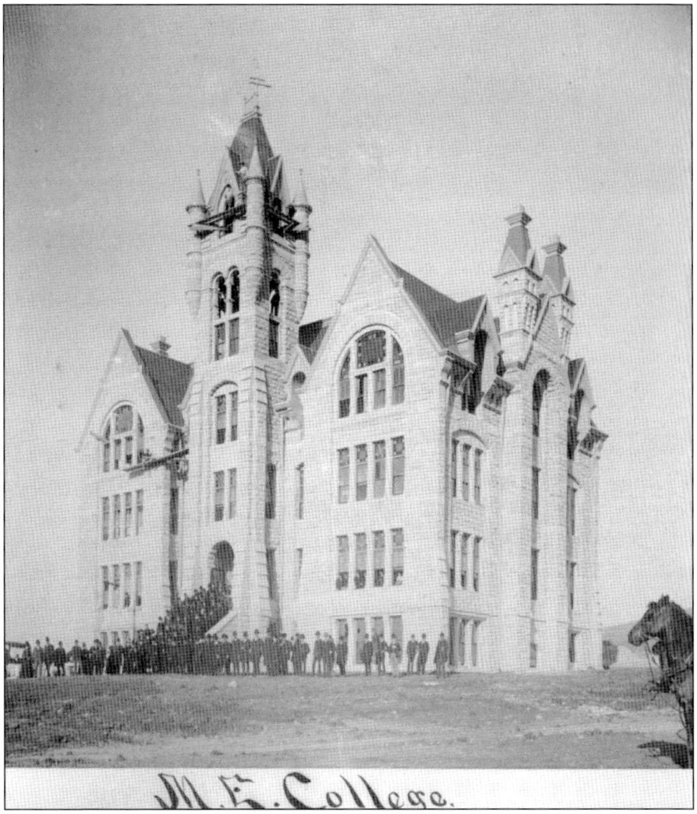

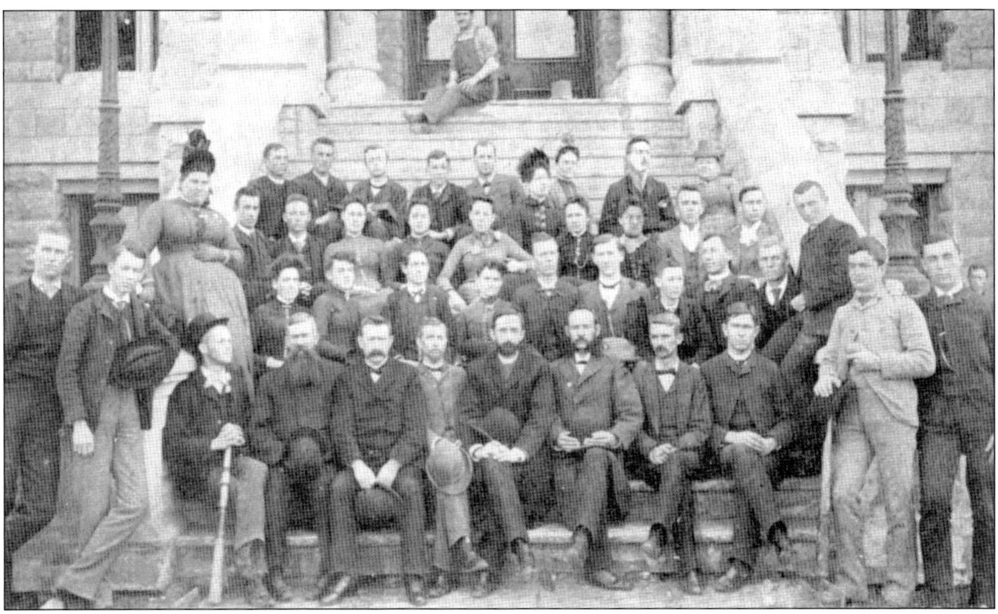

This first photograph of the school, showing students and faculty, was taken in 1888. President Earp, with beard, is in the center of the first row, surrounded by faculty members. His wife, Ella, is in the fourth row, third from the right. Note the school handyman at the top of the stairs.

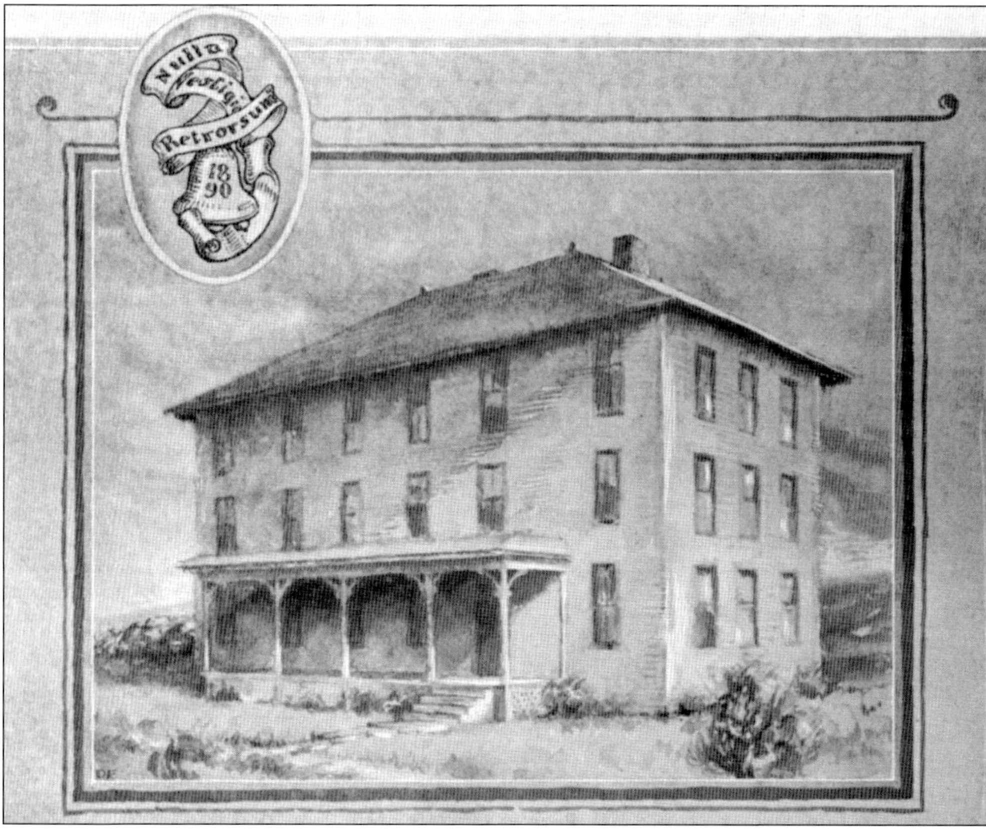

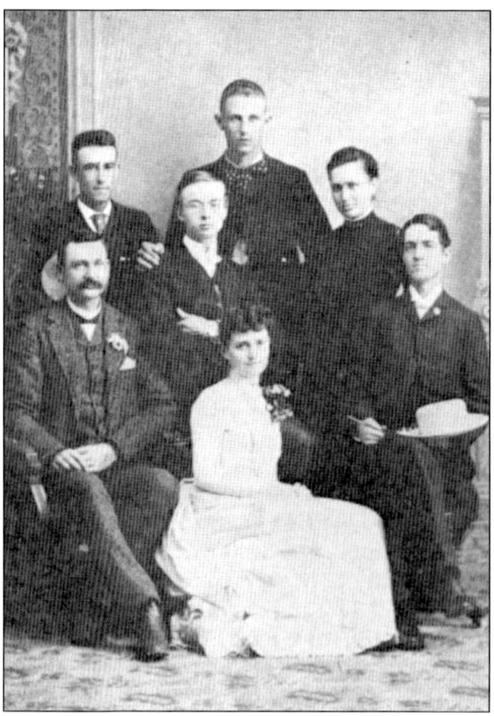

The Ladies Boarding Hall, popularly known as the "Dorm" by students, was opened in the fall of 1888. Housing 30 students, the building stood in the area to the immediate east of today's Deets Library. A mysterious fire destroyed the structure in the summer of 1894. In those early days, board was $2.50 per week, and one room cost 25¢.

Shown here is the staff of the *College Times*, which began "an era of Southwestern Journalism" with its publication in 1889. The *Times* was not the first student paper, but it was the first sustained venture. The staff members are, clockwise from lower left, Fred G. Wilber, Hugh Owen, Joseph Earp (the president's son), J.R. Cottingham, Pearl Van Doren, Alvah Graham, and Amy Barnes.

Pictured here are the first three graduates of the collegiate department of Southwestern College. They are Amy Barnes of McPherson (left), Alvah John Graham of Winfield (center), and Olive P. Stubblefield of Winfield. The graduation ceremony took place on June 3, 1889, at 2:30 p.m. in the assembly hall on the third floor of the College Building.

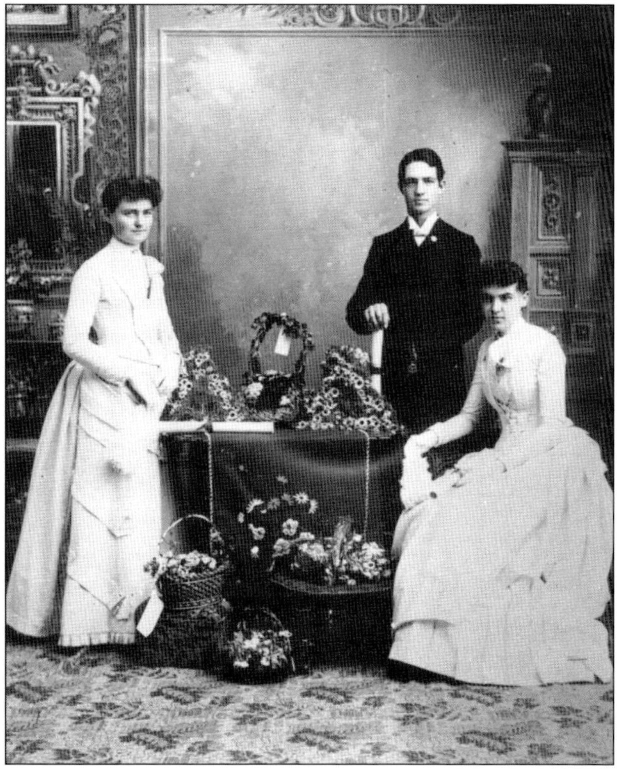

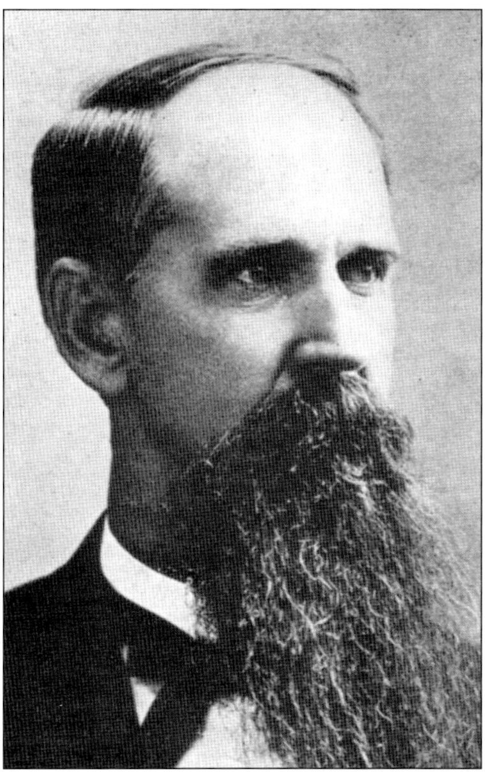

Milton E. Phillips came into office during good times. During his tenure (1890–1894), the college made exceptional progress. A Model School and a Ministerial Association for clerical students were started. An addition to the College Building was contemplated as enrollment reached 613 (a number not to be seen again until 1922). In 1893, an economic depression ushered in hard times, when the school faced increasing debt and a drastic decline in students.

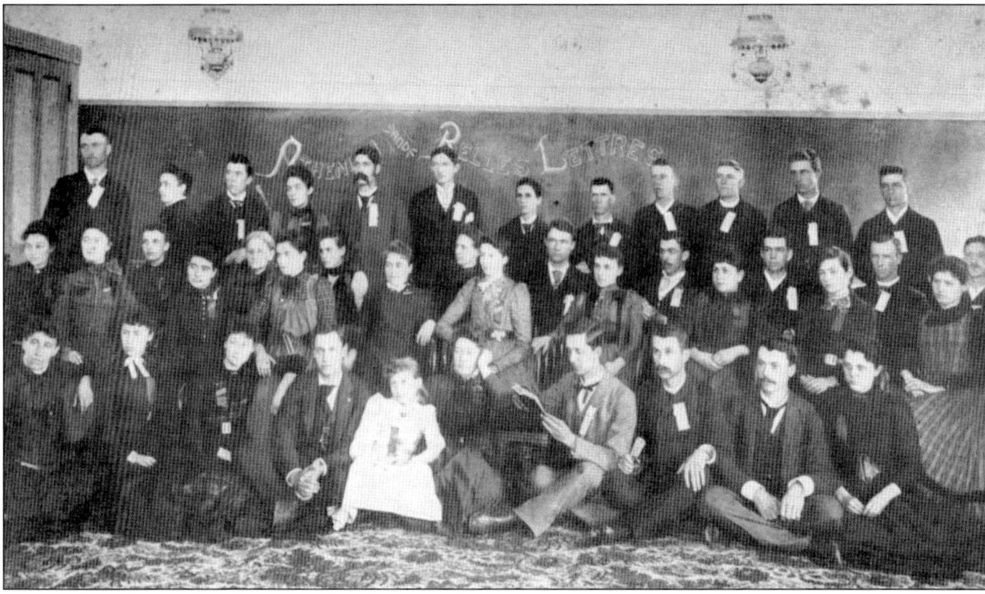

This is the first photograph of the members of the college's premier literary societies, in their meeting room in the College Building, which they themselves had furnished. The Belles Lettres women's group aimed for literary excellence and personal poise. For the men, the Athenians focused on debate and public speaking. Both groups had been organized during the 1889–1890 school year. Their organization was in the manner of the US House of Representatives, with each society presided over by a speaker.

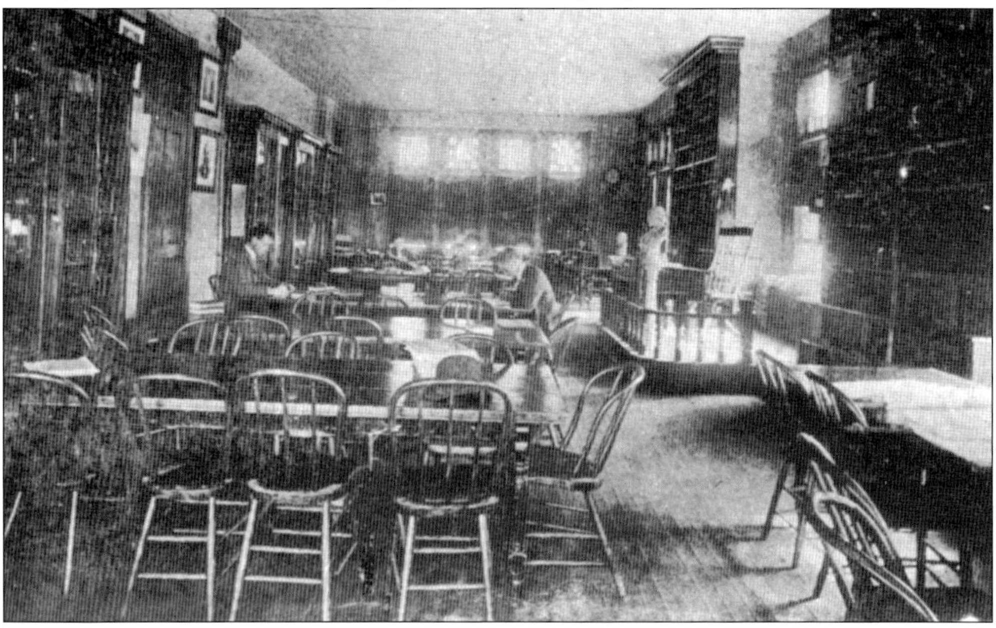

The first library was located in the College Building. In 1892, President Phillips and his wife, Magdalena, celebrated their 25th wedding anniversary with a well-attended reception. Guests were asked to bring a book. These books formed the core collection to what was known for many years as the Magdalena Phillips Library. The library was moved to the first floor of the field house in the early 1920s and then to its present location in 1951.

Shown here in the early 1890s, John Wesley Wetzel (class of 1894) was one of the college's outstanding students. The editor of the school paper, *Vox Studendium*, in 1893–1894, he was perhaps best known for his considerable oratorical skills. In 1894, he won the Kansas State Oratorical Contest with his "The Province of Faith." Wetzel went on to become a professor of elocution and oratory at Yale University.

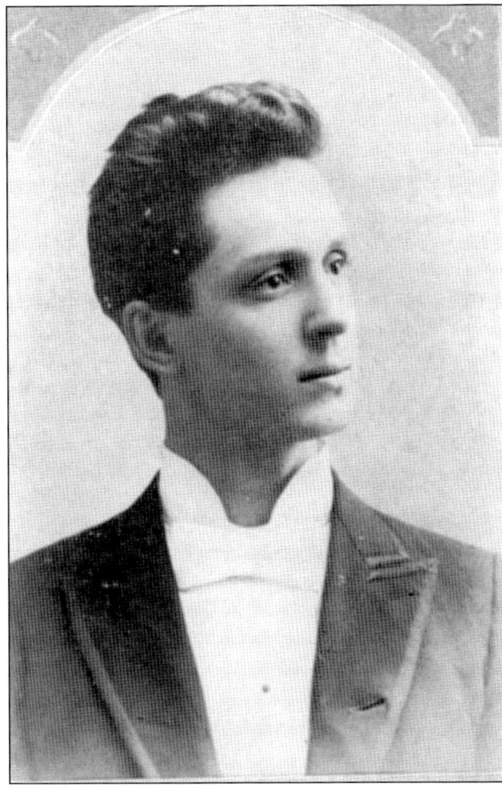

The citizens of Winfield are gathered at the intersection of Ninth Avenue and Main Street for a parade recalling pioneer days. The photograph reveals a prosperous city with fine, substantial buildings and a large and engaged population. Southwestern students often attended and participated in such city events. (Courtesy of CCHS.)

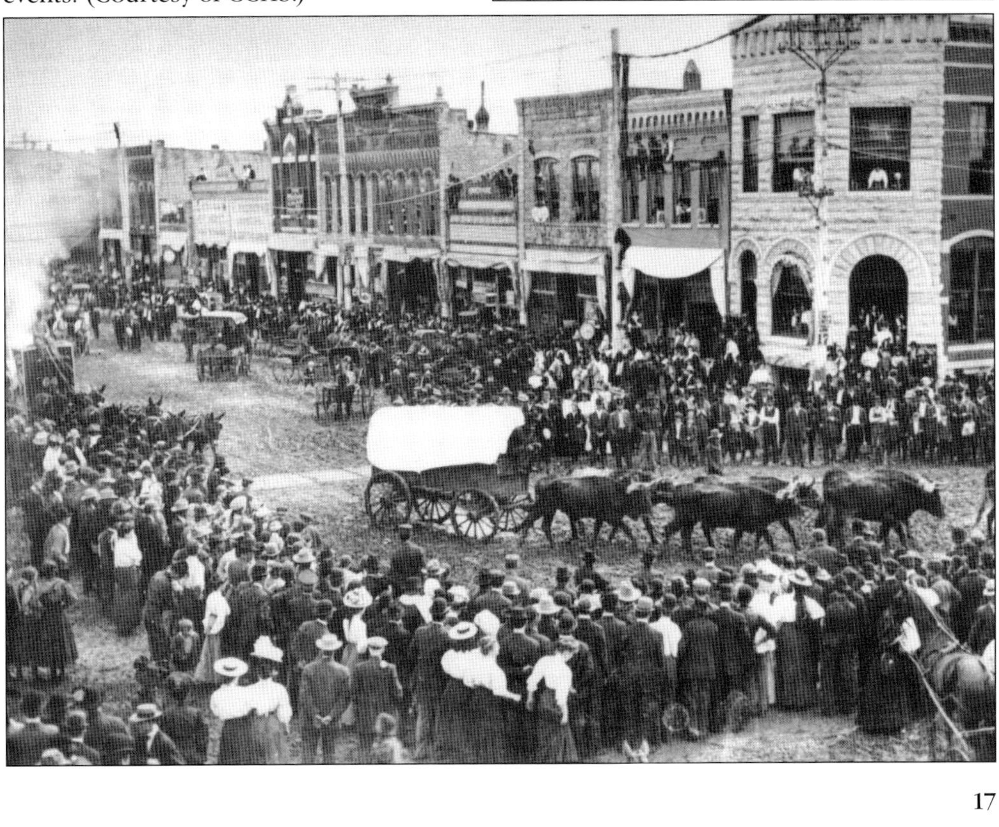

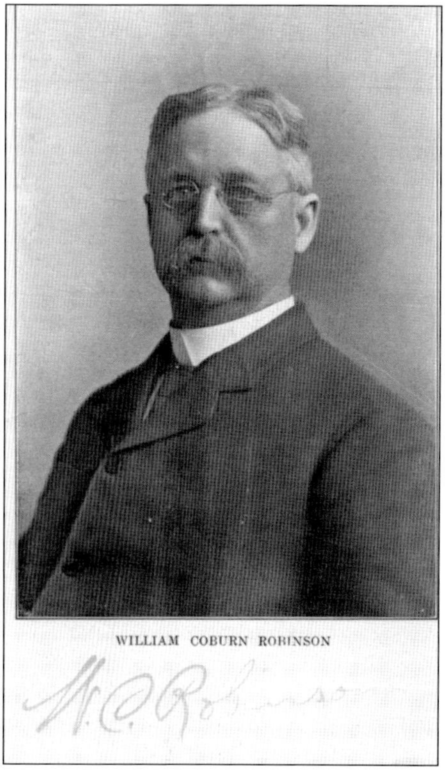

W.C. Robinson, whose brother was instrumental in obtaining the college for Winfield, was also a longtime supporter of the institution and served on its board of trustees for many years. Most important, during the financial crisis of the 1890s, Robinson stepped in to rescue the college by buying up and returning its furnishings when sold off to pay debts. He also purchased and held the college's bonded debts for several years. Of W.C. Robinson, it can be said, he saved the school that his brother had brought to Winfield.

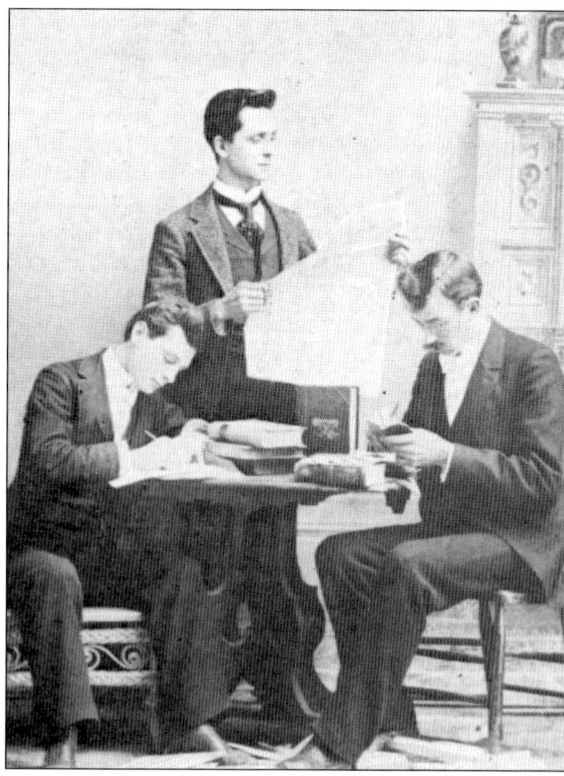

Members of the student newspaper, *Vox Studendium*, are shown here in 1983. Staff members included W.W. Van Pelt (left), John W. Wetzel (center), and Carrie Wood. In the following school year, the paper appeared as the *Southwestern Collegian*. Its editor was Leroy Weeks.

Chester A. Place, a strong, capable man, assumed office during a time of severe financial stress. As the economy improved, Place stabilized and rebuilt the college, increased enrollment annually, and paid down debt. Notably during his tenure (1895–1899), a controversy arose over a Sigma Nu fraternity branch on campus. The issue ended with Place and the trustees banishing the fraternity and its unrepentant members from campus and forever outlawing future fraternities.

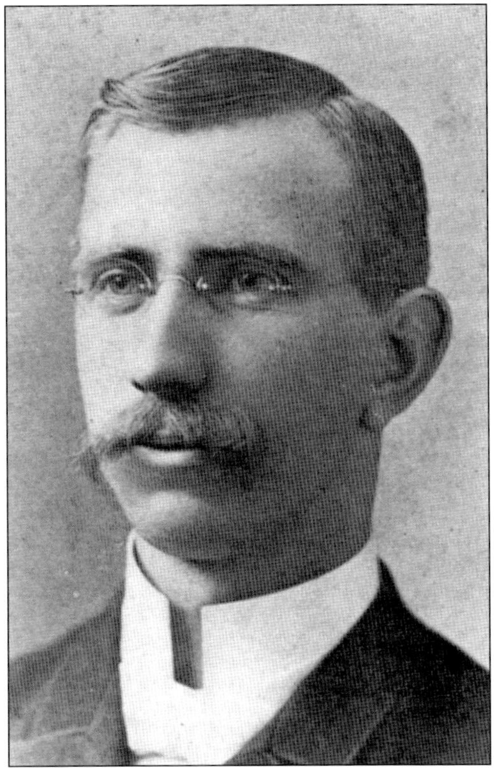

Throughout its history, music has played a prominent part in the culture of Southwestern. Zeno Nagel, music department director and an accomplished musician, organized the Ladies' Glee Club (first row, center). The club made its debut in the college chapel on February 2, 1900. The group soon became one of the college's most popular organizations, receiving frequent praise. It was considered the best-trained glee club in the area. Pride in and support for the college's musical groups remain strong.

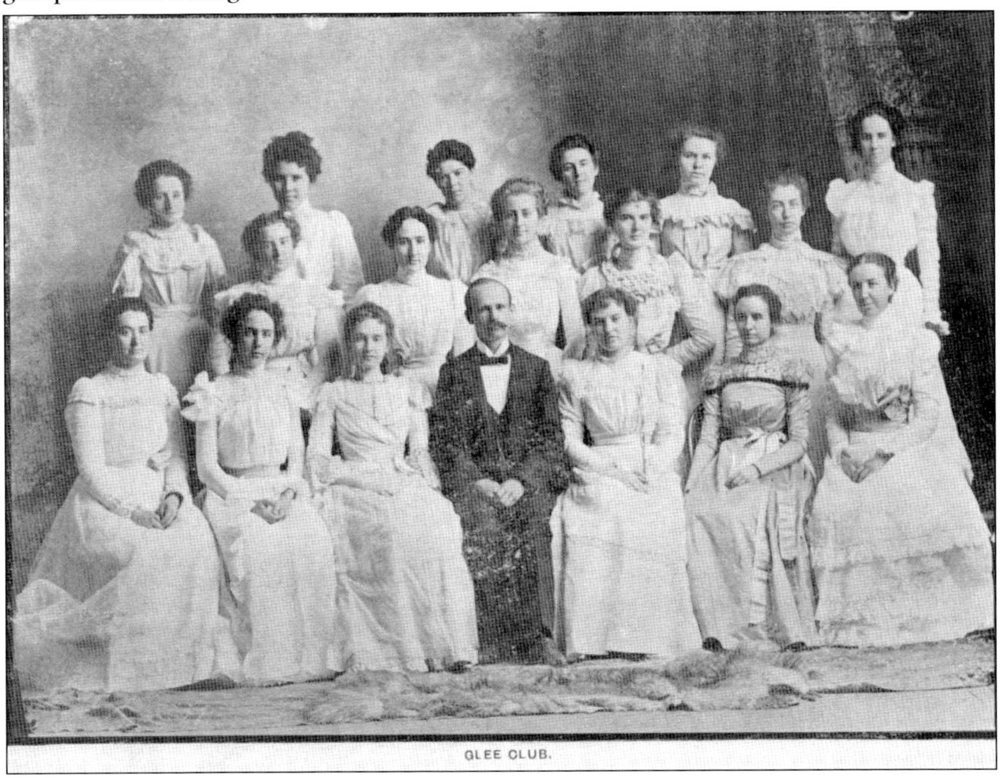

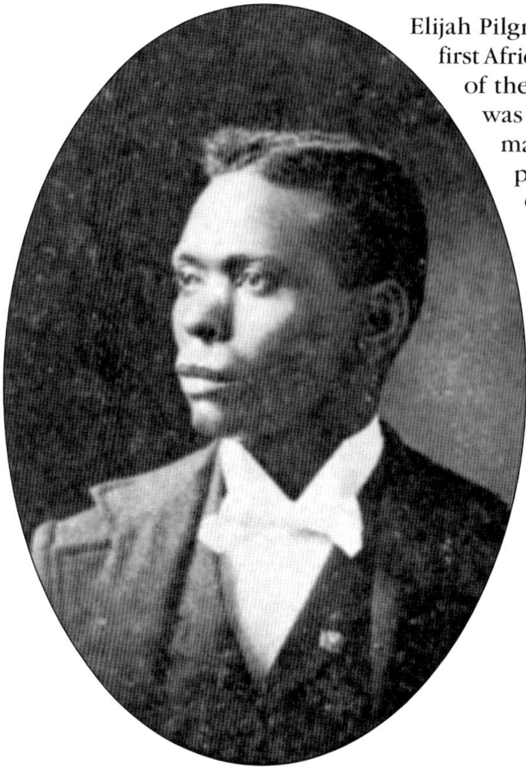

Elijah Pilgrim Geiger (class of 1899) was the college's first African American graduate. Geiger was a member of the prestigious Athenian Literary Society and was described by his contemporaries as "a man of magnificent brain power." He went on to become pastor of the African Methodist Episcopal Church in Guthrie, Oklahoma. As President Strohl wrote, "From the beginning, young people of every race and creed . . . were welcomed to [Southwestern's] campus."

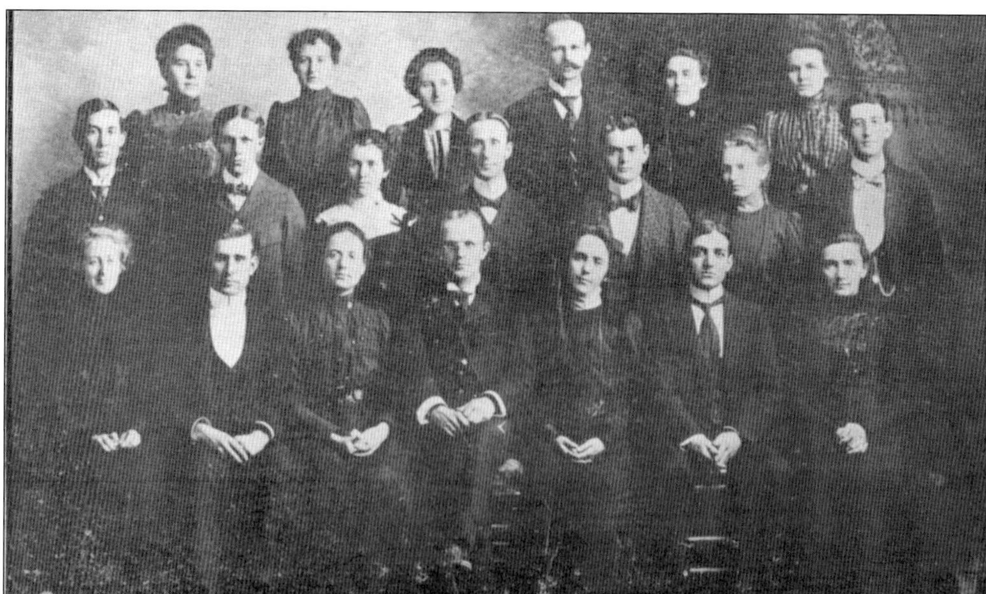

The college offered courses in the classical languages, Latin and Greek, as well as modern languages. Shown here is the German Club with its 19 members. Seated in the first row, fourth from the left, is Prof. Peter A. Claassen, who taught German and French. He came to the United States at the age of 16 from West Prussia.

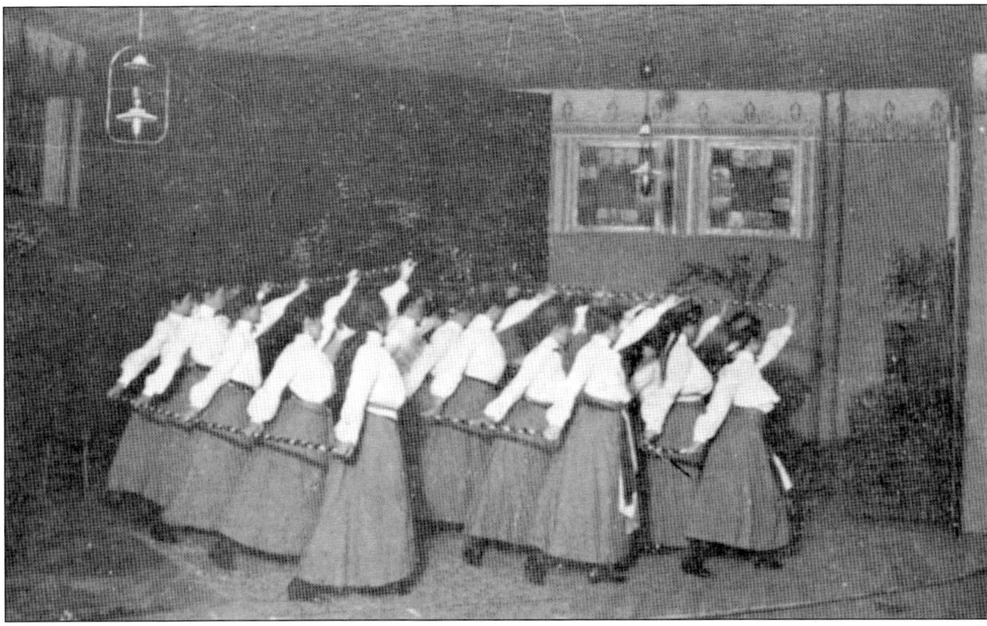

The ladies of the Belles Lettres Society rehearse the first May Fete in the college chapel in 1898. The actual program took place on the day of Adm. George Dewey's great victory over the Spanish fleet at Manila Bay. To mark the occasion, a replica of Dewey's flagship, USS *Olympia*, was placed on stage. The May Fete became a major annual event, moving outside in 1900 and continuing until 1956.

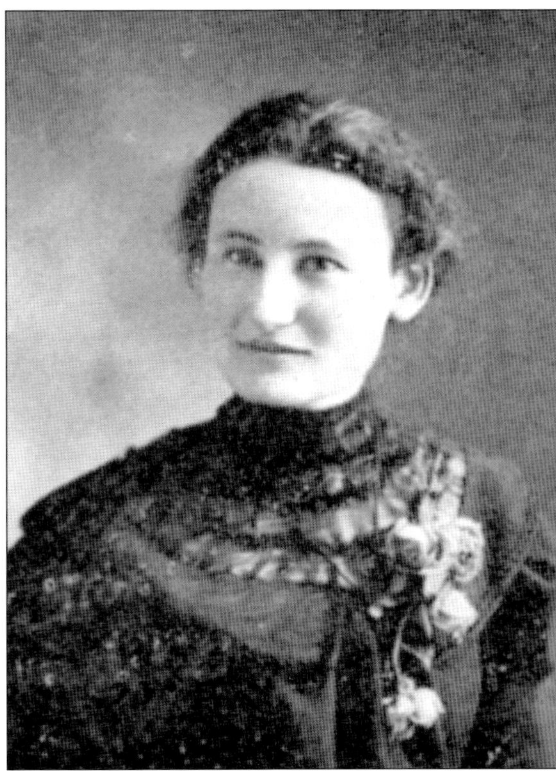

Mabel Madeline Southard was chosen in 1898 for the college team to debate against Fairmount College (now Wichita State University) in the first intercollegiate debate. President Place said that she was chosen for her ability, "regardless of sex." After being ordained a Methodist minister in 1925, she went on to become noted in her field. She preached throughout the United States as well as in the Philippines and India, and she was a founder and president of the International Association of Women Preachers, working tirelessly to advance women in the church. Southard was twice a delegate to the General Conference of the Methodist Church.

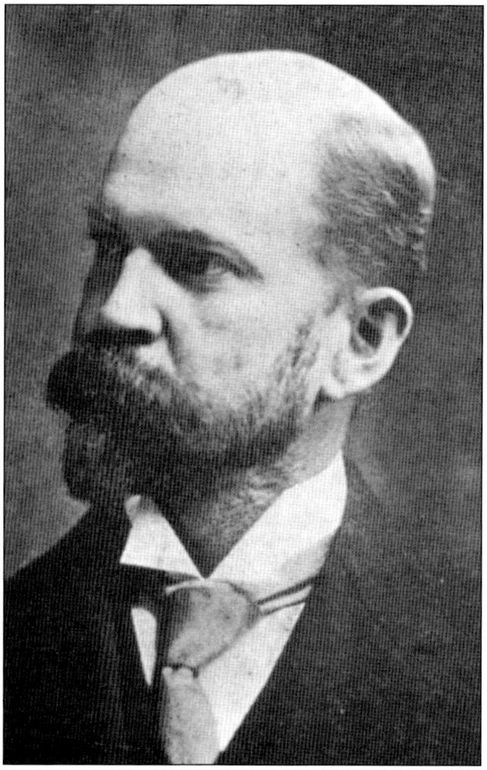

Pres. Frederic Coe Demorest continued the work of rebuilding the college and putting its finances in good order. A $100,000 proposal was made in April 1903, with the Southwestern Methodist Conference providing $75,000. The remaining $25,000 came from the citizens of Winfield and Cowley County. During Demorest's tenure (1900–1903), the Student Volunteer Band, a group of students interested in foreign missionary work, was organized.

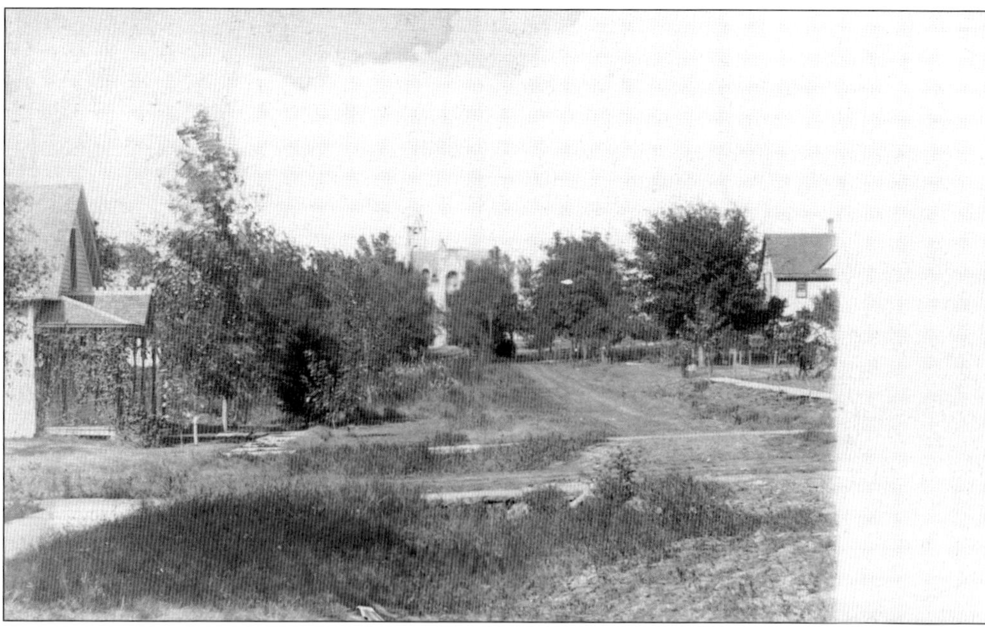

This late-19th-century photograph offers a distant view of the College Building and campus. It was taken looking north, up Soward Street at the intersection with Janes Avenue. The area around the school was gradually being settled, but it was still very much a rural, peaceful place. Male students often boarded at homes near campus. Many of the surrounding street names honored Methodist bishops.

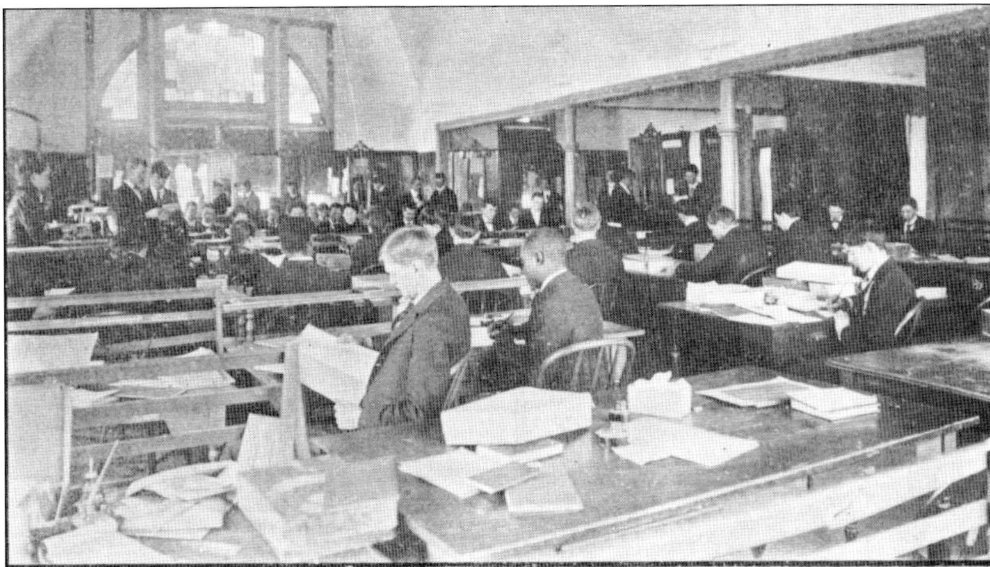

SCHOOL OF BUSINESS TRAINING.

Said to be "one of the best of its kind in the west," the School of Business was separate from the college and offered certificates. Class work emphasized actual business dealings. Students could develop skills in stenography, typewriting, and telegraphy, which were much in demand. "A shorthand writer," it was said, "who can typewrite his own notes would be safer from poverty than a great Greek scholar."

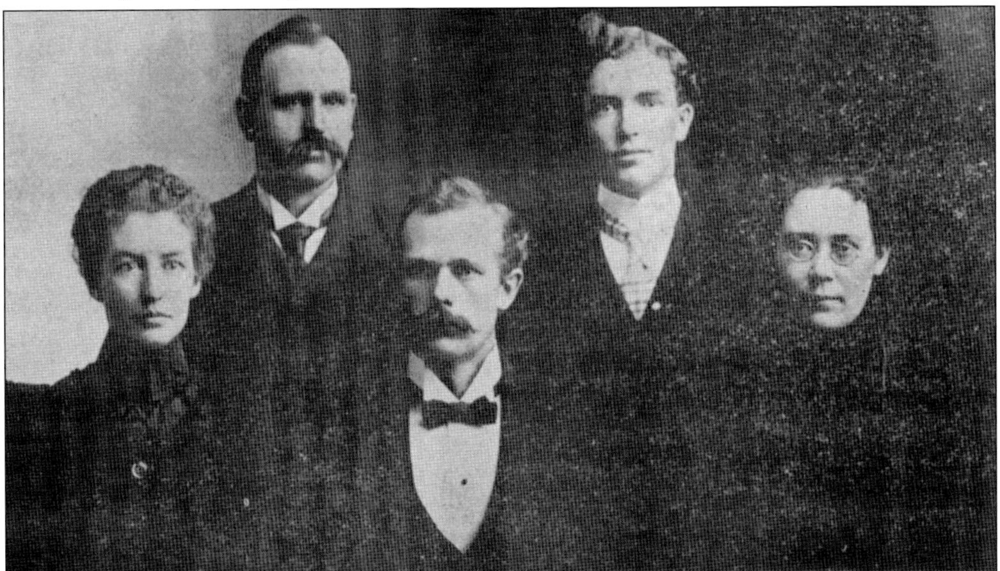

GRACE ROSE, J. W. DIBBENS, PAUL J. WHITE, FORREST H. ROSE, CLARA GILMER,

The senior class of 1900 consisted of five students. They are, from left to right, Grace Rose, J.W. Dibbens, Paul J. White, Forrest H. Rose, and Clara Gilmer. The two Roses were brother and sister. This small group had its origins in the depression year of 1896, when the college was at its low point. There would not be a graduating class of more than 10 individuals until 1904.

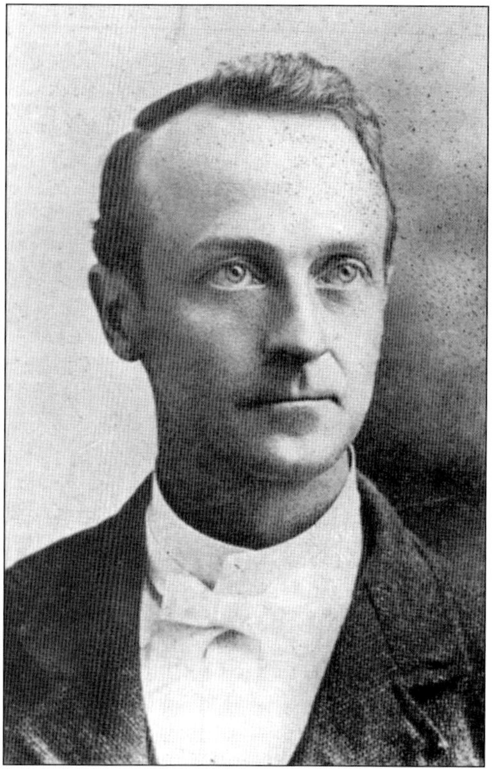

Pres. George Fox Cook (1903–1905) was quite popular with students and faculty. Cook came to education from a background in the law. His early teaching had involved work with black students at Philander Smith College. He continued to hold Southwestern on a steady course. Most important, the board of trustees tasked him with fundraising, a skill for which he felt himself unsuited, and this led to his resignation.

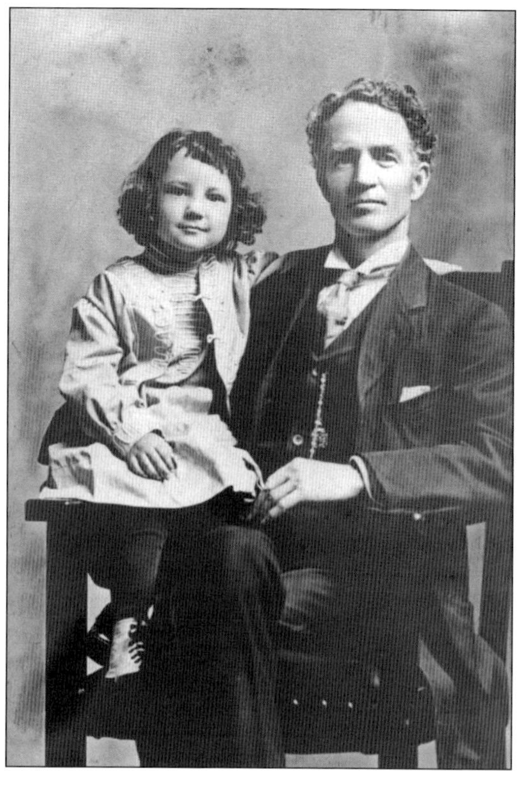

Alvah Graham was one of the first three graduates of Southwestern College in June 1889. He poses here with his young daughter Helen. Alvah Graham was the founder of the Southwestern alumni association and remained active in its affairs until his death in 1953. Helen would graduate from the college in 1919 and become the legendary and longtime head of its drama department. The Helen Graham Little Theatre was named in her honor.

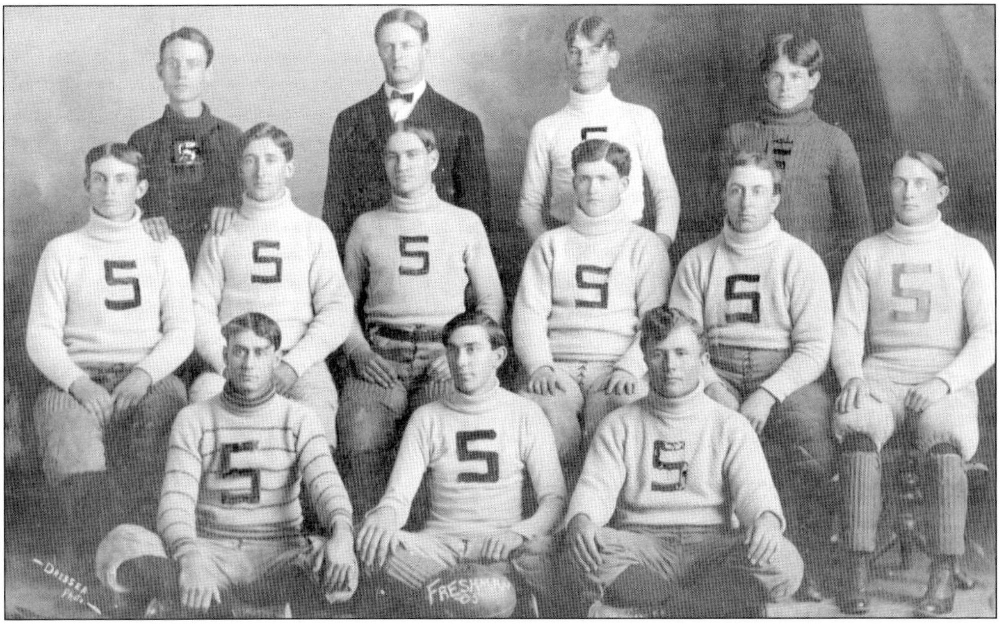

Southwestern College's freshman football team poses during the 1905 season. The players make for a handsome photograph in their "S" sweaters. At this time, football had yet to create the frenzy among students as in later years. At the beginning of the 1906 season, getting enough players to constitute a team was difficult.

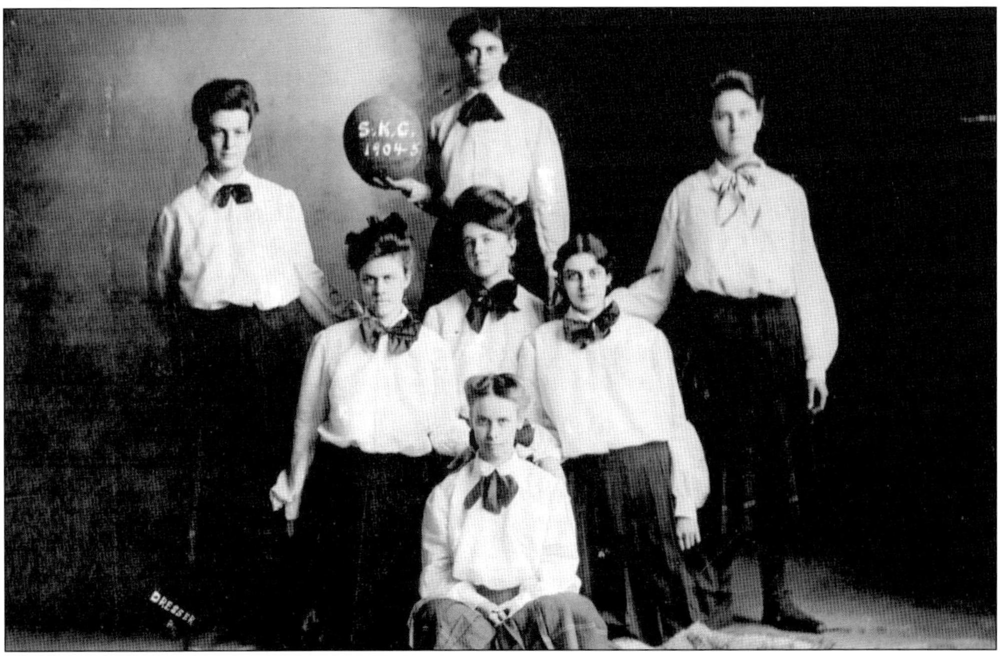

These young ladies made up the college's first girls' basketball team, in 1904–1905. They are, from left to right, (seated) Florence "Tommy" Thomas; (kneeling) Maude Marshall, Mabel Richards Garter, and Josephine Bell; (standing) Clara Randall, Stella Wells, and Pearl Barnhill. Without a gymnasium at the time, the players had to practice and play their games outdoors.

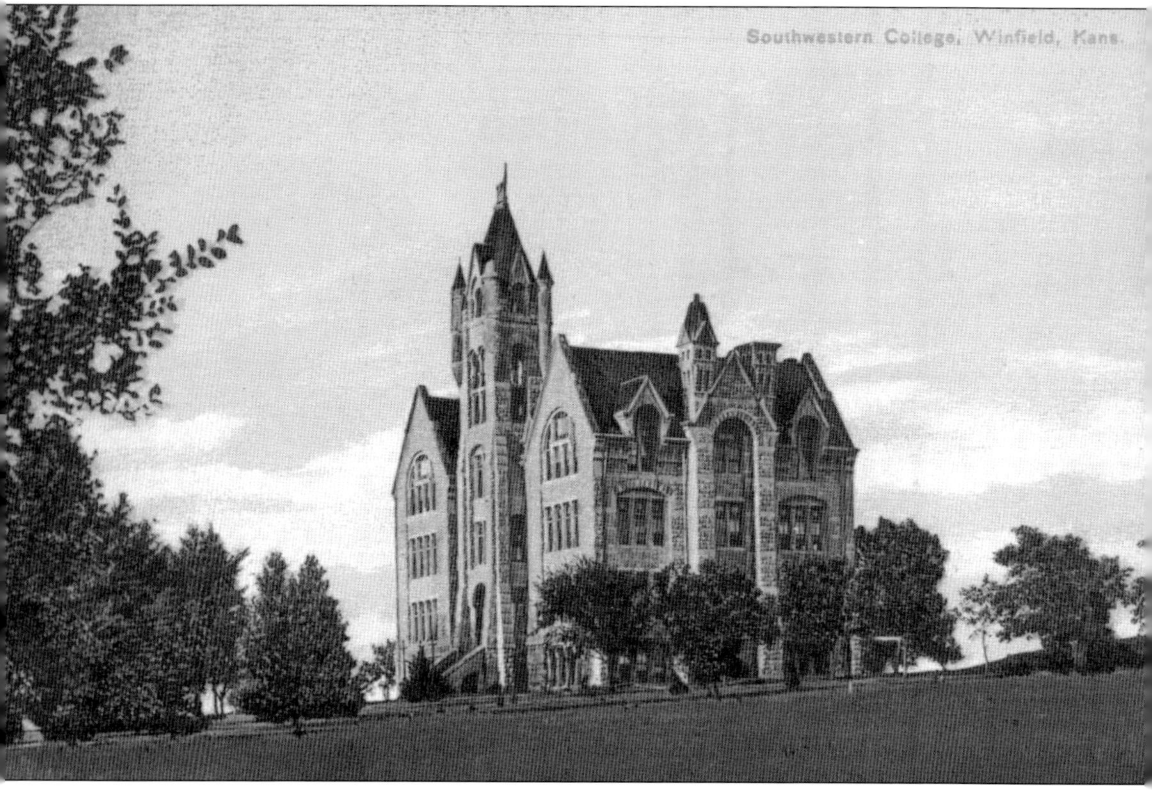

This turn-of-the-century postcard shows the College Building in its glory days. The crises of the 1890s had passed, and a new day would soon be coming to Southwest Kansas College of the Methodist Episcopal Church, including a shorter name: Southwestern College. The new, shorter name would make good school yells possible and more adaptable to cheers. One tower was missing on the south side, and eventually, the main tower would be removed, out of fear it might collapse.

Two

BUILDING A MODERN COLLEGE 1906–1928

Between 1905 and 1928, Southwestern College was transformed from a 19th-century country college into a modern, 20th-century educational institution. Pres. Frank E. Mossman oversaw the first phase of this transformation, which lasted from 1905 to 1918. He was a young man of 32 years, full of energy and ideas, and enthusiastic about the school's future. He easily captured the hearts of the college community.

A man of action, he began at once to advocate for a "greater Southwestern." Mossman soon added five acres to the campus and secured a 20-acre athletic park. A skilled fundraiser, he established a $100,000 endowment. "Never has the school seemed so possessed with throbbing life," the *Collegian* observed.

Mossman's legacy would be cemented in the construction of a new college, physically and academically. Among his greatest achievements was the erection of the imposing Richardson Hall. While creating new buildings and refurbishing old North Hall, he also reduced debt and grew the school's endowment. Mossman expanded the faculty while improving its quality and implementing a modern curriculum.

Fundamentally, Mossman refocused the nature of the institution by creating a college in the modern sense. He abolished the academy and subsumed individual departments, such as the normal school and business department, into the overall college curriculum. After 13 years, Dr. Mossman departed Southwestern for Iowa's Morningside College in October 1918.

Pres. Albert Emmanuel Kirk followed Mossman in January 1919 and continued the latter's work in modernizing the school during the exuberant 1920s. Kirk was an intelligent, well-educated, charismatic man, who stood out in any crowd. He, too, was popular; not only on campus, but also on Main Street. Under his leadership, construction continued with the charming Smith Hall, a dormitory for girls, and the standout Steward Field House. Notably, he also pushed the development of the School of Liberal Arts.

The college also became more democratic, with all-school events taking the place of society-sponsored activities. Kirk's tenure was well regarded by his contemporaries. But, below the surface, the institution's finances and enrollment eroded. Dr. Kirk left the college in October 1928 for a position within the Methodist Church bureaucracy.

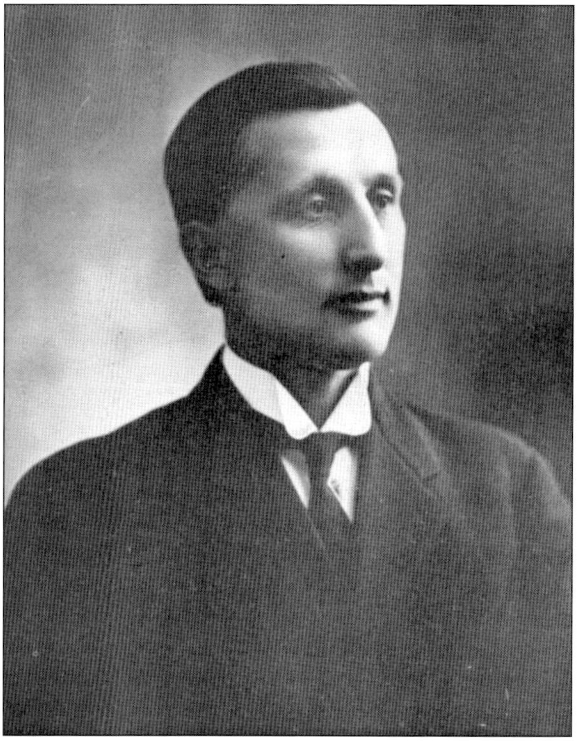

Frank E. Mossman became Southwestern's sixth president on August 8, 1905. He came from Morningside College, where he was its financial agent. At 32, he was the nation's youngest college president. A bright, capable, and likable man, he would modernize the school's organization and curriculum, establish sound finances, and significantly upgrade the campus. The *Collegian* spoke of him as "the man who does things." Mossman left in 1918, only to return again in 1931.

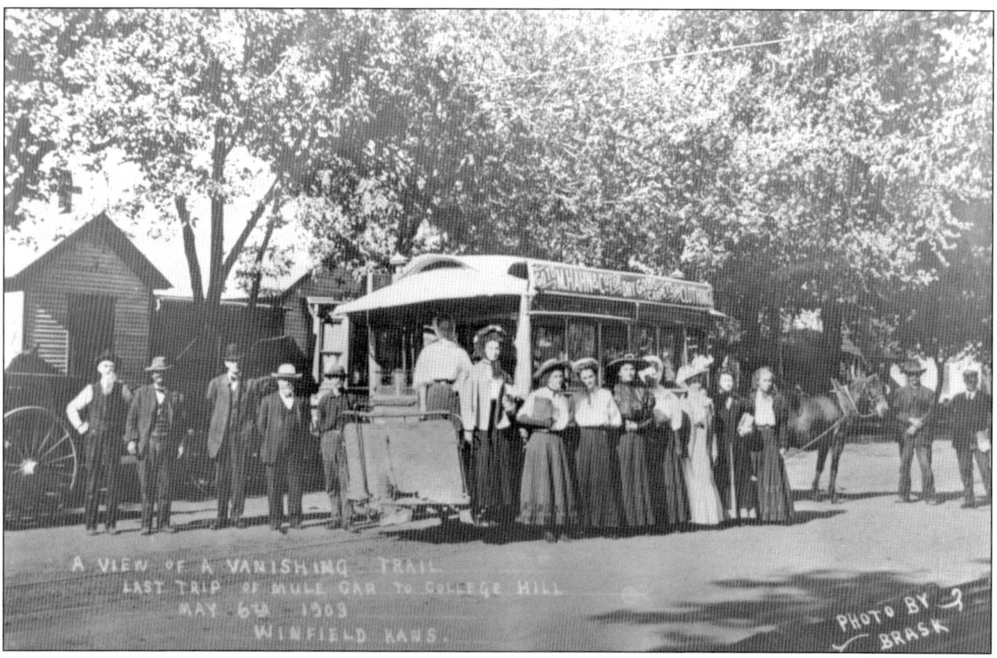

In 1886, a mule-car transit service was organized to provide transportation to the college and elsewhere. By 1900, the system included 10 miles of track and six cars. The fare was 5¢. Mule cars on the College Hill line were replaced on May 6, 1909, by electric trolley cars, which continued to operate until May 1926, when city buses replaced them. While irksome at times, the mule cars were dearly loved by many passengers.

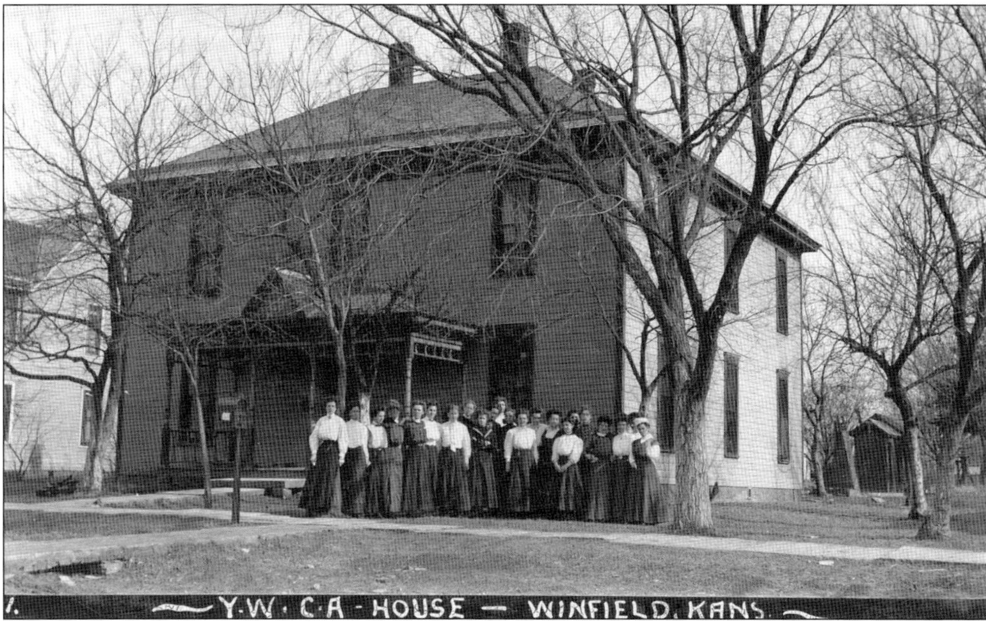

The Young Women's Christian Association was a popular organization on campus since 1899. The YWCA provided a program of recreational, educational, and spiritual activities for members, like those shown here around 1907, in front of their Newman House. "It is the plan of the Y.W. girls to make this house truly a home for all the girls that enter Southwestern, and a place where they are welcome at all times." (Courtesy of Beverley Olson Buller.)

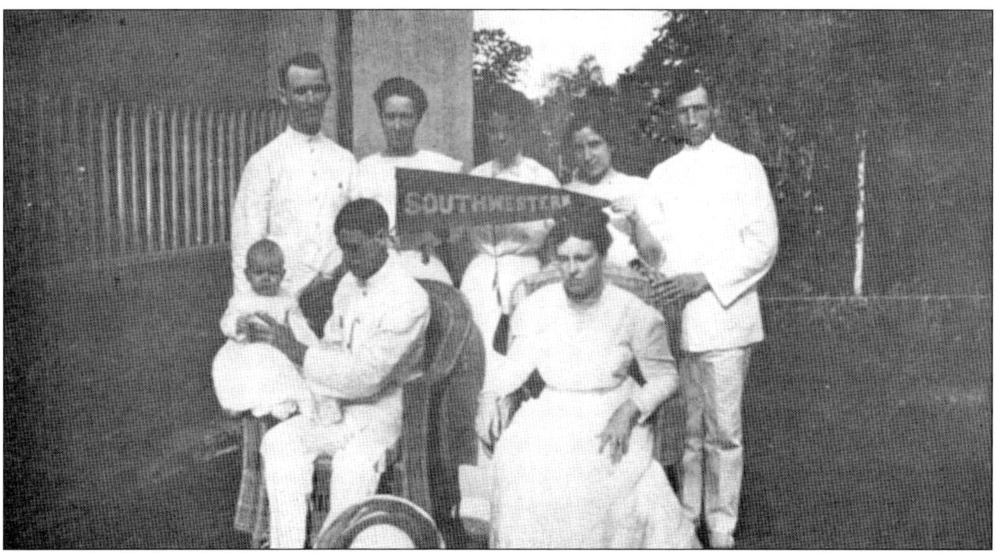

This group of Southwestern alumni, holding a college banner, is serving in Malaysia. Mr. and Mrs. Ambrose Wells, the couple seated, were Southwestern graduates. The school would send its graduates out as missionaries to China, the Philippines, India, Latin America, and Africa. Students interested in mission work joined the Student Volunteers for Foreign Missions, whose motto was "Evangelization of the World in this Generation."

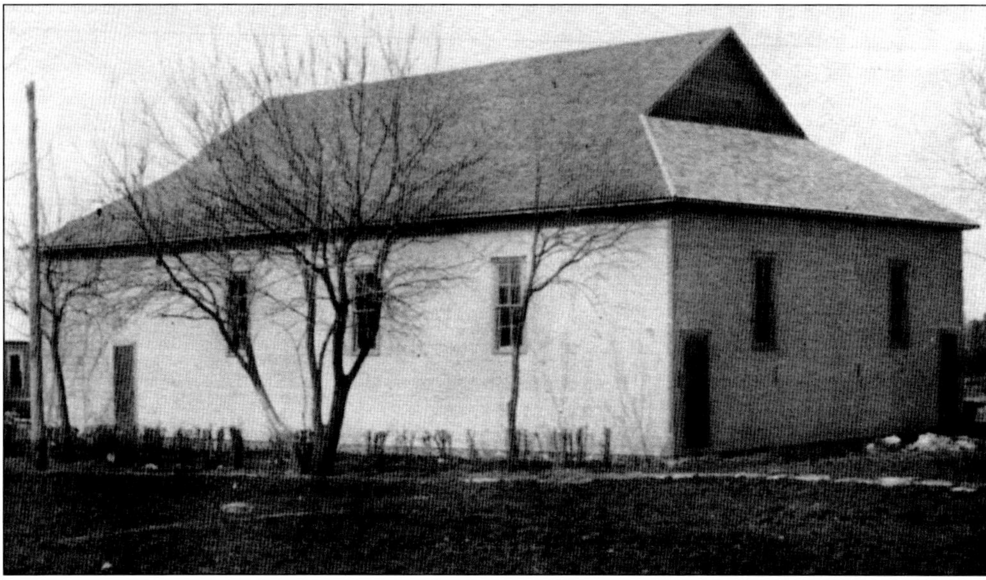

With its wall decorated with 300 college pennants, Southwestern's new gymnasium, known as the "Prexy's Barn," was dedicated in February 1910. The 40-foot-by-80-foot building was meant to be a temporary structure until a proper gym could be built. Having a gym in which to practice and play gave a positive boost to the school's athletic program. Both men and women would now have gym class. Men, however, were forbidden to watch the women practice basketball.

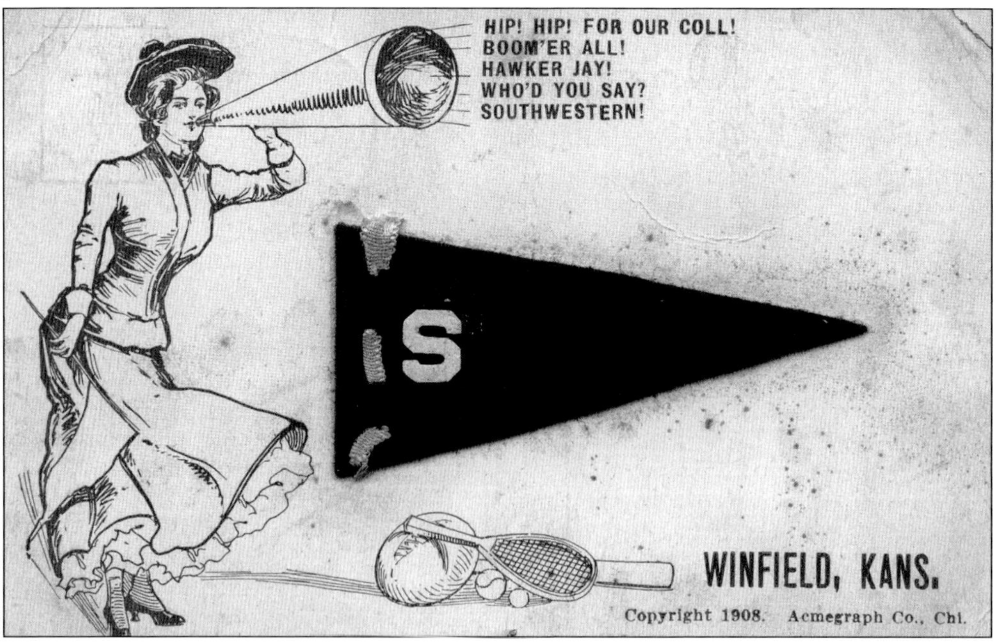

In the new century, sports began to play a more prominent role in the school's life, reducing somewhat the interest in debate and oratory. School yells and pennants became commonplace. Since 1906, Southwestern had been a participant in the Kansas College Athletic Conference, which worked to secure uniformity in athletics. Popular sports of the day included football, basketball, baseball, and track and field. (Courtesy of Beverley Olson Buller.)

May Henninger, a Southwestern junior from Winfield, has a victory smile on her face. In the 1911–1912 basketball season, she was a member of the girls' team, playing guard. The team was described in the *Moundbuilder* as "one of the most successful in the history of the school and set a record for games won, winning nine games." Its one loss, to Fairmount (now Wichita State University), kept them from the state championship.

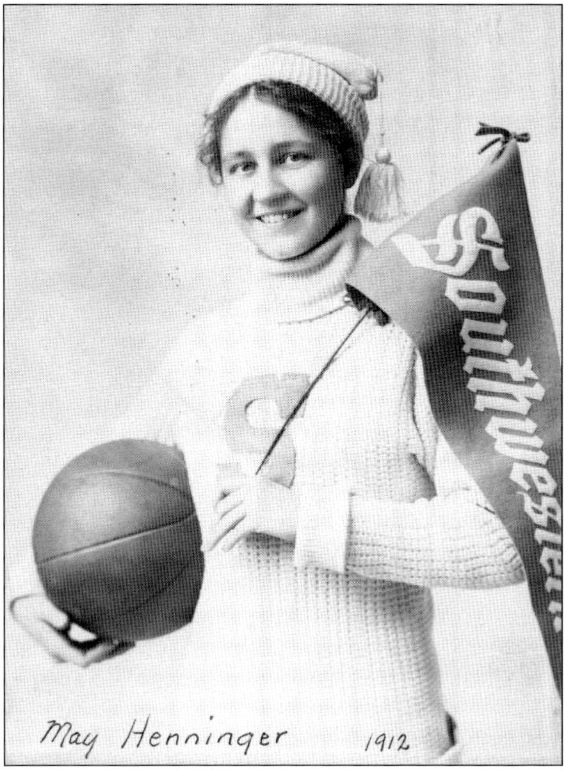

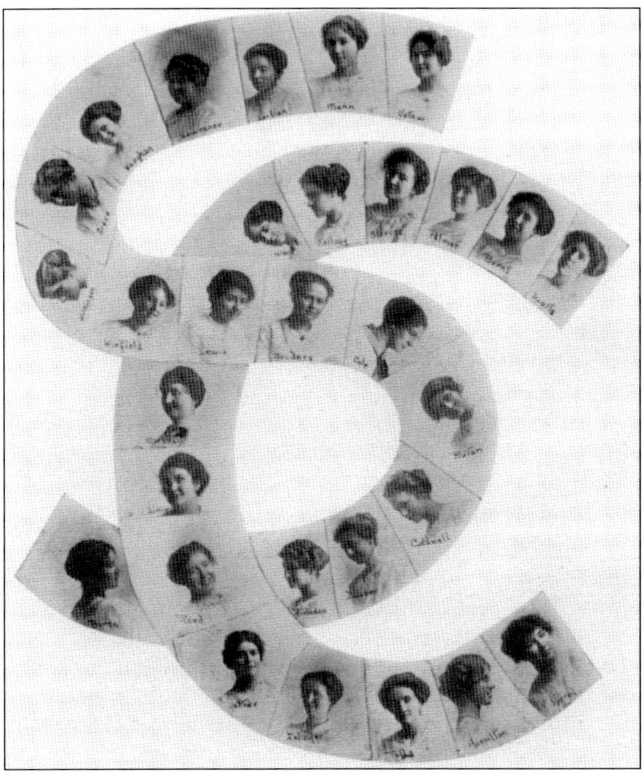

This is a clever use of the new "SC" motif to show off the ladies of the 1913 Southwestern Girls' Glee Club. This new design was made possible by the school's 1908 name change, when the Southwest Kansas Conference College of the Methodist Episcopal Church became simply Southwestern College. This change notably simplified college sports yells.

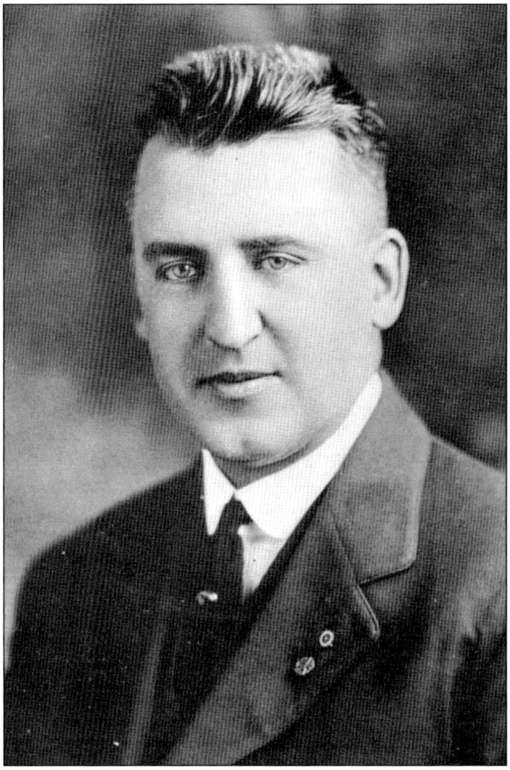

Coach Willis S. Bates was highly regarded by students, as described in the *Moundbuilder*: "[He] is one of Southwestern's greatest assets. He is one of the best coaches in the state and much of the credit for Southwestern's success in athletics belongs to him. He is known as 'Bill' by the students and his jovial good nature has made him unanimously popular with them." He was at Southwestern from 1914 to 1925, steering his football team to 52 wins, 36 losses, and 9 ties.

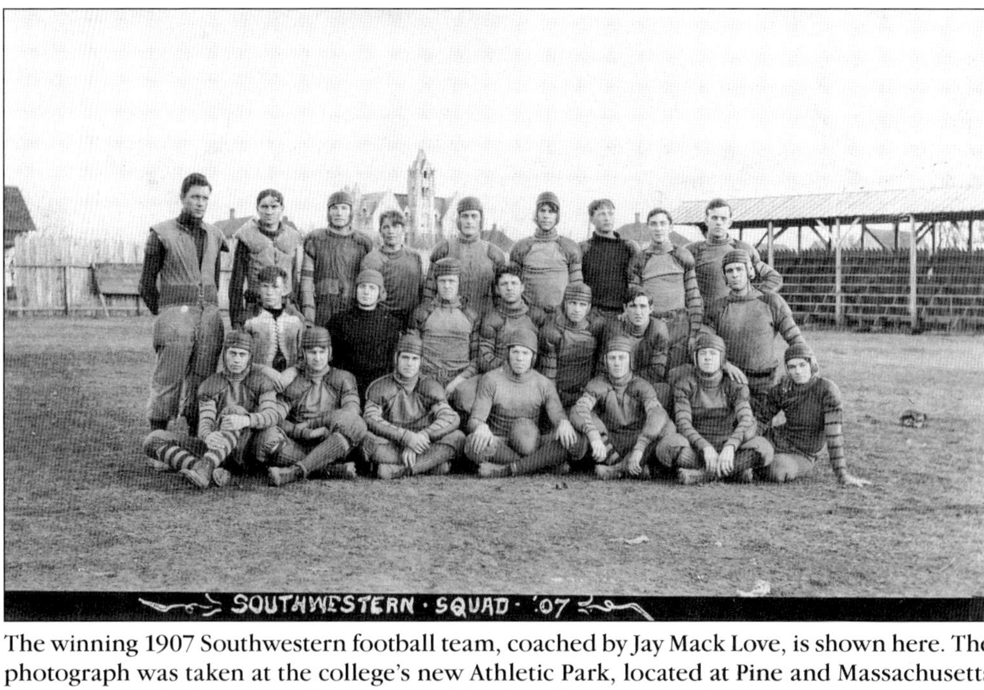

The winning 1907 Southwestern football team, coached by Jay Mack Love, is shown here. The photograph was taken at the college's new Athletic Park, located at Pine and Massachusetts Streets, which had been purchased in the fall of 1906. Note the College Building in the center background. The team played eight games: winning six, losing one to Fairmount (now WSU), and tying another. (Courtesy of Beverley Olson Buller.)

As a Methodist school, Southwestern had a strict rule against drinking alcoholic beverages. However, students will be students, and rules are sometimes broken. This student, Roy Russell, recorded himself on this 1912 postcard having a taste of what appears to be beer in his room. Note the Southwestern pennant on his wall. The other pennant is for Tonkawa, Oklahoma, located in Kay County.

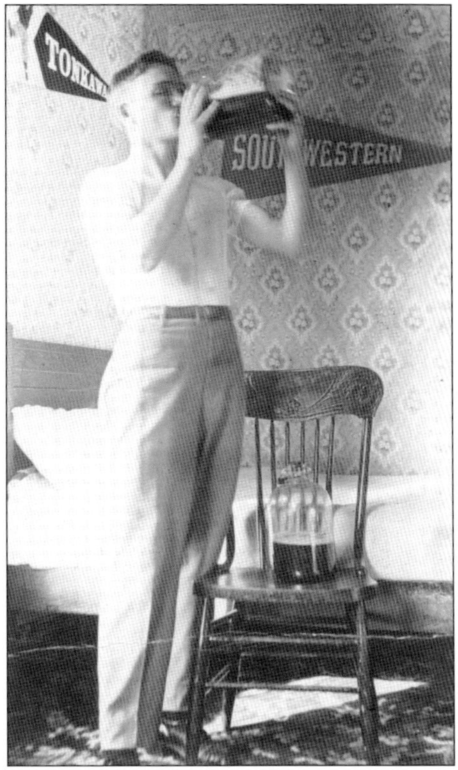

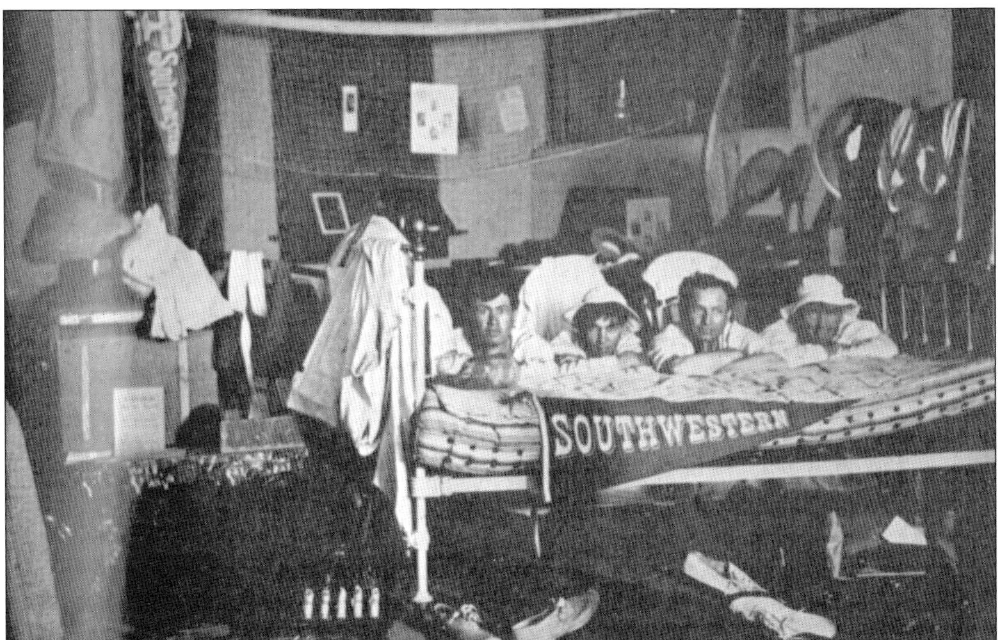

These Southwestern students occupy a messy, unkempt room—nothing unusual here! Note the tennis net and racket. These gentlemen seemed to have been members of Southwestern's gospel team, which went out recruiting students for the college. Shown here are, from left to right, Ralph Krantz, possibly Herbert Vaughan, George Cavit, and an unidentified student.

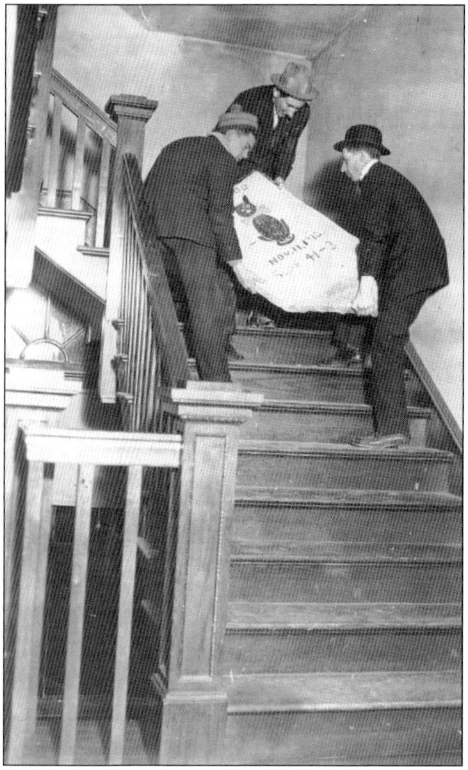

The Jinx, "a smug, black cat, wearing a black bow tie," is the proverbial bad-luck black cat. It first appeared in 1912, when Moundbuilders painted the Jinx on a slab to celebrate their great victory over Fairmount. The Jinx, students said, brought bad luck not to them, but to their opponents. Here, Moundbuilders take down the Jinx stone from its hiding place; rivals often tried to steal it, probably to use its magic powers against an opponent.

The school quickly took to the "Hoodoo" Jinx, and it became a popular item with students. Today, it remains a unique symbol of the college's prowess in sporting affairs. On this postcard, Moundbuilder women pose in their granny garb, along with "Jennie Jinks." Written on the card at the bottom is "We defend the Jinks from its foes."

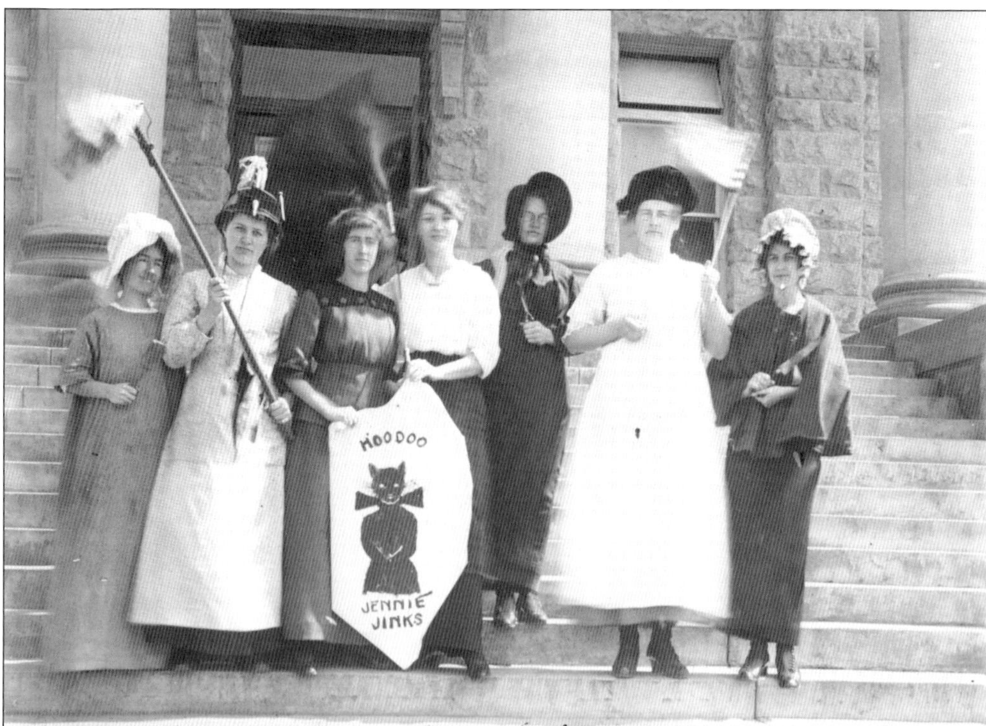

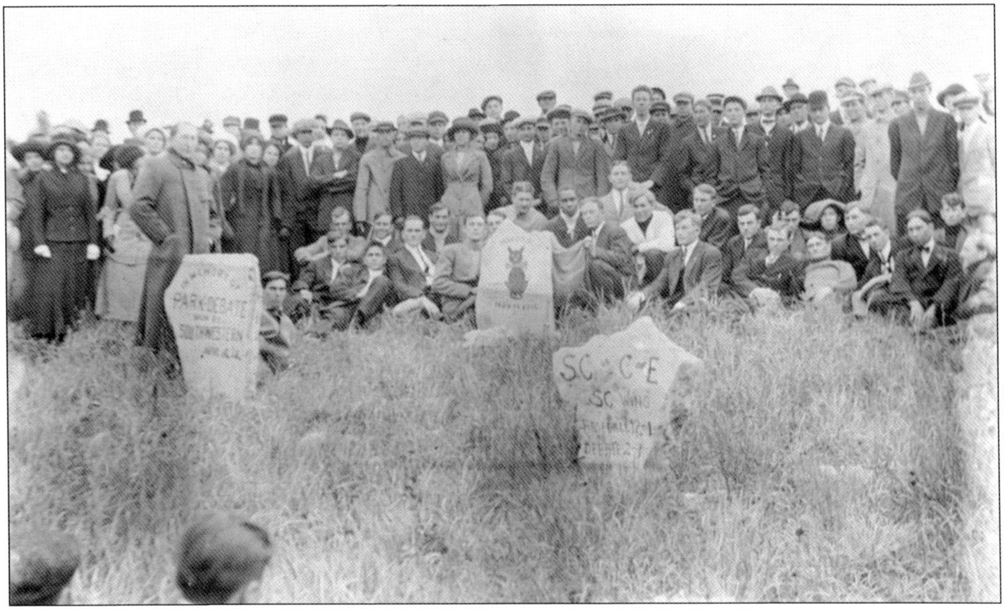

The Jinx stone, seen at center, soon made its way into the Southwestern Cemetery, where it was the focus of all eyes. The cemetery, dreamed up by student Leonard Bacon (class of 1912), dated from 1910. When Southwestern defeated an opponent in a sporting event or other competition, a mock funeral was held for the defeated, and a tombstone was erected to mark the victory.

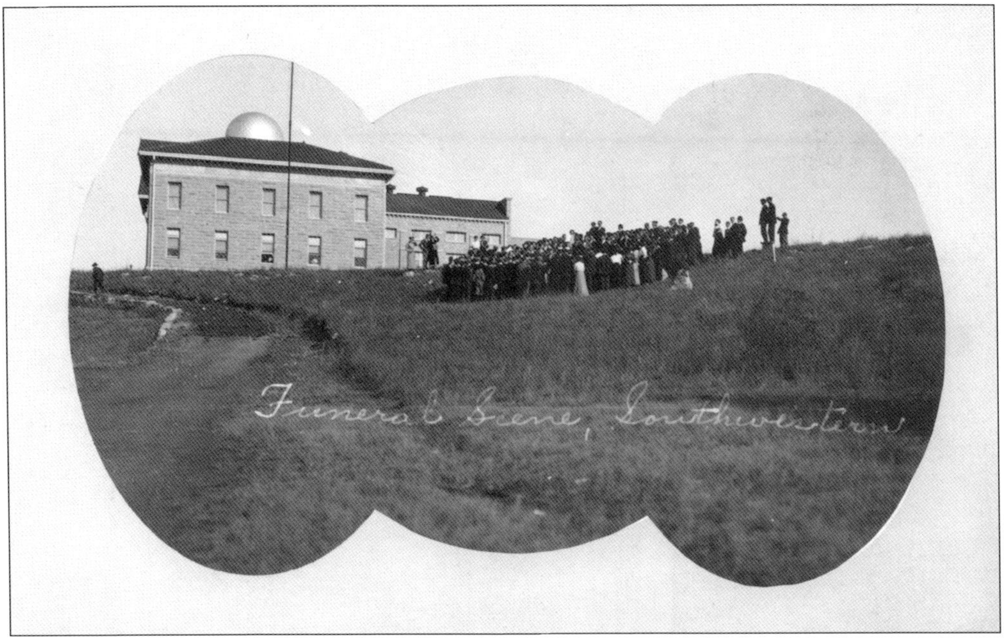

This postcard shows a burial ceremony of a defeated opponent in the college's "Boot Hill." The graveyard was located near the site of today's Student Union. A road ran beside it, and when opponents drove up it, they saw their fate. Southwestern's cemetery came to an end in 1936. At the time, Dean Leroy Allen wrote, "We have room here for nothing dead! Let our rivals bury their own dead on their own campuses!"

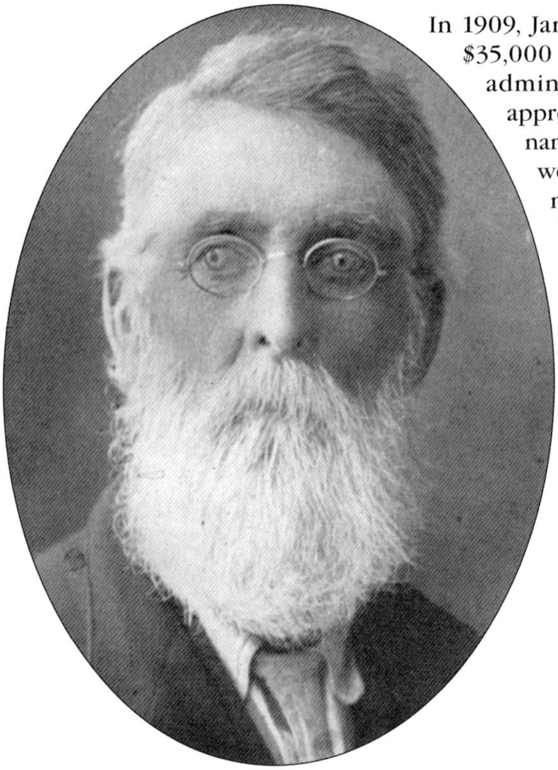

In 1909, James H. Richardson gave Southwestern $35,000 toward the construction of a modern administration and classroom building. In appreciation, the new building was given his name. Richardson, a 78-year-old bachelor and wealthy landowner, was not a Methodist, nor a member of any church, but he believed in the young and in the value of a Christian education. Richardson Hall is no more, but he is still memorialized in Christy's Richardson Auditorium.

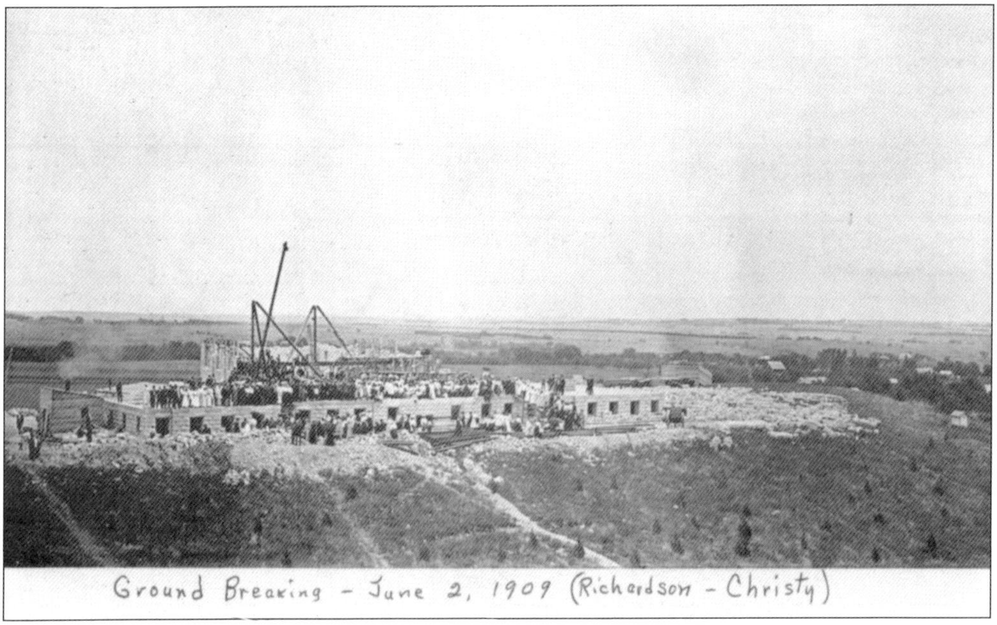

On June 2, 1909, President Mossman laid the cornerstone for the magnificent Richardson Hall, and the college song received its public debut. This building was key to Mossman's plan for a modern college that could accommodate up to 800 students. The hilltop land had been donated to the college in 1906. The board of trustees had pushed construction forward. Mossman successfully raised the $60,000 necessary for its completion.

This is the famous Richardson Hall dome under construction. The dome was silver in color, rather than gold. Some speculate that this was to honor William Jennings Bryan's silver crusade, which appealed to Southwestern's constituency. The dome, lighted at night, was visible for miles around Winfield. To the regret of many, Christy, built to replace Richardson Hall, did not have a dome.

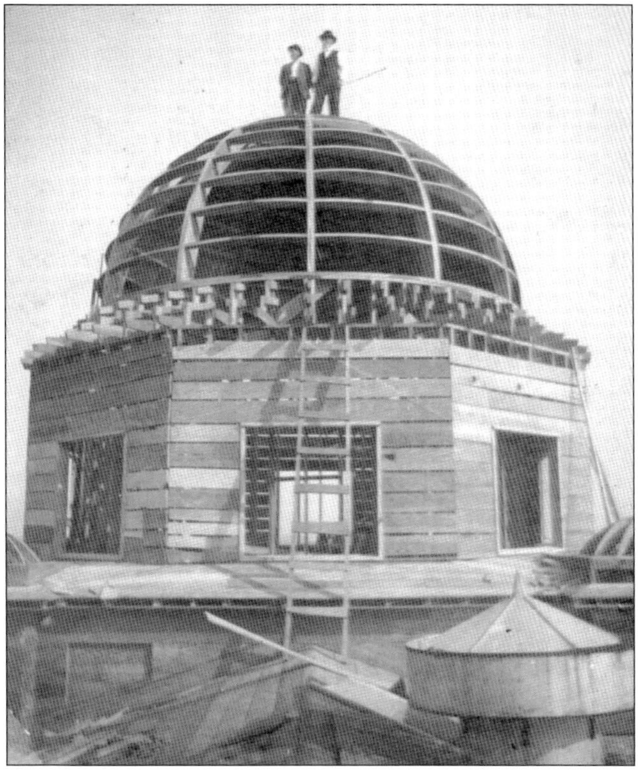

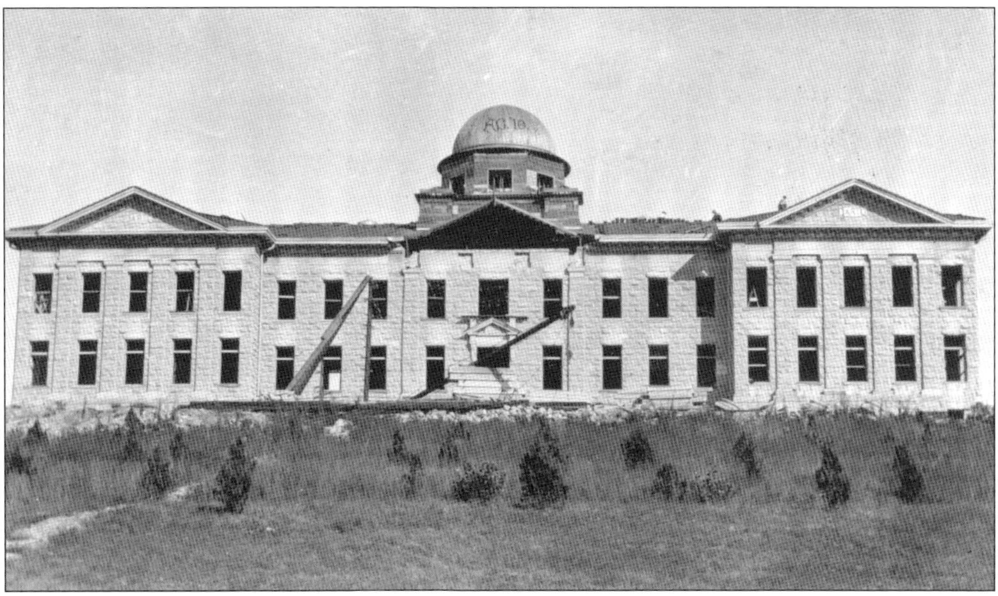

Construction on Richardson Hall nears completion. H. Eilenberger & Co. of Chicago was the chief contractor. Work had begun on December 1, 1908, and moved ahead quickly, except for delays due to lack of steel. During construction, one worker, Henry Hoel, was accidentally killed. On May 31, 1910, Bishop Wilson Seeley Lewis of Fuzhou, China, dedicated Richardson Hall before a large and happy crowd. Prof. J.A. Wood, the oldest faculty member, who had been brought in by President Earp, also spoke.

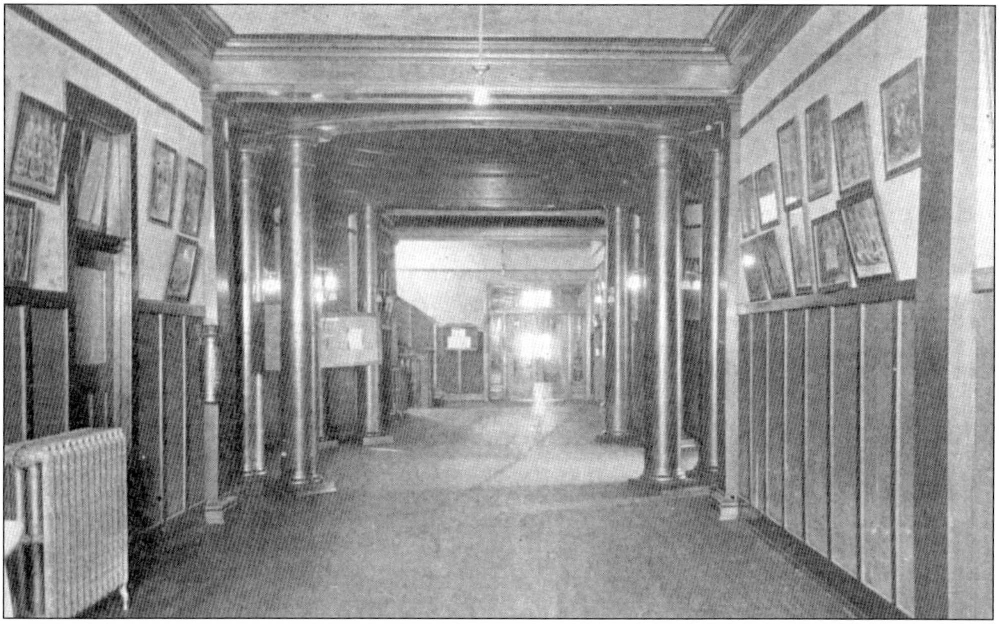

This photograph reveals the beautiful interior of Richardson Hall. The rotunda area, where students would gather between classes, can be seen in the distance. The building's walls were decorated with pictures, many relating to the history of the college, and other memorabilia. Numerous glass cases held trophies and historical objects, such as Peter Cartwright's Bible, all of which would be lost in the 1950 fire.

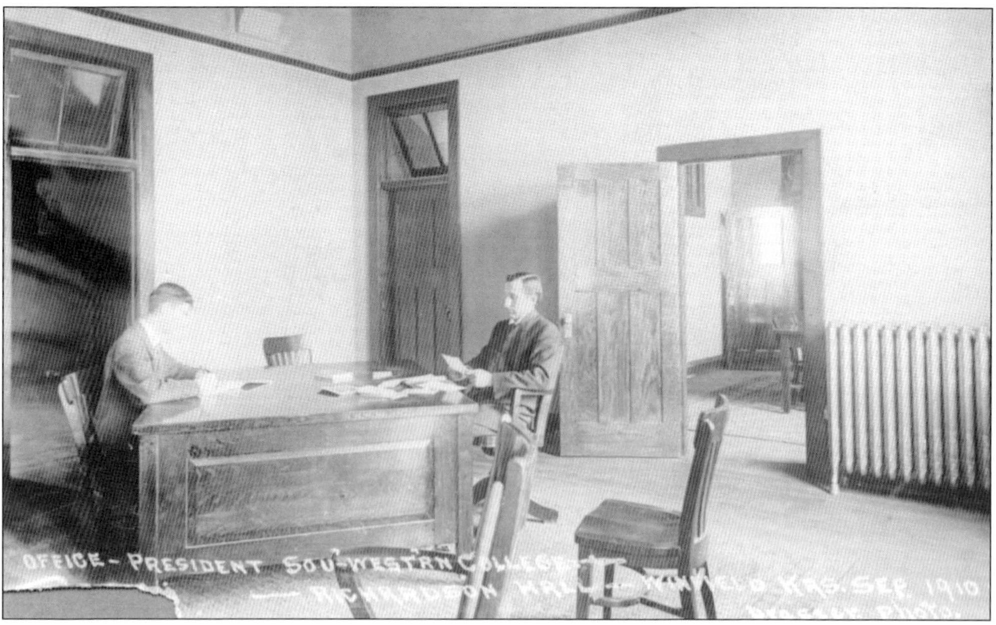

Pres. Frank E. Mossman (right) sits at his office desk in the newly opened Richardson Hall. His secretary sits across from him, taking dictation. There are no photographs as yet on his walls, which, like all the walls in the building, are painted robin egg blue. Mossman most likely considered the funding and construction of Richardson his greatest achievement, and it would serve as the centerpiece of the new college he was putting in place.

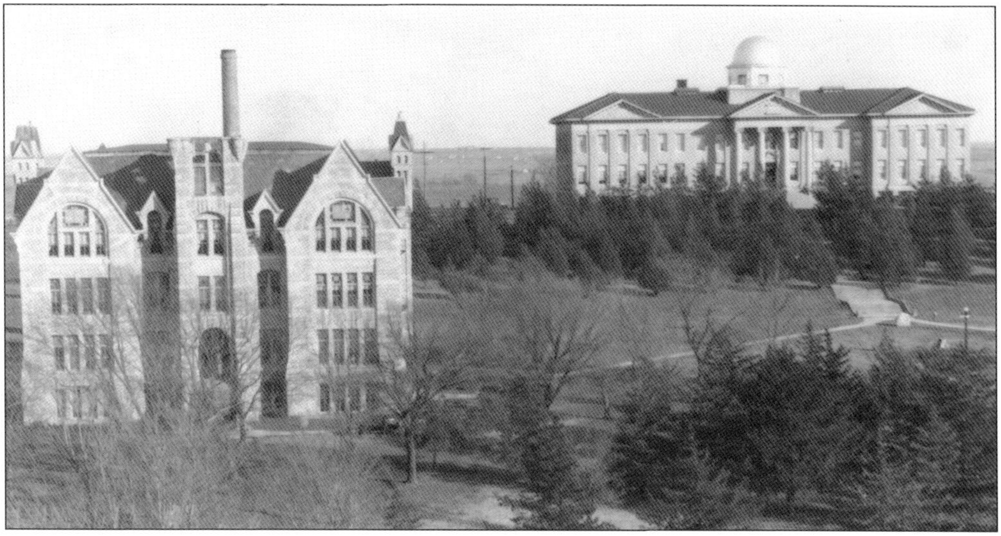

Richardson Hall (right) served as the home of the college's administrative offices, classrooms, and auditorium. North Hall, formerly known as the College Building, primarily housed the science department. The structure was 24 years old in 1910, and once Richardson was completed, North Hall underwent an extensive reconditioning.

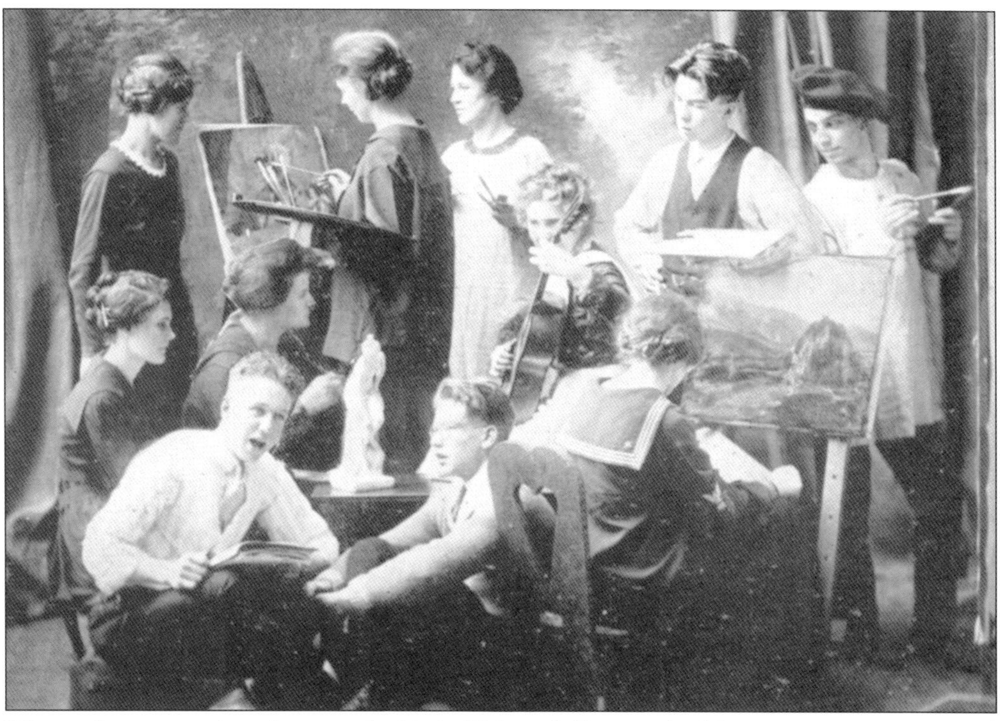

What a clever, creative photograph this is. This artfully posed tableaux composition, staged by Southwestern students and teachers, represents an idealized vision of the fine arts, with each "artist" displaying an affinity toward music, drawing, sculpting, and acting.

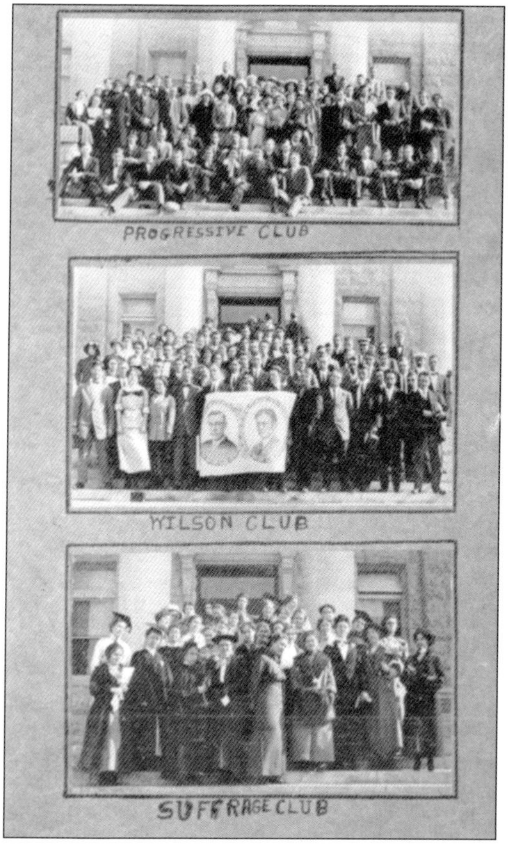

The 1912 presidential election featured three candidates: William Howard Taft (Republican), Woodrow Wilson (Democrat), and Theodore Roosevelt (Progressive). As shown here, student support was divided between Roosevelt and Wilson, with poor Taft having little or none. Women, who did not have the vote, had their own pro-suffrage organization. The students wanted a president who would use government effectively to address problems and create a wholesome society.

Downtown Winfield is seen during the Mossman years. Automobiles are not yet present on the streets, but electric trolley cars have replaced the mule cars. The large building houses the First National Bank (now CornerBank). It was designed by Willis A. Ritchie, who also designed the College Building. W.C. Robinson, who headed the bank, was a longtime trustee of the college and had helped to save it during the crisis of the 1890s. (Courtesy of CCHS.)

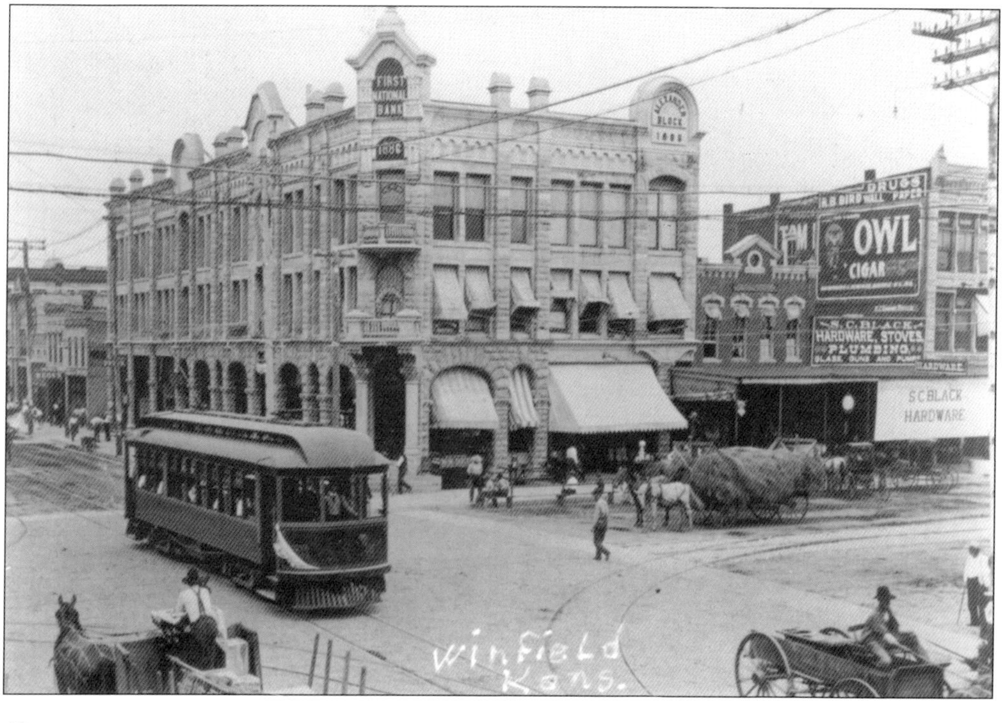

Southwestern sent gospel teams to reach out to the children of the school's constituency. These teams put on programs of music and sales talk aimed to interest young people in attending Southwestern. President Mossman, like his predecessors, was also frequently on the road, preaching the value of a Southwestern education to farm and small-town families.

The United States entered World War I in April 1917. President Mossman advised students to "hold steady" and wait to be called. In the fall of 1918, Southwestern established a Student Army Training Corps (SATC) unit to train officers. On October 1, 1918, 93 students were inducted into the Army. The unit was preparing to send out its first trainees when the war ended. The men were discharged on December 20, 1918. The SATC members held a 50th-anniversary reunion at Southwestern in 1968.

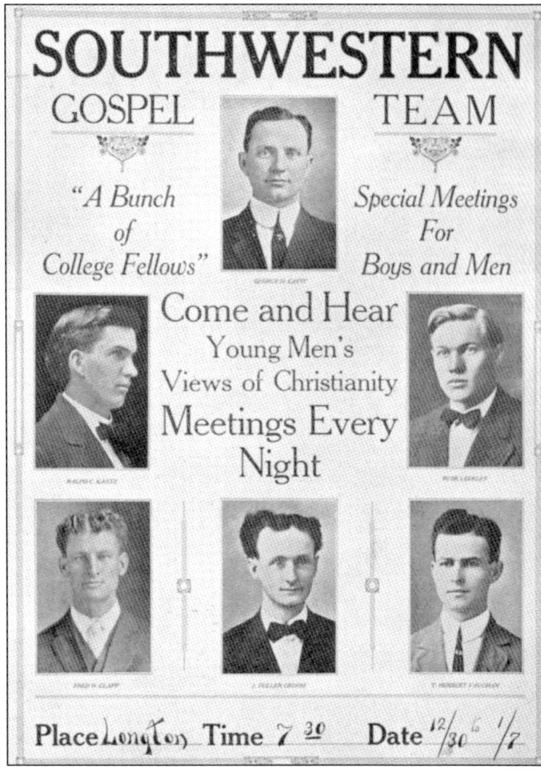

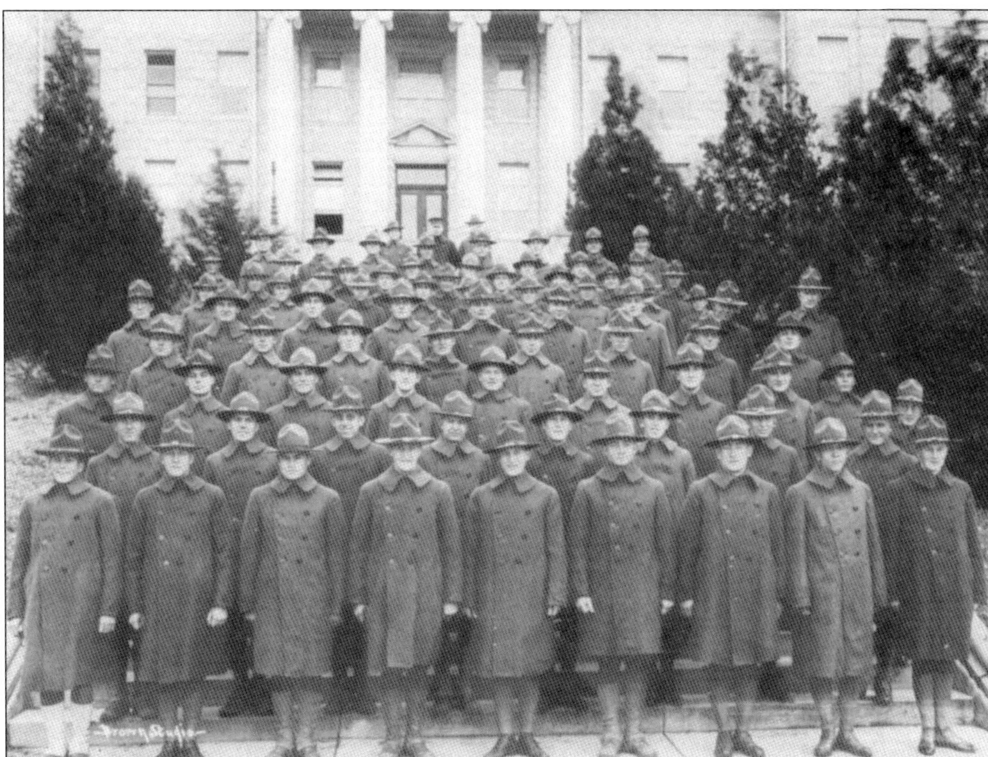

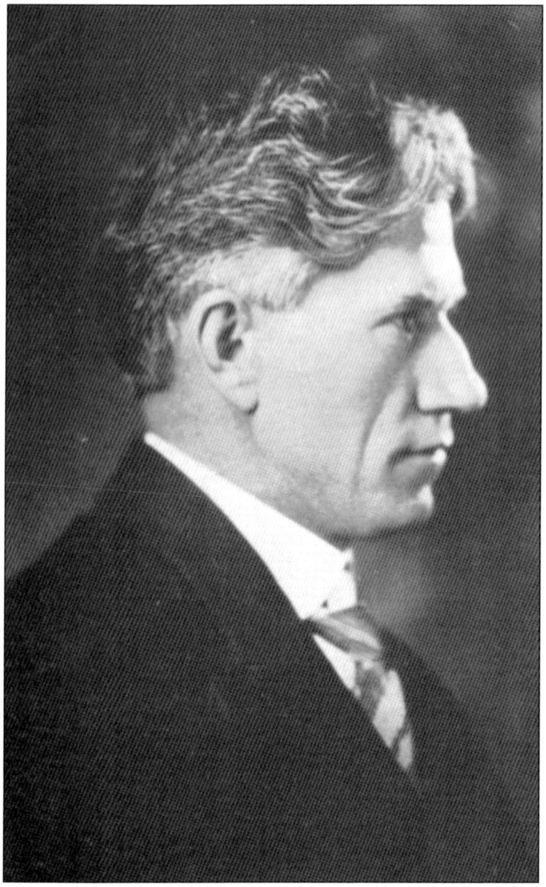

Pres. Albert Emmanuel Kirk was an impressive man. He was a scholar, theologian, and educator with a charismatic personality. He came to the college on January 1, 1919. The war was over, and America was moving into the most exciting and creative decade of the 20th century—the 1920s. It was the decade when modern America came alive, and Southwestern College was at high tide. Sensing, perhaps, that it was time to "skidoo," Kirk resigned in October 1928.

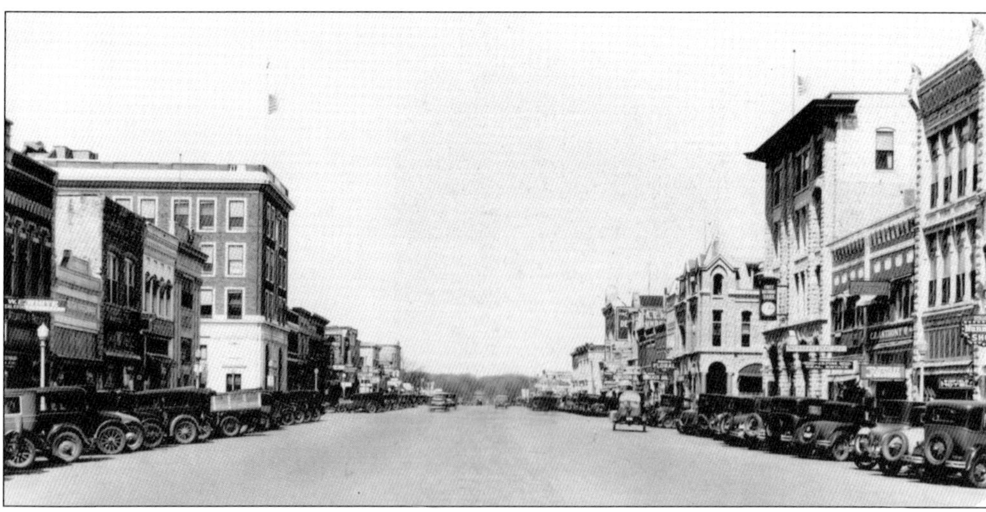

Main Street in Winfield, Kansas, is seen here in the mid-1920s. Winfield, like the nation, was booming in the Calvin Coolidge years. There was money to spend not just on the necessities of life, but also on its pleasures. Indeed, many Winfielders could now afford to send their children off to college, and many chose Southwestern. Winfielders would also generously support the college's building program. (Courtesy of CCHS.)

This drawing, dated August 1919, shows a general plan for the development of the Southwestern campus. The plan called for two new educational buildings on each side of Richardson Hall, along with a sports field, stadium, and new gymnasium. Also proposed were a new administration building across from North Hall, a YWCA facility, and another girls' dormitory. A "greater" Southwestern was clearly in the works.

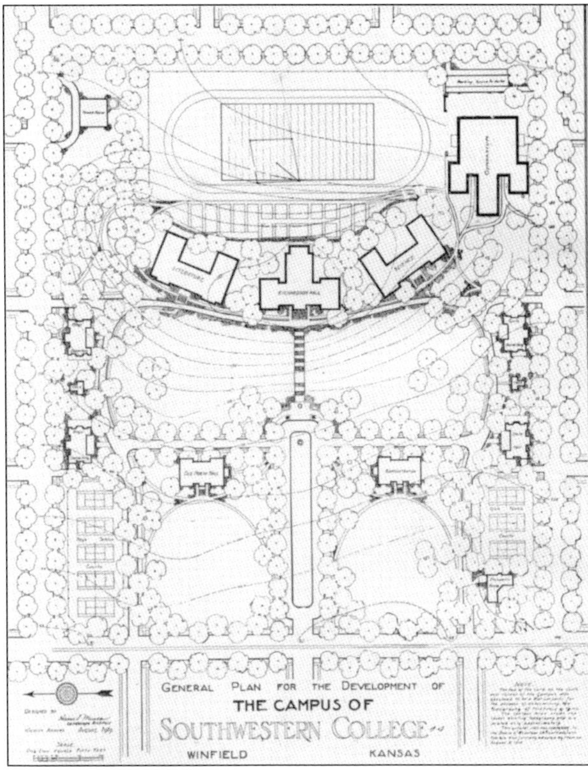

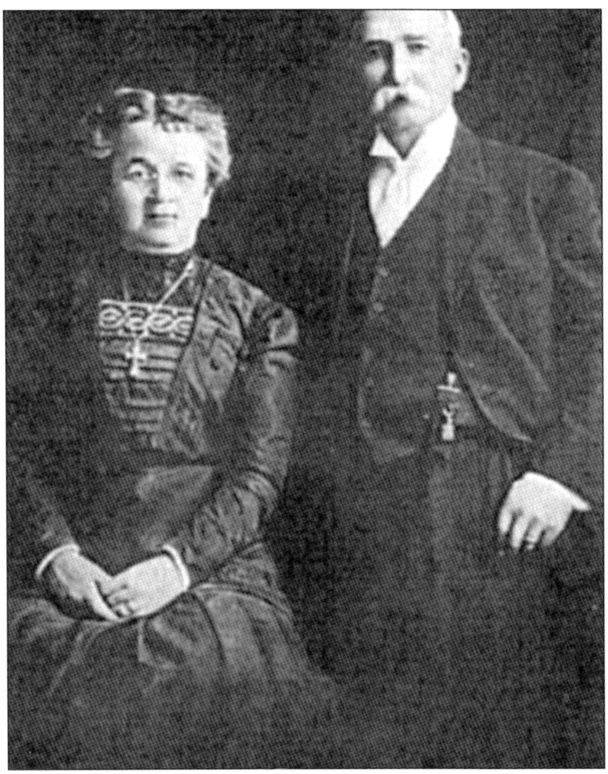

Levi and Ella Smith of Kinsley, Kansas, provided Southwestern with an annuity of $50,000 that was used to build a dormitory with a cafeteria that served as a women's residence for over 40 years. Influenced by the cottage style of architecture, with green gables, high chimneys, and sheltered doorways, it was said to be "the finest dormitory in the Central West." In the Smiths' honor, the dormitory was named Smith Hall upon completion in January 1921.

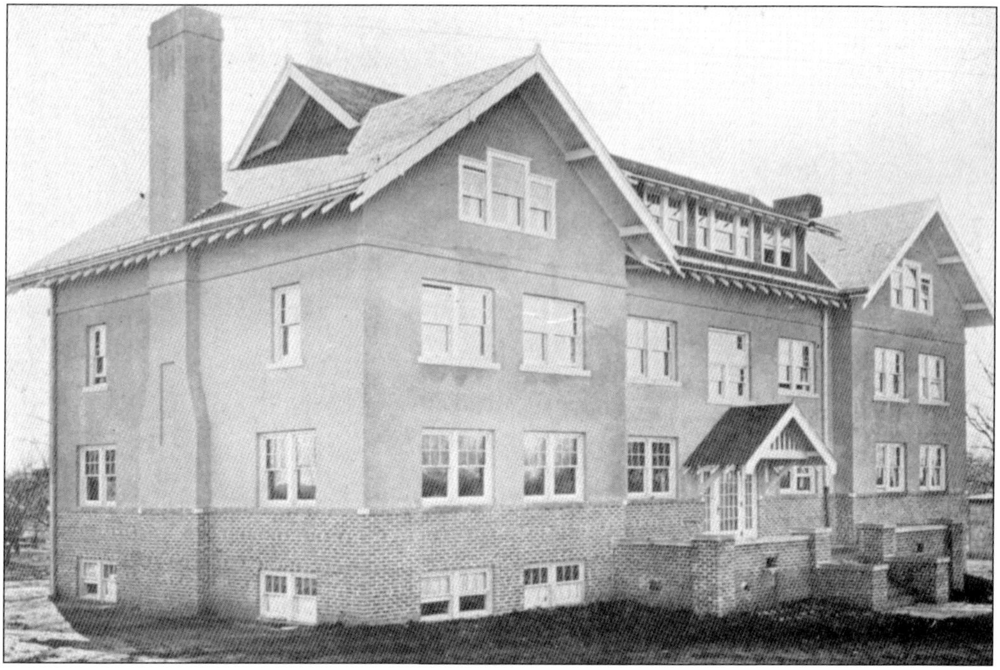

Smith Hall is seen here when it was fresh and new. The building of tile, brick, and stucco cost $55,000 and could accommodate 60 women. It was described in the *Moundbuilder* as "modern in its conveniences and beautifully furnished." The basement area served as an eating facility that could handle 200 students. Smith Hall was seen as the first of a group of dormitories built to accommodate both men and women.

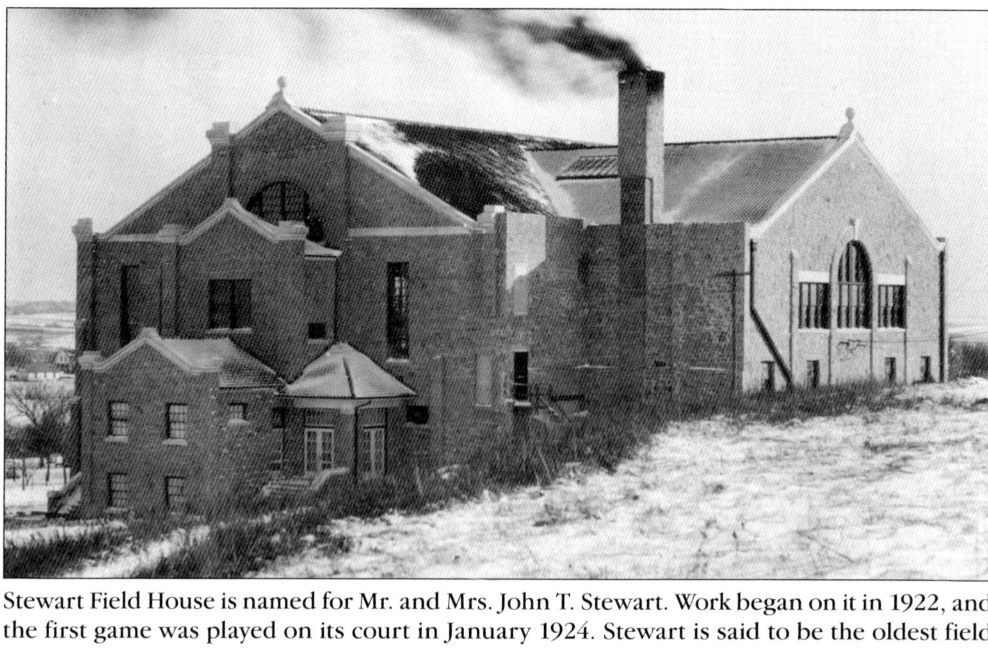

Stewart Field House is named for Mr. and Mrs. John T. Stewart. Work began on it in 1922, and the first game was played on its court in January 1924. Stewart is said to be the oldest field house west of the Mississippi River still in use for basketball play. The gym was described on a sports website as "a true landmark within college basketball in America." The facility was built at a cost of $132,490. In 1998, it underwent a $1.5 million renovation.

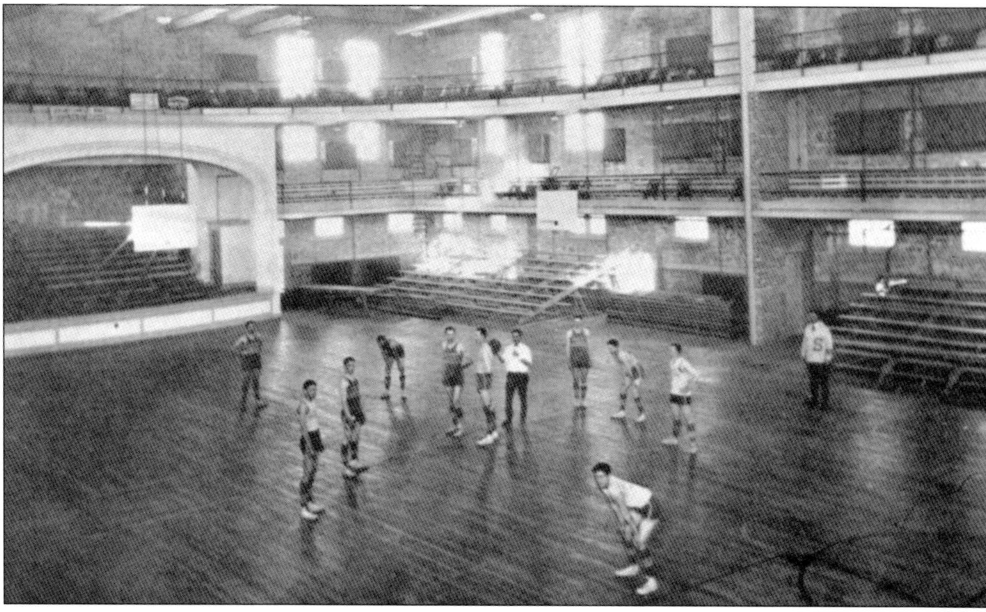

Southwestern players practice basketball on the new field-house court. The court is still in use 90 years later. Note the stage and bleachers on the sides. Besides athletic events, the court area has been used for school and public events, including assemblies, graduation exercises, class registration, speeches, lectures, and musical programs.

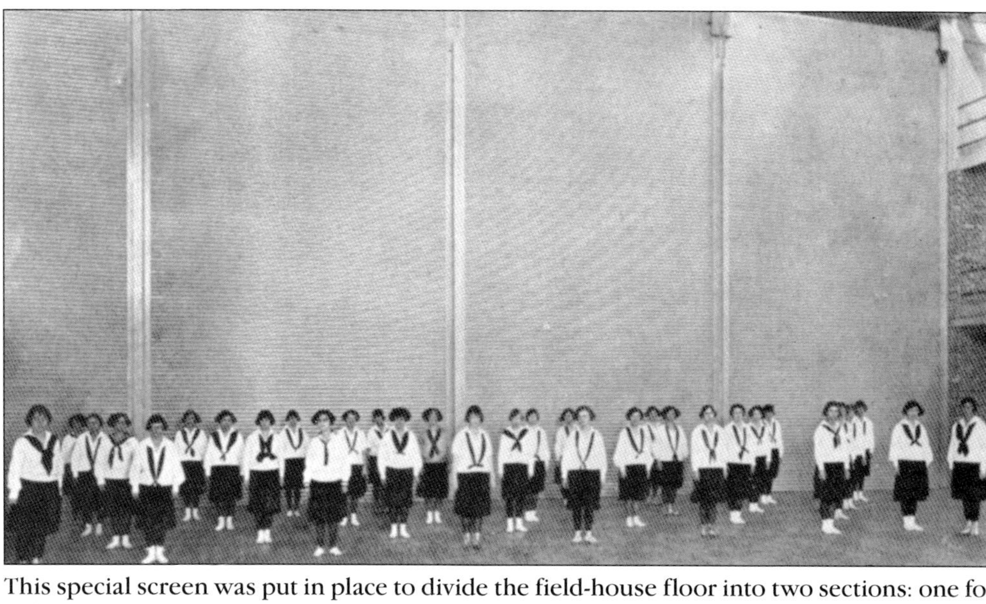

This special screen was put in place to divide the field-house floor into two sections: one for girls' physical education classes, the other for the boys. Since the days of Prexy's Barn, male students had been prohibited from watching the girls practice basketball. Thus, the heavy, mesh screen prevented the boys from watching the girls as they exercised—and vice versa. During World War II, physical education classes at Southwestern became coeducational.

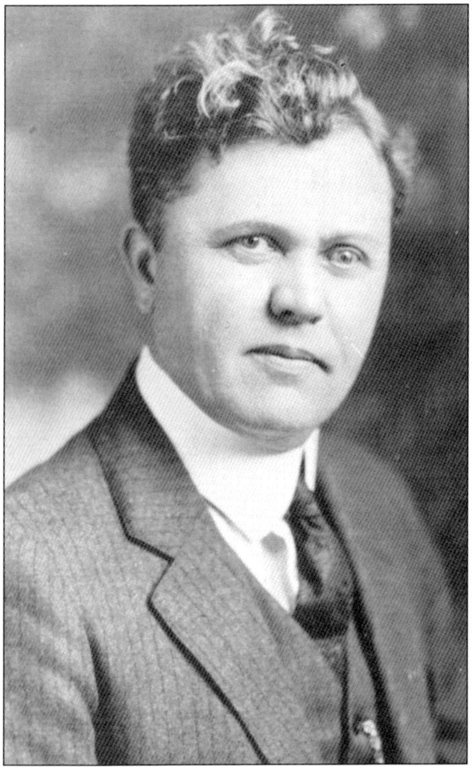

Leroy Allen came to Southwestern as a professor of economics in 1922. He became dean of the College of Liberal Arts in 1925 and held that position until 1939. From that time until his death in 1947, he taught religion and speech. Dr. Allen gained national prominence as the founder of Pi Gamma Mu, an international honor society in social sciences. He is probably best remembered for the "Building of the Mound" ceremony. In addition, he coached many of the championship debate teams.

The Moundbuilding ceremony, one of Southwestern's great traditions, was the product of Leroy Allen's fertile imagination. The ceremony was first held at night on September 8, 1927. Students and faculty placed rocks on the Mound, in the center of which was a time capsule. Prof. Dewey Short presided, President Kirk gave an inspiring prayer, and Allen spoke on the new concept of "moundbuilding." The program was described as "impressive and beautiful."

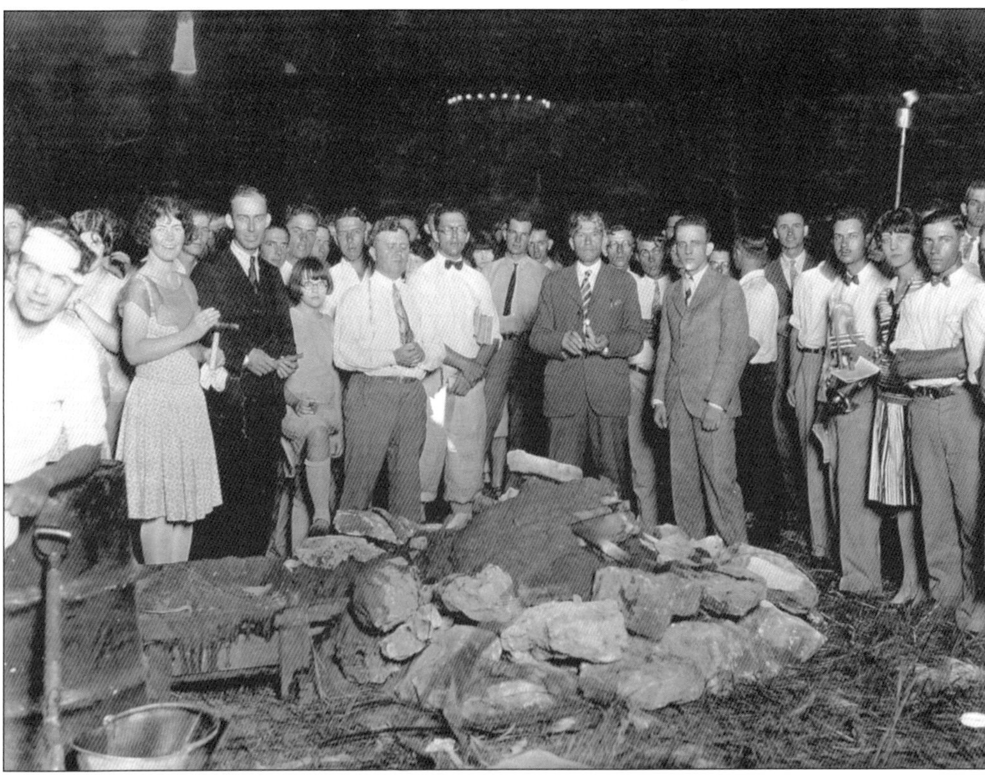

Students pose for a photograph celebrating the May Fete ceremony in the early 1920s. At this time, the May Fete, which had been a Belles Lettres and Athenian event since 1898, became an all-school affair. May Fete was a popular annual event, enjoyed by students and the public. As a spectacle, it would reach its high point in the late 1930s.

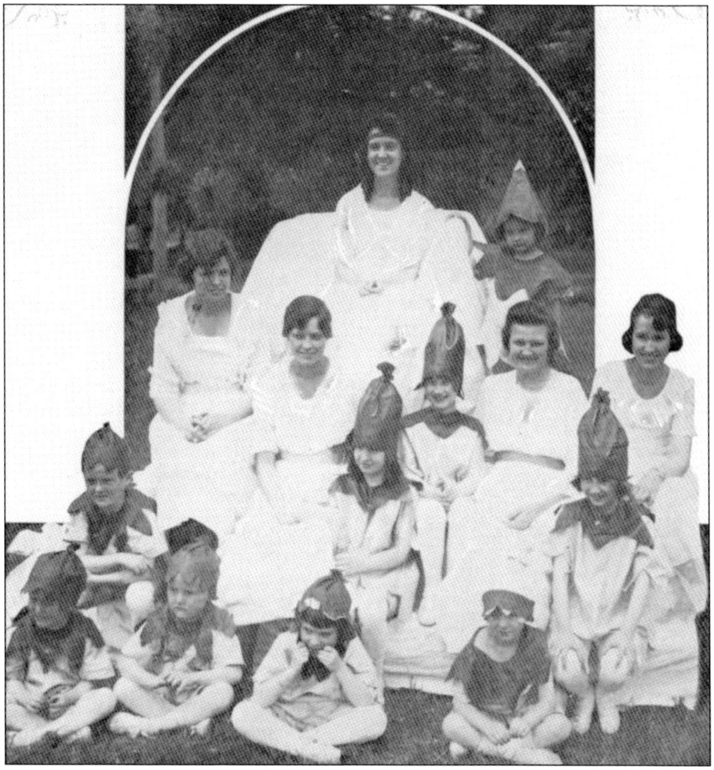

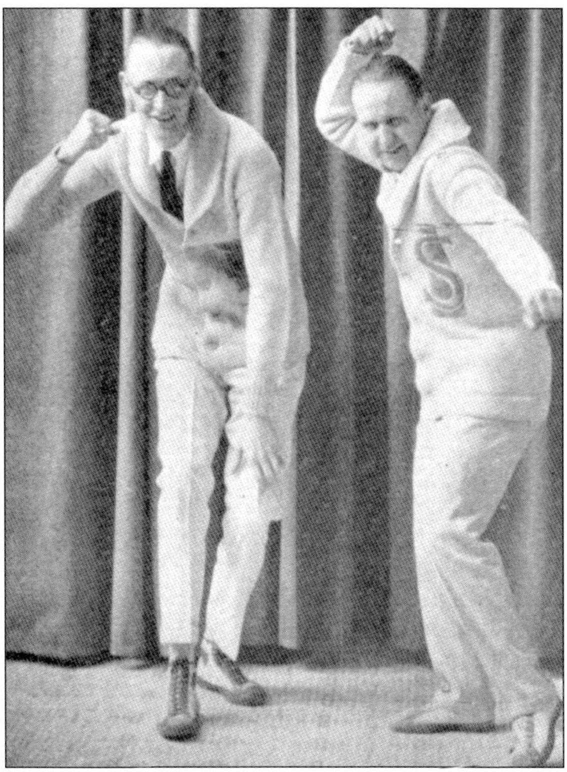

Southwestern had male cheerleaders in the 1920s. Here, two "yell leaders," Glen Witherspoon, '25 (left), and J. Buren Linthicum, '22, display their limber moves and fierce Builder spirit. Intense competition was the rule of the day; students were vigorously loyal to their friends, their class, and their college, and they fought mightily to prove their convictions.

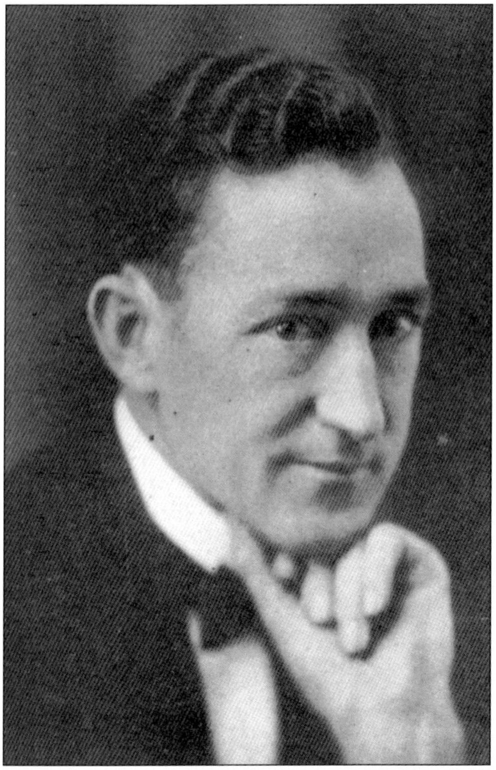

William M. Goldsmith, who had come to Southwestern in 1920, was a popular professor of biology. His specialty was eugenics, of which he was a noted advocate and had written a textbook on the subject. Goldsmith is best remembered as the creator of the Omnibus tours. His wife, Amy, was an instructor of domestic science. The Goldsmiths left the college in 1930 after a disagreement with the administration.

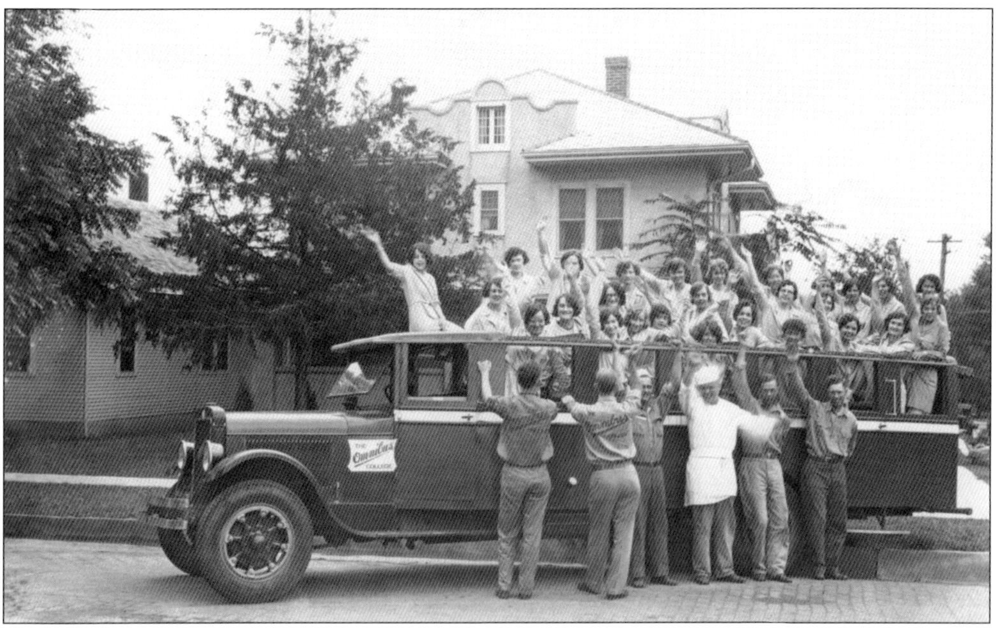

Passengers and staff of the Omnibus are ready to depart for a study tour lasting several weeks. Southwestern students and groups of Kansas primary- and secondary-school teachers camped out on these journeys to various regions of the country. In the summer of 1925, Southwestern students took a month-long field trip through the Southwestern states, which included "studying the Cliff Dwellings of the West."

Antiwar sentiment was strong on campus in the spring of 1924. Southwestern students gained national attention when they proposed that the Methodist Episcopal Church's General Conference in Boston adopt an antiwar resolution, which was interpreted by some as supporting pacifism. The newspaper headlines of the day illustrate the widespread attention the issue received. Dr. Kirk rushed back from Boston to Winfield to calm the trouble waters.

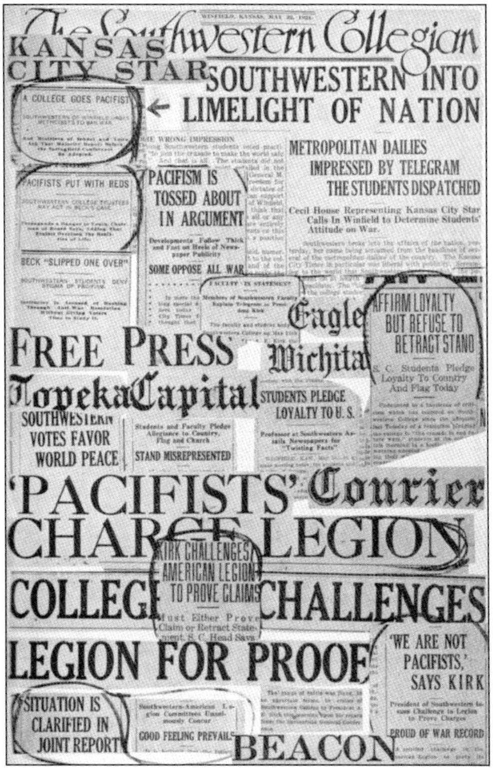

This is the Athenian and Belles Lettres meeting room in Richardson Hall in the 1920s. The room is well furnished—note the bust of Homer on the stand and a fine piano. In the college's early days, the exclusive Athenians and their female counterpart, the Belles Lettres, had dominated. But now, the number of societies had increased to eight as part of an effort to open up society life to all.

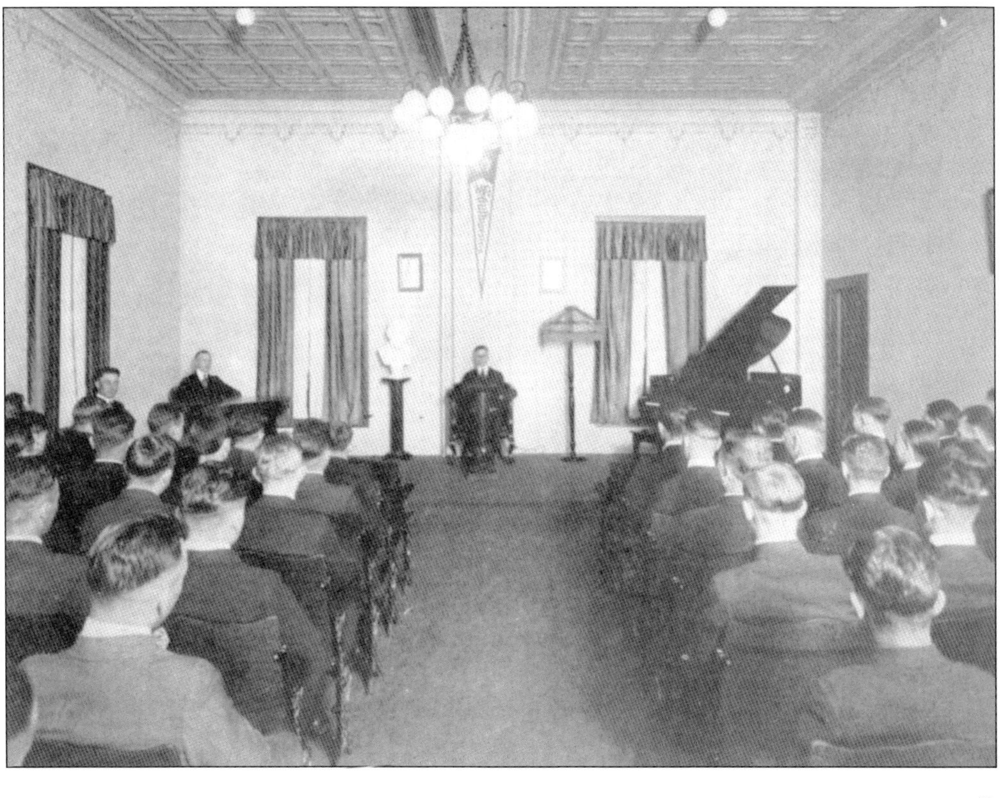

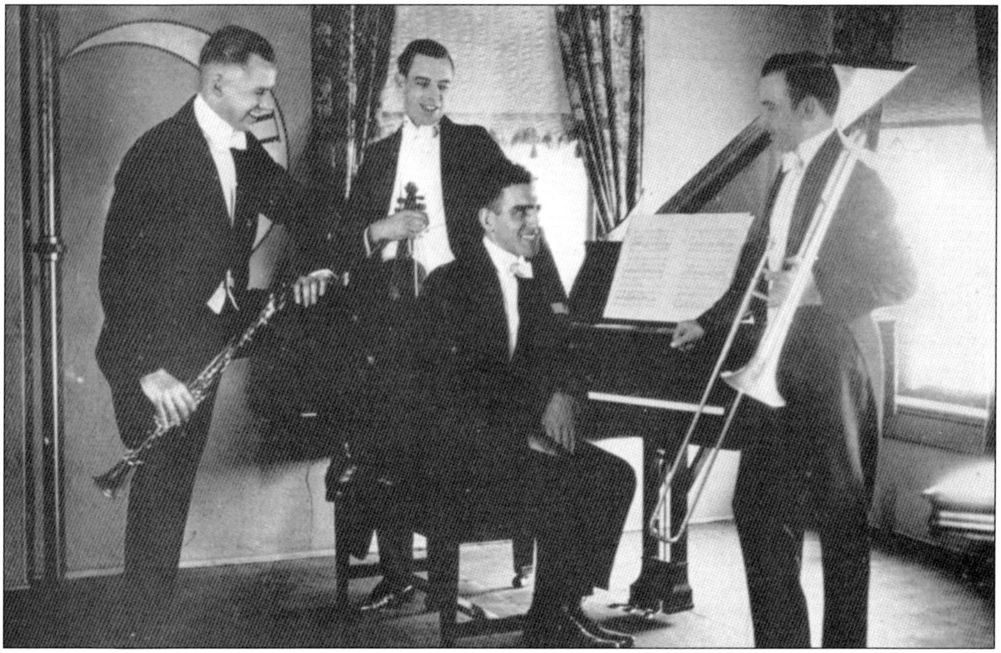

This tuxedo-clad, all-male quartet entertained students in one of the society rooms in Richardson Hall. Popular music of the day included the "S-O-U--Southwestern Blues," written especially for the college, and the latest Rudy Vallee tunes, including his signature song, "My Time Is Your Time."

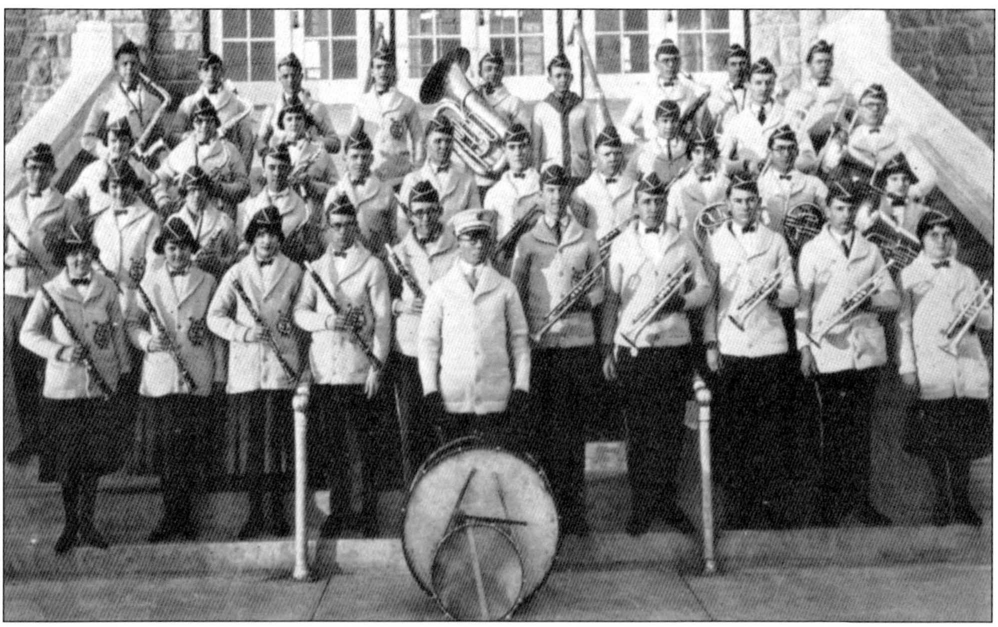

The Southwestern band, under the direction of C.O. Brown, was very popular with students and Winfielders. The band worked hard to inspire Builders at sporting events. The band also marched in parades, notably the ones for homecoming and Christmas, and the spectators along Main Street were quick to applaud. In 1927, the band was given a two-hour period on the regular class schedule; doing so was a rarity among colleges at the time.

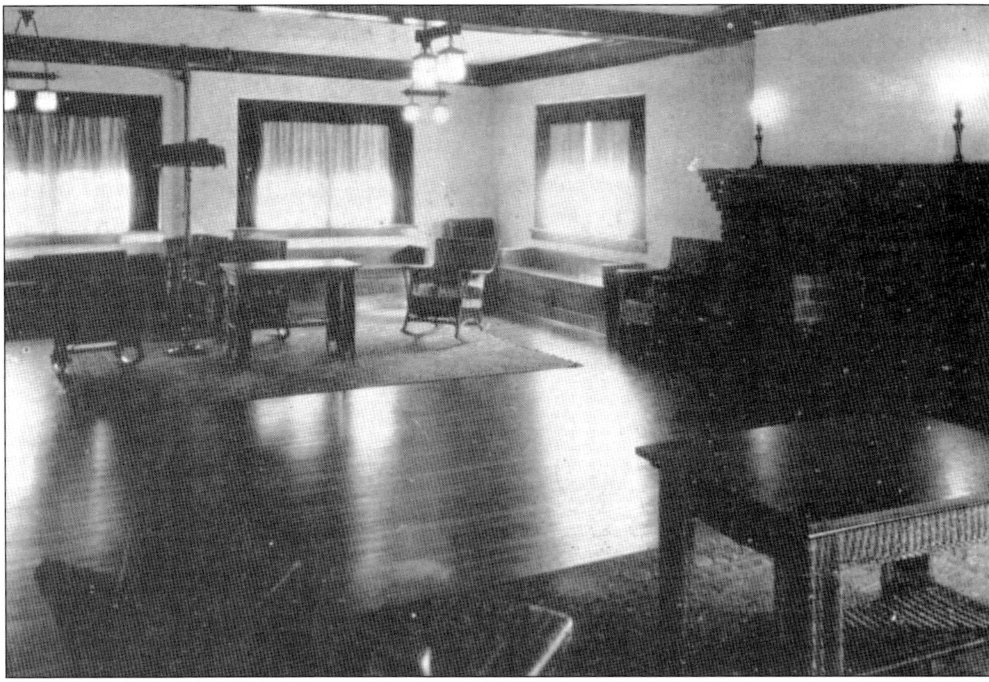

This is the parlor of Smith Hall in the early 1920s. The parlor was a warm, welcoming space where young ladies could entertain their gentlemen friends. It was certainly a room filled with happy memories, often of personal significance.

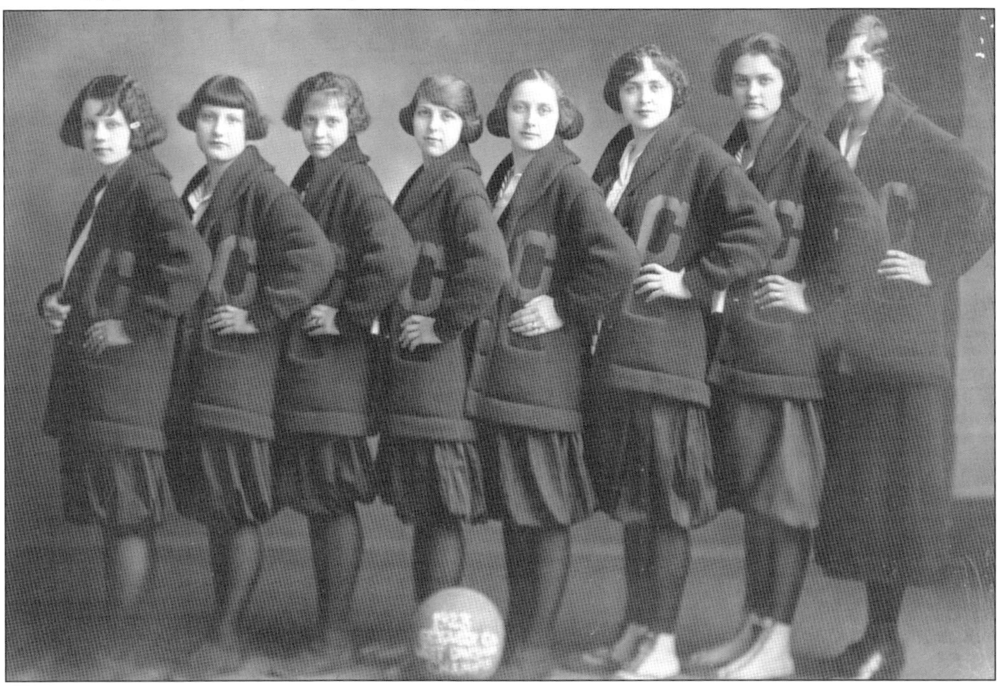

From shortest to tallest, the Southwestern girls' basketball team lines up with coach Lillian Cloud (far right). In the 1920s, girls' basketball was an extremely popular sport, enjoyed by all. Years later, the team became known as the Lady Builders.

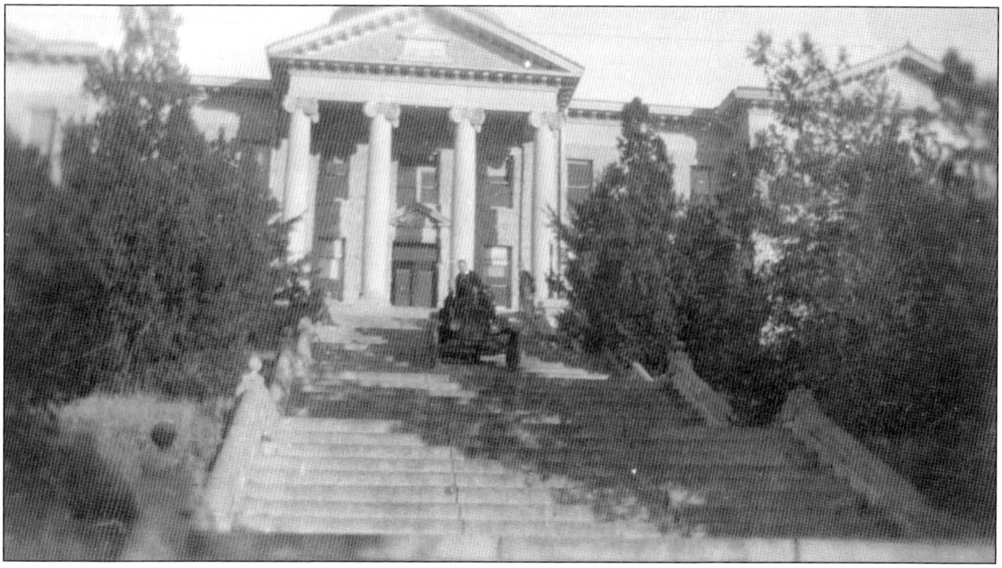

Zany happenings were common on campus in the boisterous 1920s. In 1922, as documented for posterity in this photograph, a courageous student drove a Model T Ford down the 77 Steps. If nothing else, this exercise proved that a Model T could take almost any punishment. A note accompanying the photograph indicates that school officials were not amused by this wacky prank.

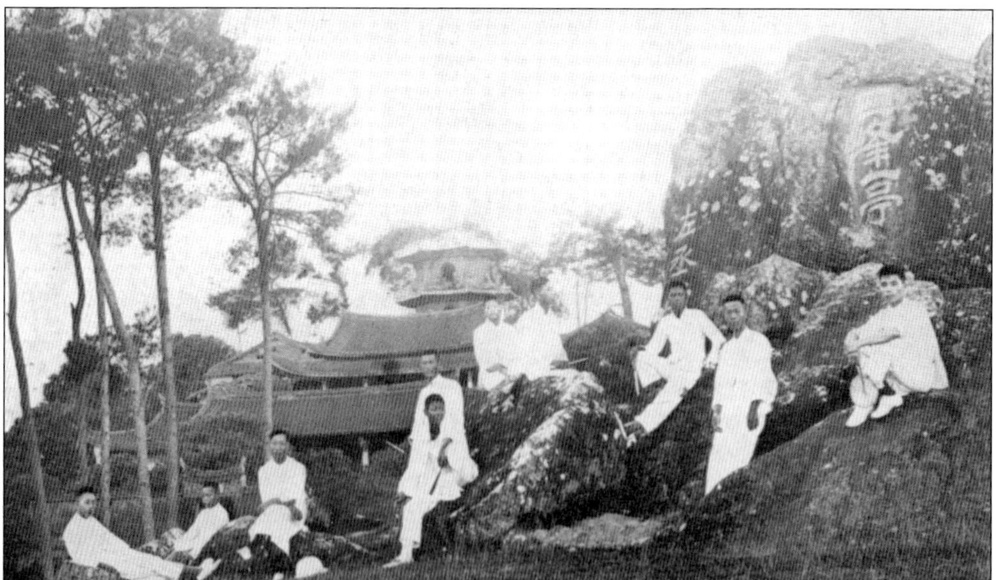

A group of students in China gather to send off a friend, Kang W. Huang (third from left), to study at Southwestern College. In the early 20th century, a large number of Chinese students attended Southwestern. After graduation, some furthered their education in the United States, while others went back to China, where they pursued careers in education. As published in the 1925 history *The Story of Southwestern*, "Seldom have a group of students been enjoyed as have Southwestern's friends from China, bringing with them oriental courtesy, application and fine arts new to the careless West."

Three

Depression and War Years 1929–1949

In October 1928, Dr. Ezra T. Franklin became Southwestern's president. The trustees had chosen Franklin, known as a "college economist," to bring fiscal order to the school, which, after years of exceptional growth, faced challenging budget and endowment problems. Franklin acted forcefully to address these concerns, but regrettably, his actions inspired opposition and dissent rather than cooperation, and the situation only worsened. Lacking the confidence of the college community, President Franklin resigned on January 14, 1931.

In this hour of crisis, the trustees turned to a proven leader: Frank E. Mossman. It had been 13 years since his departure from Southwestern, but he returned on June 1, 1931. Over the next 11 years, Mossman would work to restore and stabilize Southwestern by balancing its budget, cutting its debt, and growing its endowment. This was hard work, indeed, during these years of austerity—but he did succeed. President Mossman retired in the spring of 1942 to the plaudits of all, after faithfully serving the college for 24 years.

During World War II, Southwestern was presided over by Charles E. Schofield. For a time, the school participated in Navy training programs, which kept men on campus, but as these programs expired, males became quite scarce due to the draft. Of necessity, football ended. In a Christian spirit, the school leadership, after overcoming some opposition, offered young Japanese Americans the opportunity to complete their education. Eventually, thinking and planning began about Southwestern's future in the postwar world. Dr. Schofield resigned in December 1944. Mearl P. Culver succeeded him in May 1945, as the war approached its end.

Culver presided over the college's peacetime transition. Notable was the arrival of veterans on campus, thanks to the GI Bill. They were mature young men, many married with families, and they brought a distinct change of atmosphere to the campus. Most of the old Methodist bans on dancing, smoking, and card playing passed into history. The school secured former military barracks for use as classrooms, dormitories, and apartments. President Culver resigned in June 1949 and was followed that fall by Dr. Alvin W. Murray, who would soon face the challenge of a lifetime.

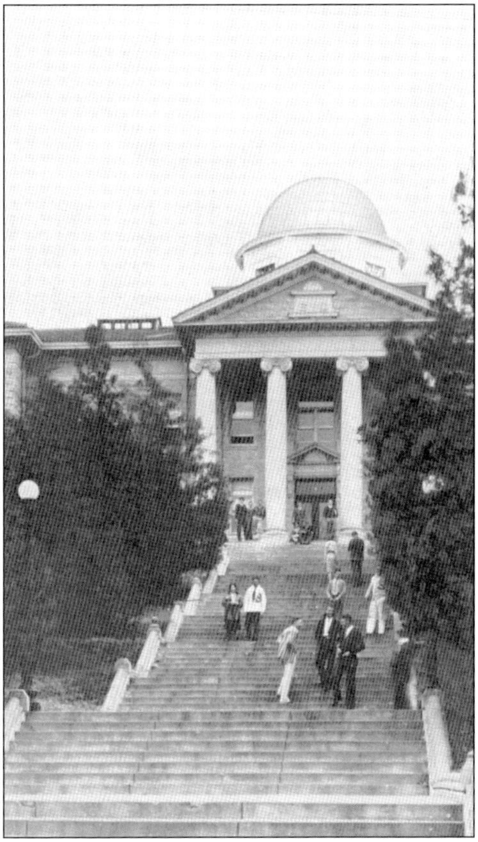

It is fall in the late 1920s. Southwestern students gather and chat on the 77 Steps, as had their predecessors and as would their successors. President Kirk is gone now, and a new man is in charge. The world itself is on the cusp of profound changes. These students have no inkling that the heady days of the Roaring Twenties are passing and that a time of depression and world war await them.

Ezra T. Franklin, a businesslike man, is seen here at his desk, ready to take on the financial challenges facing Southwestern College. Franklin identified the problems and proposed solutions, but he failed to gain the support of the board, faculty, and students in implementing them. There was discord, and Franklin eventually had enough. He packed his grip and departed.

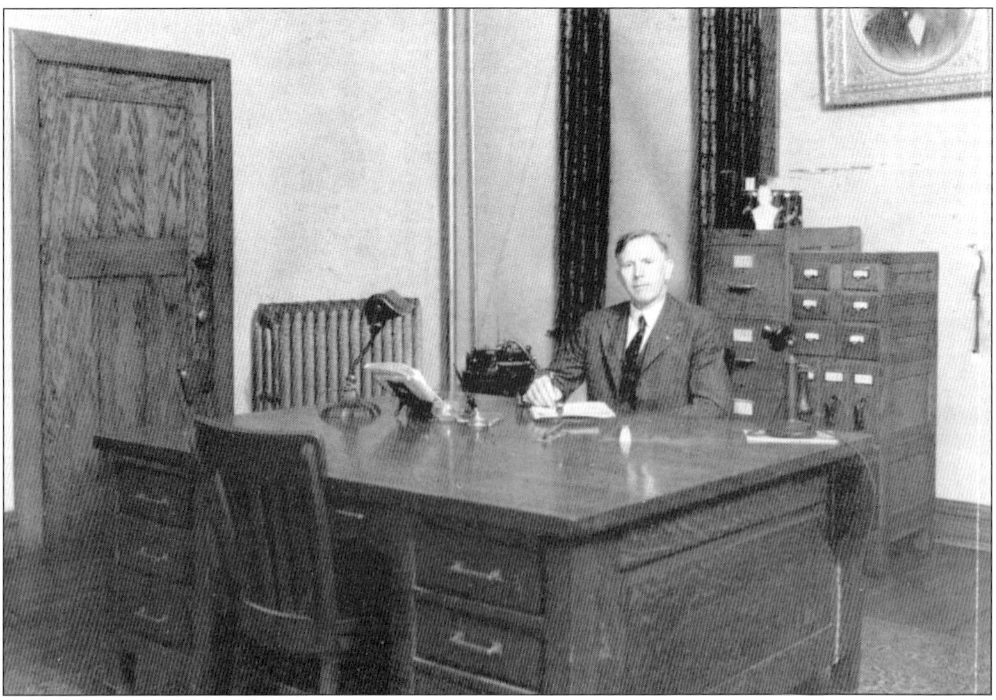

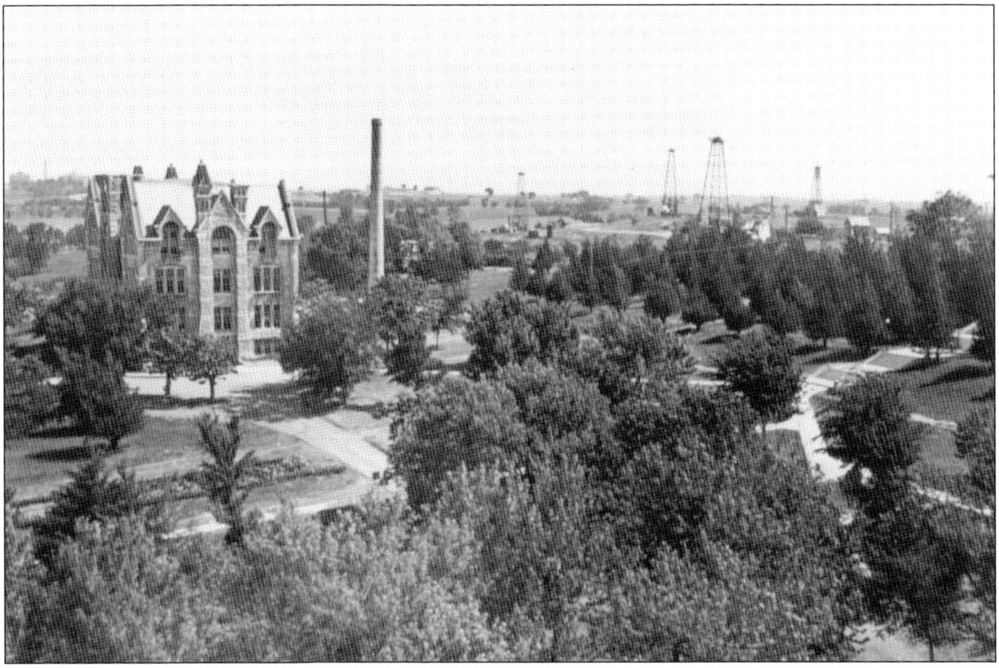

This photograph of Old North Hall and environs was taken from an oil derrick located near the President's House. Oil had been discovered early in the century in Cowley County; by the 1920s, it had been found around Winfield. Visible on the right are five oil wells, located to the northeast of the college campus. For several years, these derricks were actively pumping the "liquid gold."

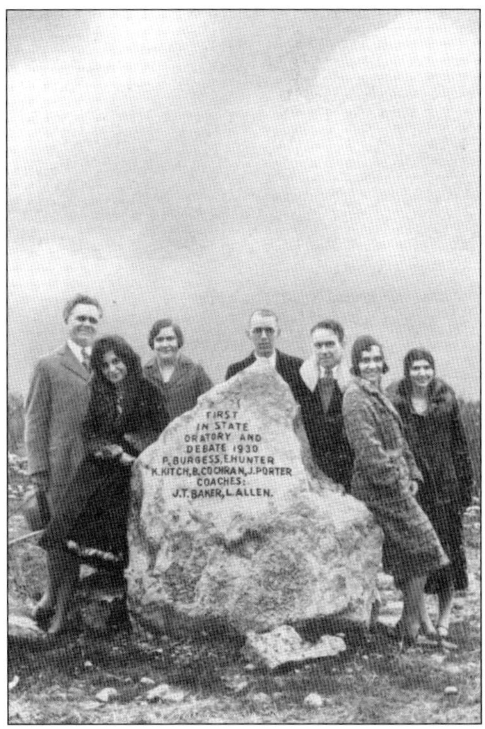

Dean Leroy Allen (far left) poses here with victorious Southwestern debaters, home from a decisive match. The group stands in front of a large rock commemorating another great win. Debate had long held a prominent place at Southwestern, especially in the years before sports came to prominence. When the school was young, literary societies encouraged debating and produced several exceptional debaters.

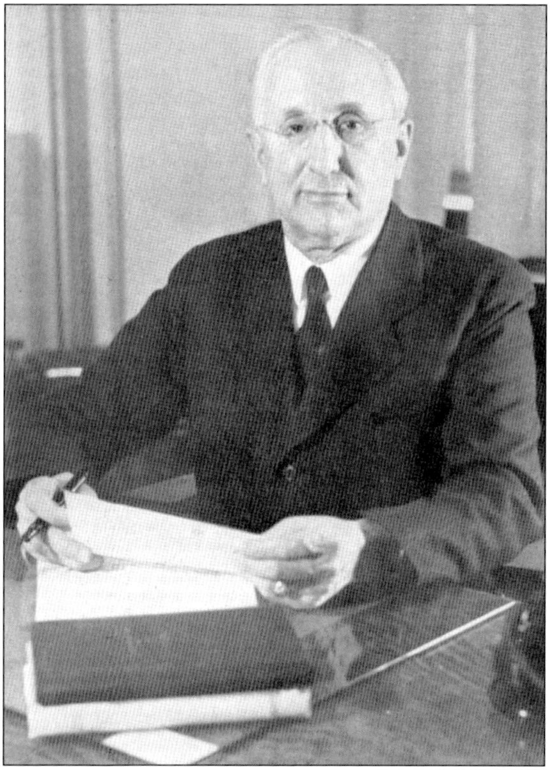

President Franklin may have left the college, but the problems he faced remained. With a critical financial situation that was damaging the school's academic standing, the board of trustees turned to former president Frank E. Mossman. He returned to the helm on June 1, 1931, and would successfully navigate the college through the lean Depression years. Mossman, who had announced his coming resignation in the fall of 1941, would resign in May 1942, his work done.

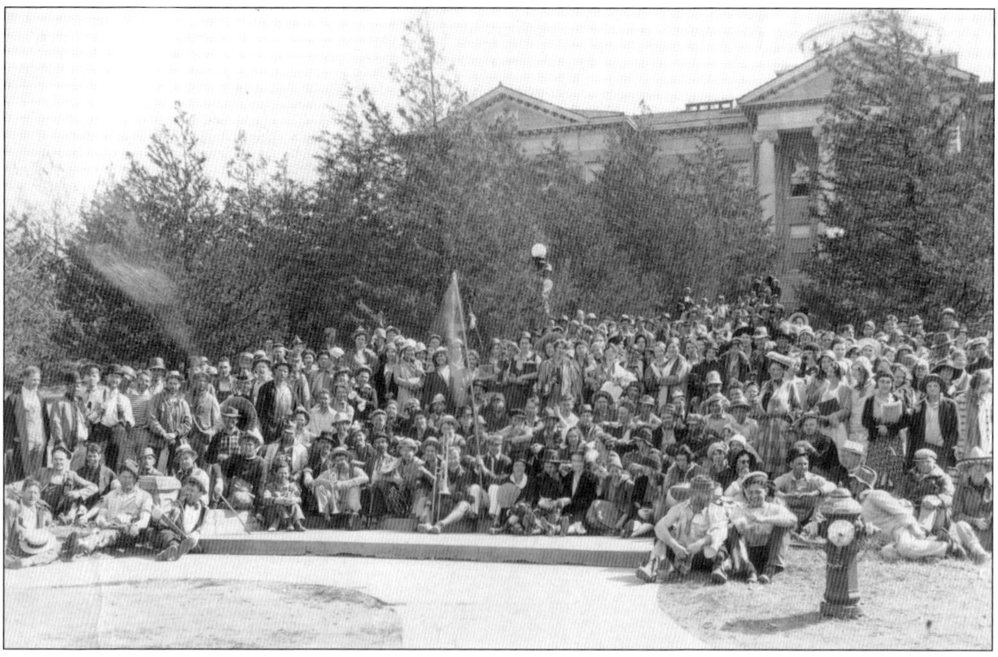

In the Depression year of 1933, students gather in front of Richardson Hall to participate in "Hobo Day." The students are dressed up in their poorest garb, looking very much like vagabond hobos ready to hop the next freight train. There is music, and all have a good time. Hobo Day became an annual event at the college for a number of years.

The May Fete took on a new elegance in the 1930s, reminding movie buffs of the grand, overly staged, and nattily costumed Hollywood movies of the era. The fete attracted large crowds from the campus and the community and featured dancing, singing, and theater performances, making it the premiere spring event. The all-school fete was directed by Lillian Cloud. The event ended in 1956 after almost 60 years.

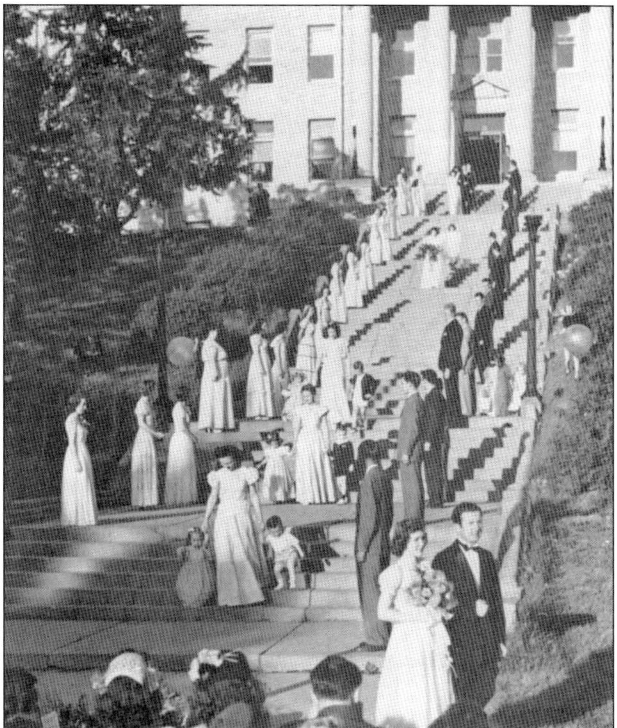

Processional . . . Annual May Day Fete

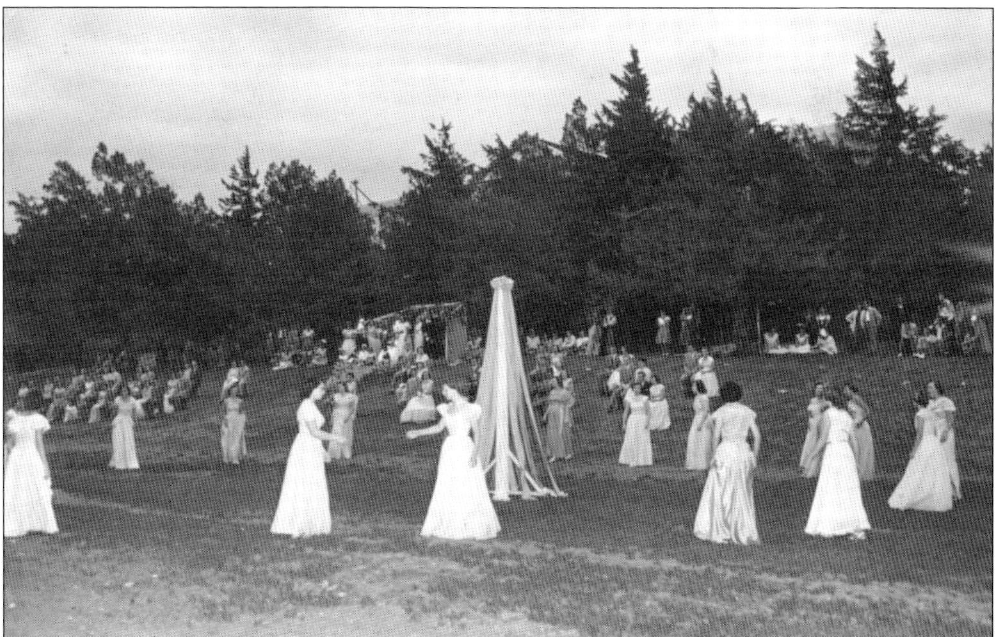

During the May Fete festivities, participants would reach the bottom of the 77 Steps and walk over to the area just east of Deets Library. There, the color-filled maypole winding joyfully took place. The mood of this formal ceremony alluded to the romanticism promoted by Dean Allen.

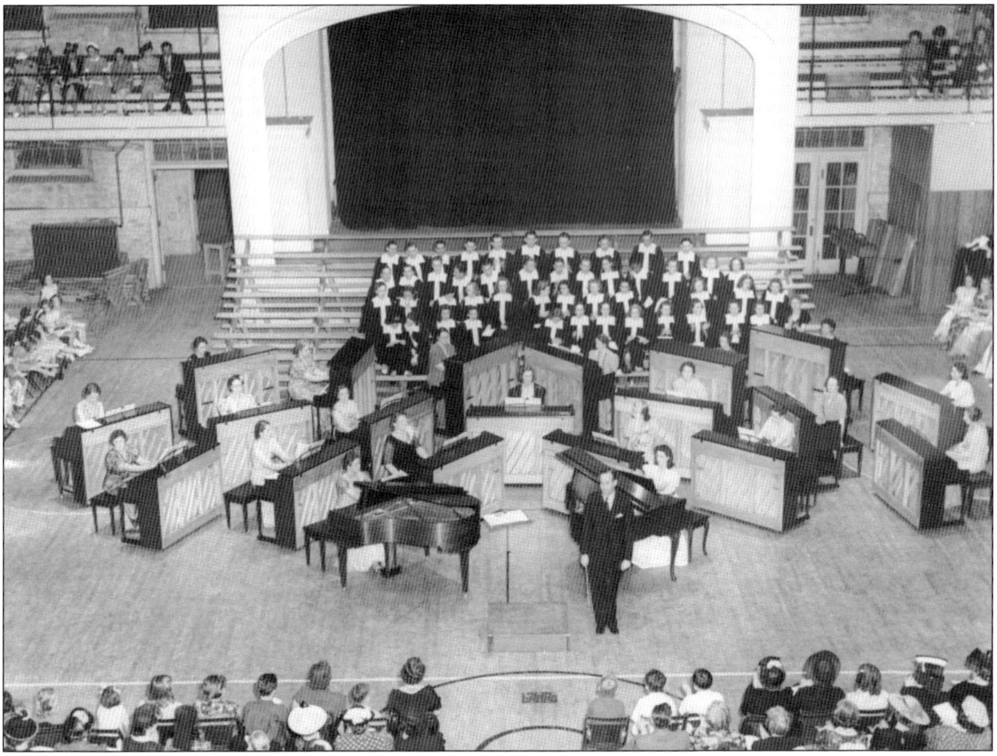

Music has always been important to Southwestern, ever since Ella Earp, the wife of the college's first president, established the music department. Here, 21 pianos were brought into the field house for a special choral concert opened to the public.

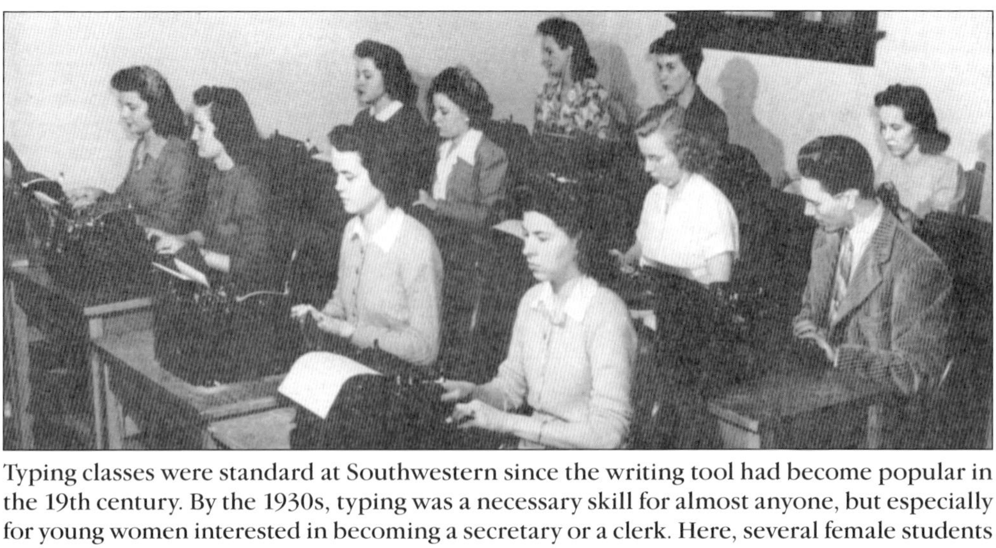

Typing classes were standard at Southwestern since the writing tool had become popular in the 19th century. By the 1930s, typing was a necessary skill for almost anyone, but especially for young women interested in becoming a secretary or a clerk. Here, several female students and a single male student pound away at their manual typewriters to master speed and error-free typing.

As the 1930s came to a close, militarism filled the air. This magnificent photograph of marching Southwestern women with their Jinx banners held high under a blue Kansas sky bears the caption: "Pageantry . . . and the battle-flags of the Builders presage victory."

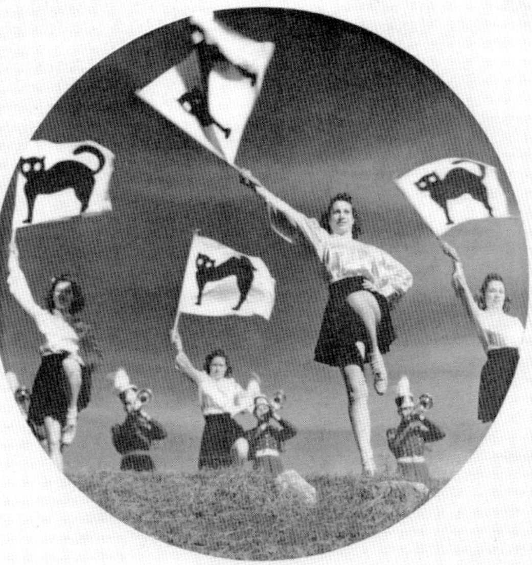

PAGEANTRY . . . AND THE BATTLE-FLAGS OF THE BUILDERS PRESAGE VICTORY

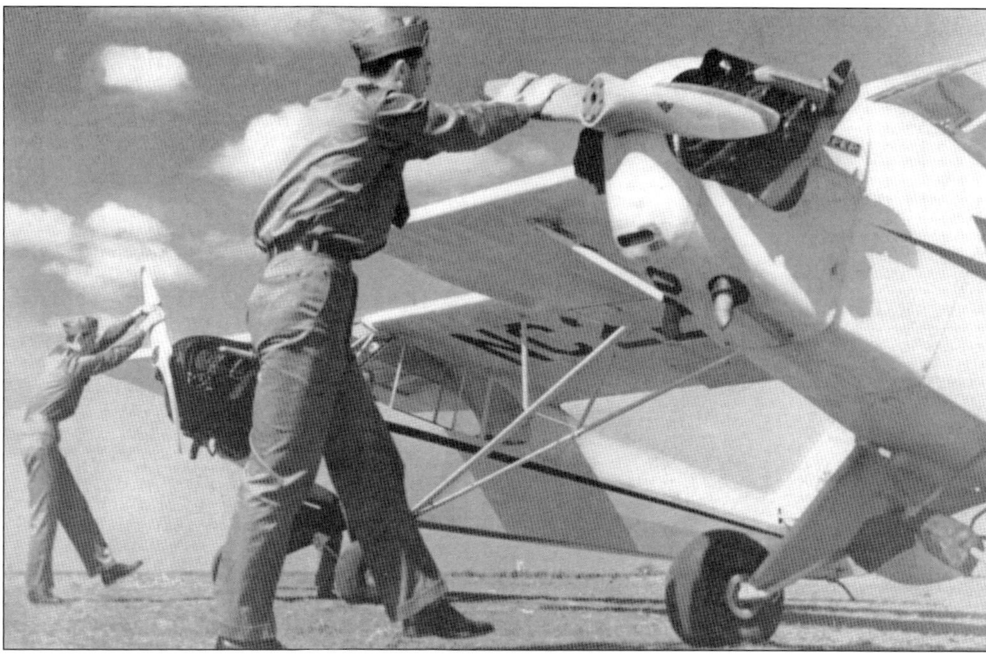

In 1939, as the clouds of war gathered, Penrose S. Albright, a popular professor, obtained for Southwestern students a government-sponsored course in civil pilot aviation. By February 1942, sixty-one men and three women had received private pilot's licenses. In this 1940 photograph, "Flying Builders" start the propellers on training aircraft at the Winfield Municipal Airport. Albright, it should be noted, loved flying, and his father, P.H. Albright, had been a trustee and a generous donor to the college.

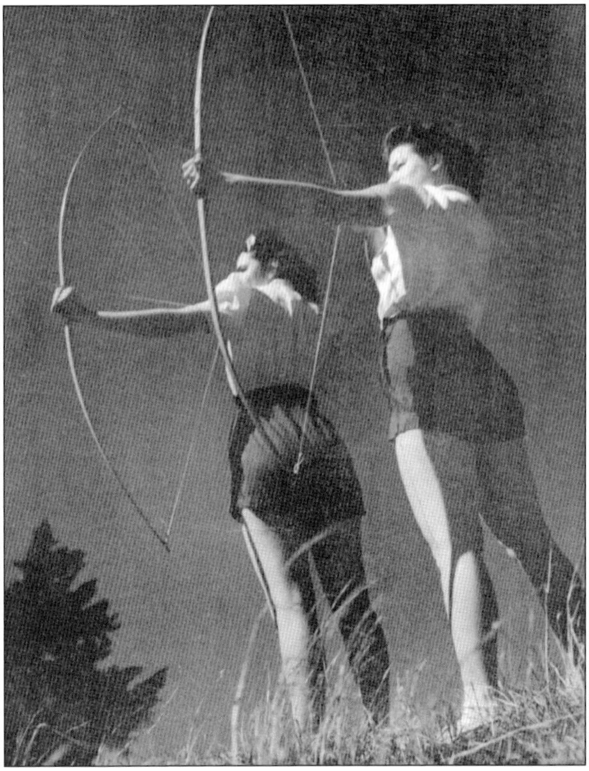

A new sport came to Southwestern in the last years of the 1930s: archery. Here, Southwestern women archers aim their arrows at the bull's-eye. Skilled archers that they are, they will undoubtedly hit the mark. This photograph is captioned: "S.C. has two aspirants to the skill of William Tell in Margaret Matthews (left) and Mary Jane Dean."

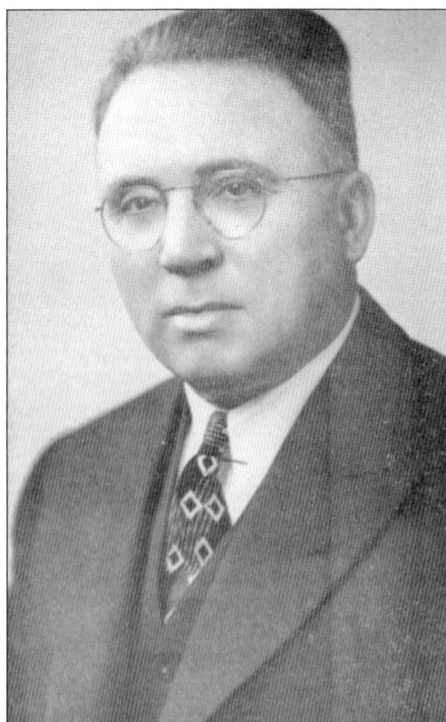

PRESIDENT CHARLES E. SCHOFIELD

In May 1942, Pres. Charles E. Schofield assumed office. The next month, the first group of naval aviation cadets arrived on campus for training. Schofield led the college through the war years, notable for the absence of men on campus and the arrival of Japanese American students. Schofield also initiated plans for the school in the coming postwar years, much of which was later realized.

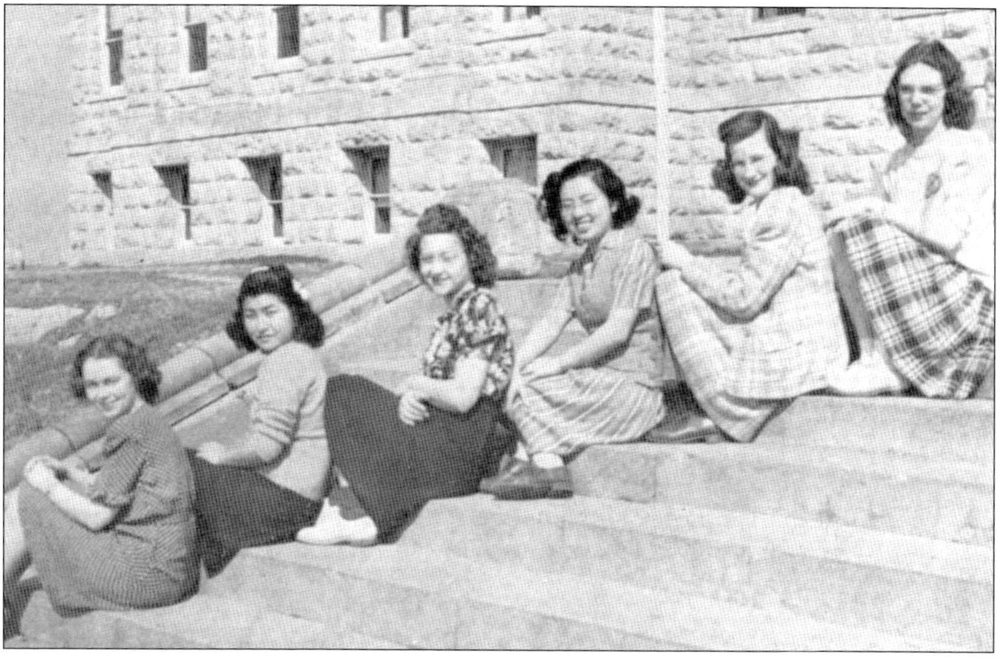

During the war, women had taken over the campus. These young ladies, seated on the 77 Steps, were given special recognition in the fall 1944 honor assembly as holders of Moundbuilder and special scholarship awards. They are, from left to right, Edith June Light, Yoshie Fujita, Ruth Akers, Masako Kamei, Doris Mossman, and Jeanette Doughty.

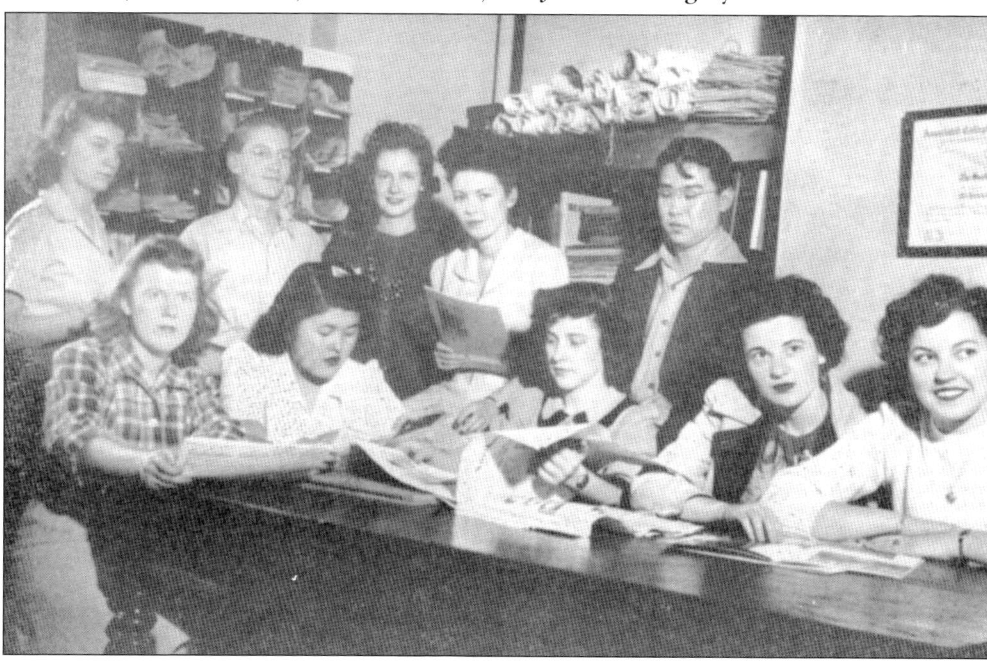

Hard at work covering the news of the day is the 1944 wartime staff of the *Collegian* newspaper. Pictured here are, from left to right, (first row) Natalie Nelson, Mary Nakahiro, Mary Miller, Neloese Johnson, and Wanda Holt; (second row) Norma Richards, Joseph Buckles, Virginia Lee Roberts, Gene Farrar, and Paul Hagiya.

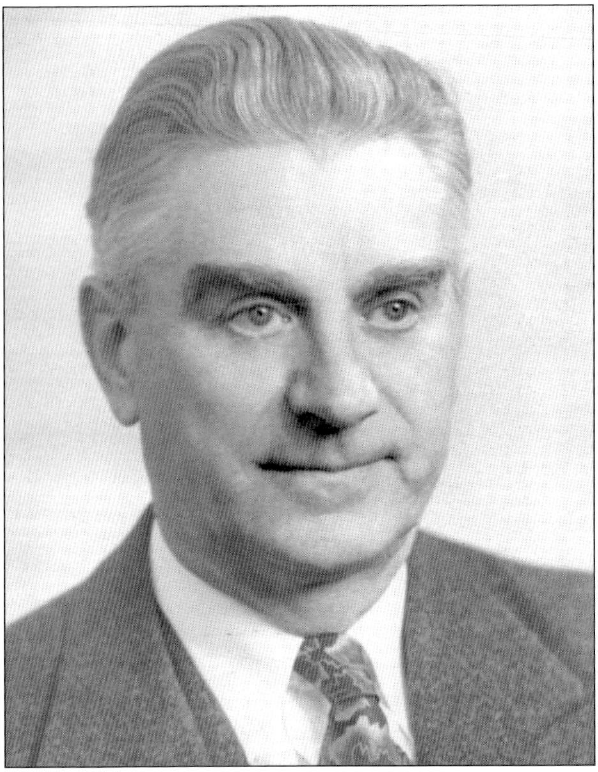

Mearl P. Culver took over the presidency of Southwestern on May 1, 1945, as World War II wound down. He would oversee the school's transition to peacetime. Planning done during war for the college's future was now implemented. Notable during this period was the building of classrooms, apartments, and dormitories using surplus Army barracks, along with other substantial upgrades in the physical plants, expansion of the faculty, and improvements in the curriculum.

The postwar years saw an inflow of foreign students onto campus, establishing a trend that continues to this day. Here, students from Nigeria, Hawaii (then a US territory), Bolivia, and Mexico line up on the steps leading into Richardson Hall in 1947.

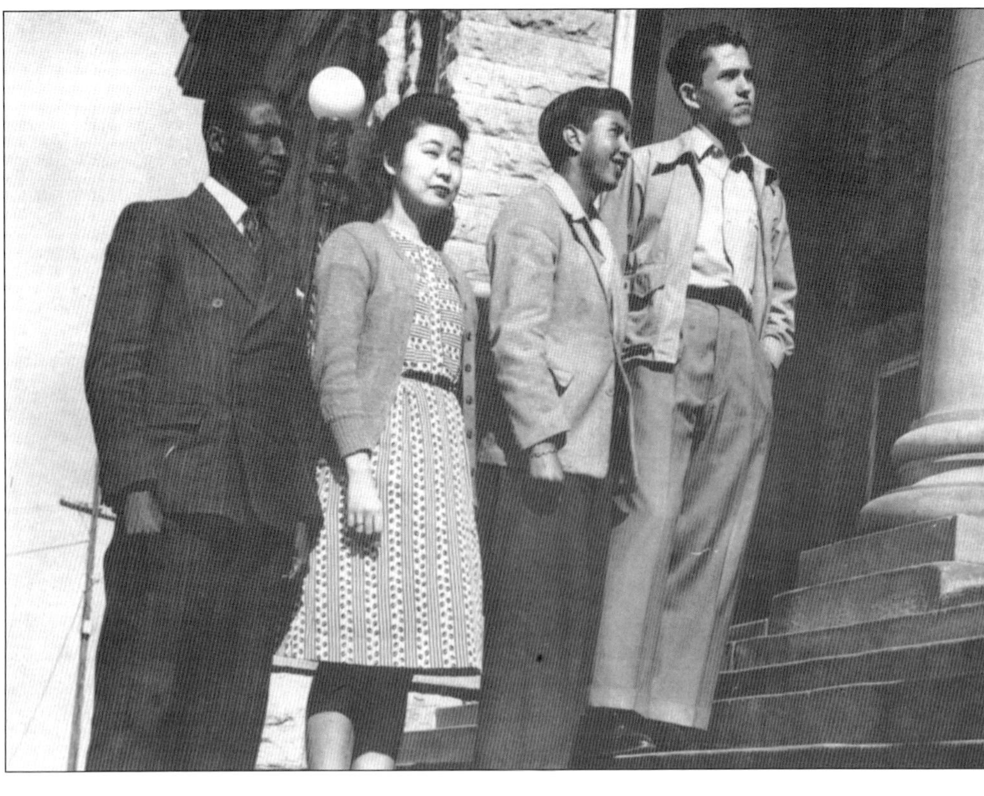

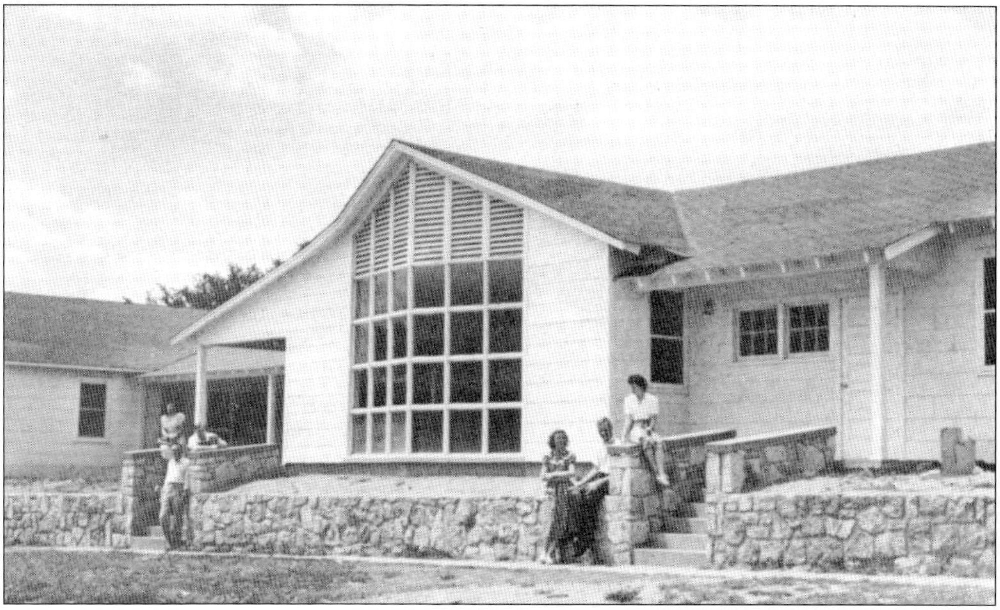

A new Student Union was a welcome addition to the campus. Constructed from military barracks, the attractive facility featured a large window in the fashionable lounge area. The building was located near the field house and was a popular meeting spot for students.

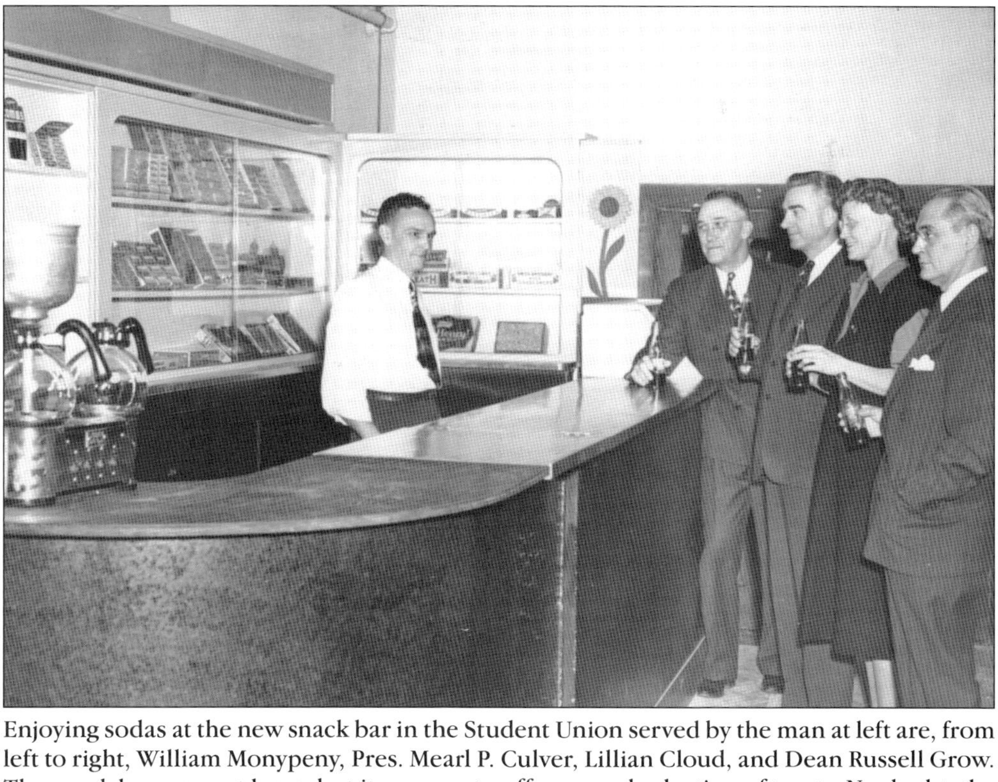

Enjoying sodas at the new snack bar in the Student Union served by the man at left are, from left to right, William Monypeny, Pres. Mearl P. Culver, Lillian Cloud, and Dean Russell Grow. The snack bar was not large, but it appears to offer a good selection of treats. No doubt, the students made good use of it.

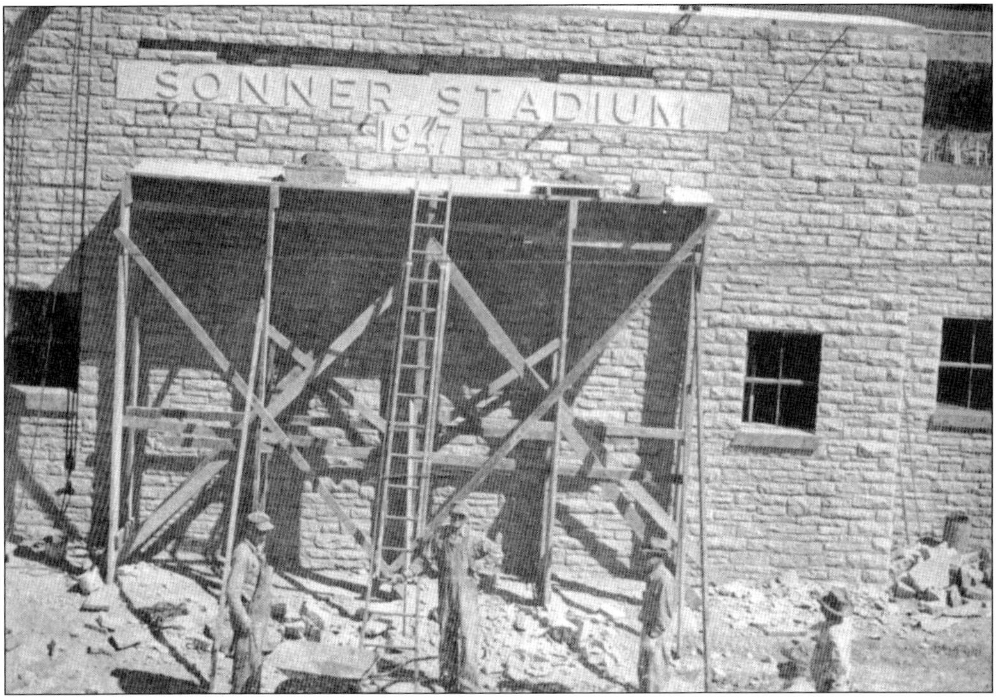

One of the major building projects of the early postwar period was that of Sonner Stadium in 1947. This much-needed facility was the gift of P.J. Sonner, a Winfield industrialist. The stadium was necessary for the development of Southwestern athletics. Seen here under construction, it would be used for many years to come.

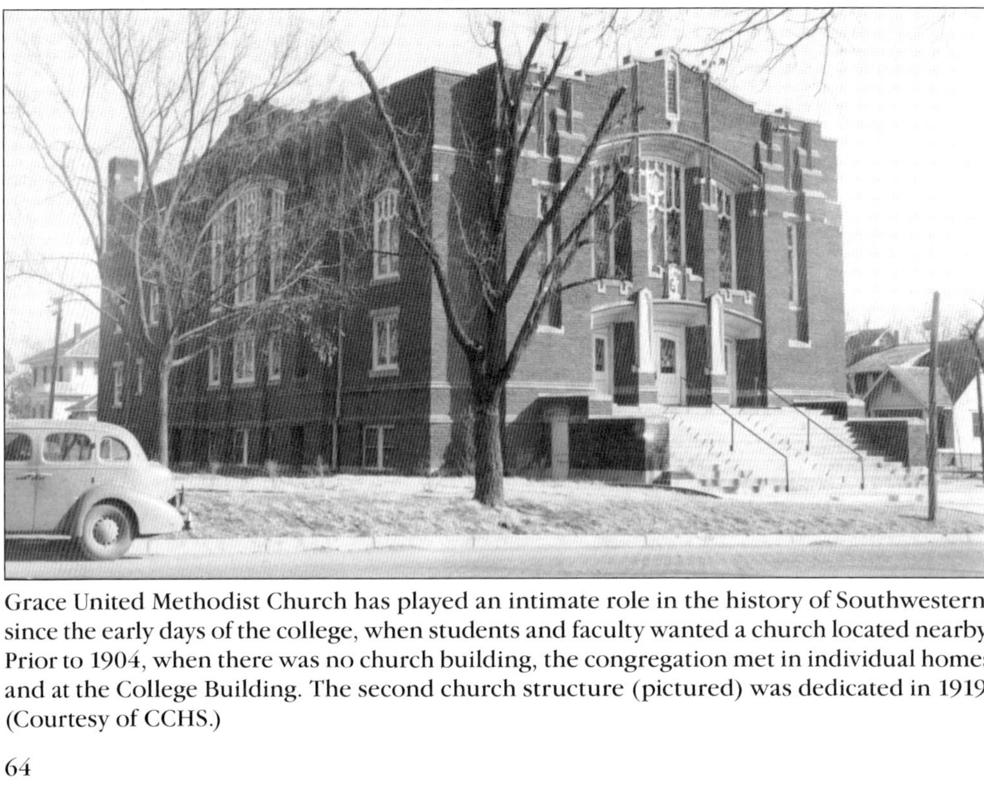

Grace United Methodist Church has played an intimate role in the history of Southwestern, since the early days of the college, when students and faculty wanted a church located nearby. Prior to 1904, when there was no church building, the congregation met in individual homes and at the College Building. The second church structure (pictured) was dedicated in 1919. (Courtesy of CCHS.)

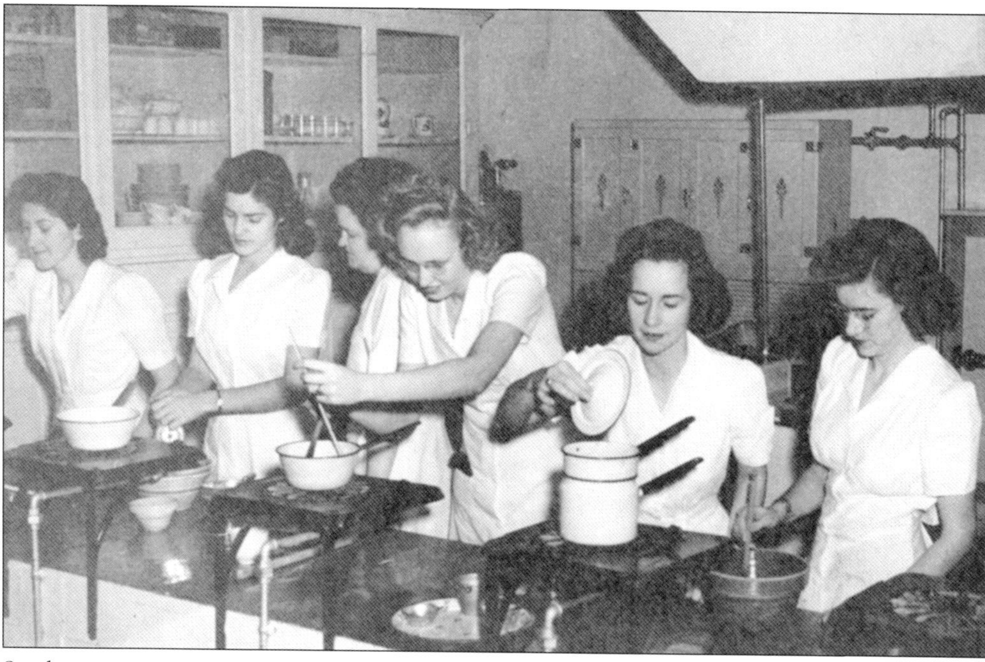

Students practice meal preparation as part of their home-economics training. In an era when most women married, had children, and oversaw their home, such training was valuable in preparing them for adult responsibilities. Home economics was an established part of the curriculum at Southwestern for many years.

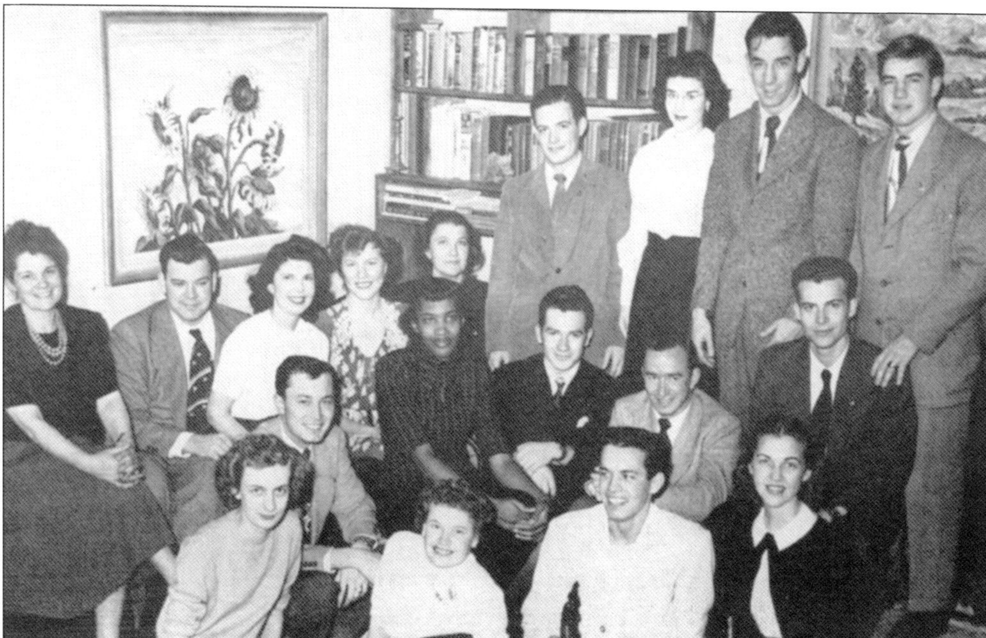

A Southwestern College art class is pictured with popular teacher Sue Jean Covacevich ('49, far left). Covacevich, an establish artist, put in place the school's art department, which was located in North Hall. One of her sunflower paintings is shown in the background. Students were members of Kappa Pi, a national honorary art fraternity.

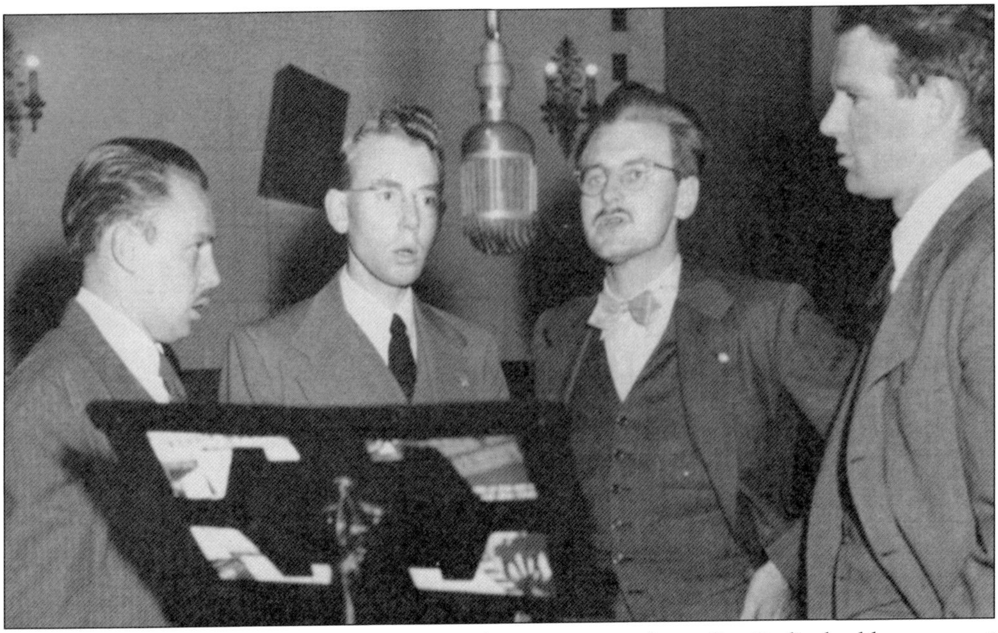

Here, Southwestern students present a vocal concert over the radio. Radio had been a part of the school's history since the early 1920s and later had its own facilities for students to study broadcasting. Leroy Allen was a regular on the radio in the 1930s. In the postwar years, Southwestern students and faculty were often on the air. In addition, school sporting events were aired. These broadcasts did much to publicize the college and its activities.

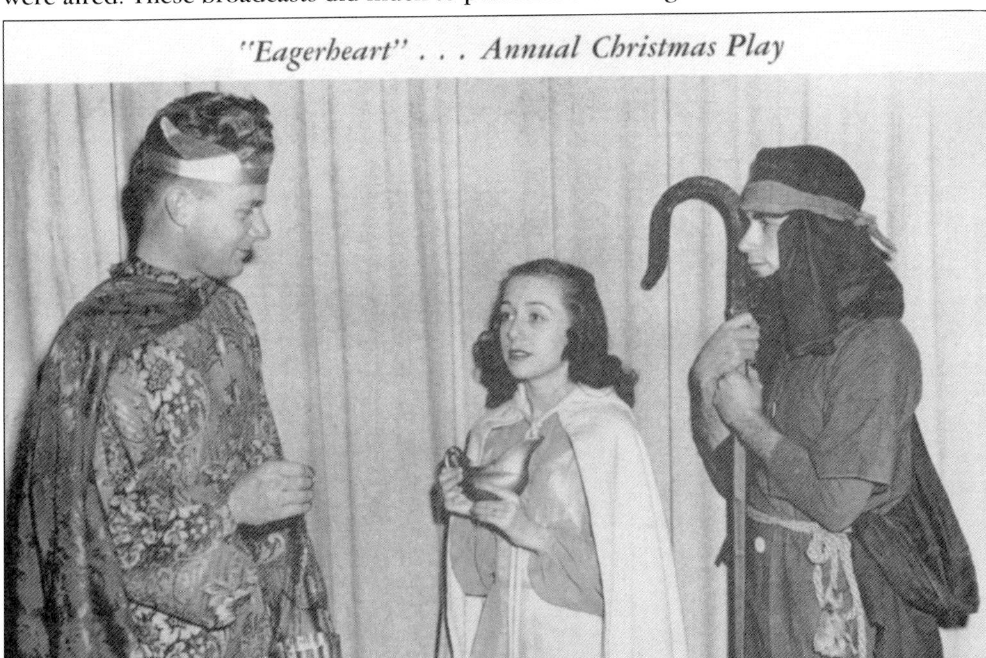

Since 1932, Southwestern students have regularly staged a presentation of *Eagerheart* at Christmastime. Shown here is a postwar presentation. The play, now a firmly established tradition, had its 82nd annual production in 2014.

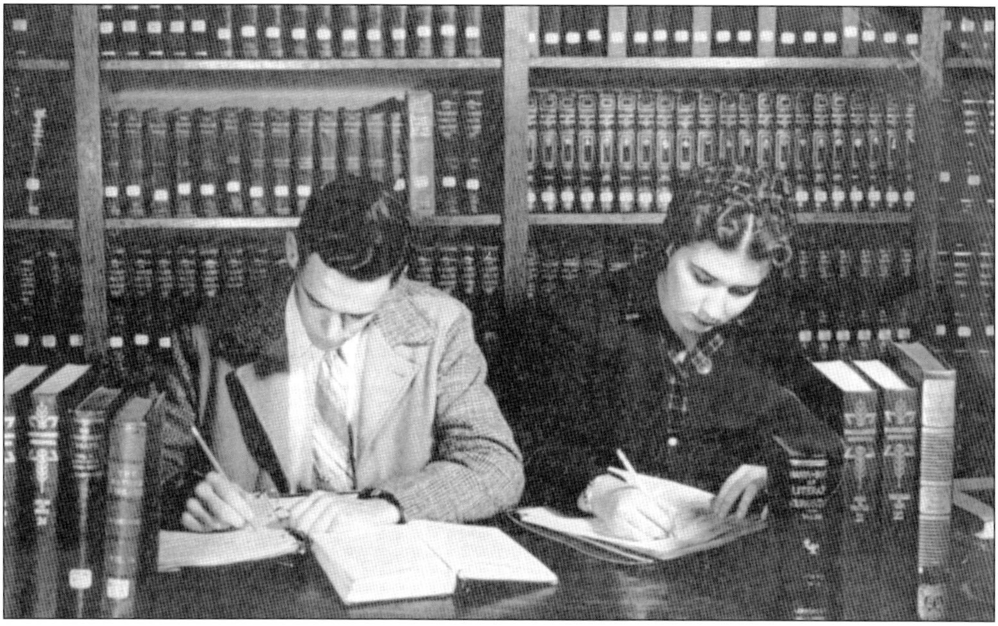

These Southwestern students are diligently researching in the library during the postwar years. At the time, the library was still located in the basement of the field house. It was supplied with a large variety of publications, which students turned to in the pre-Internet age. The science department had its own specialized library in North Hall, which included, thanks to professor Lawrence Oncley, a fine collection of chemistry journals.

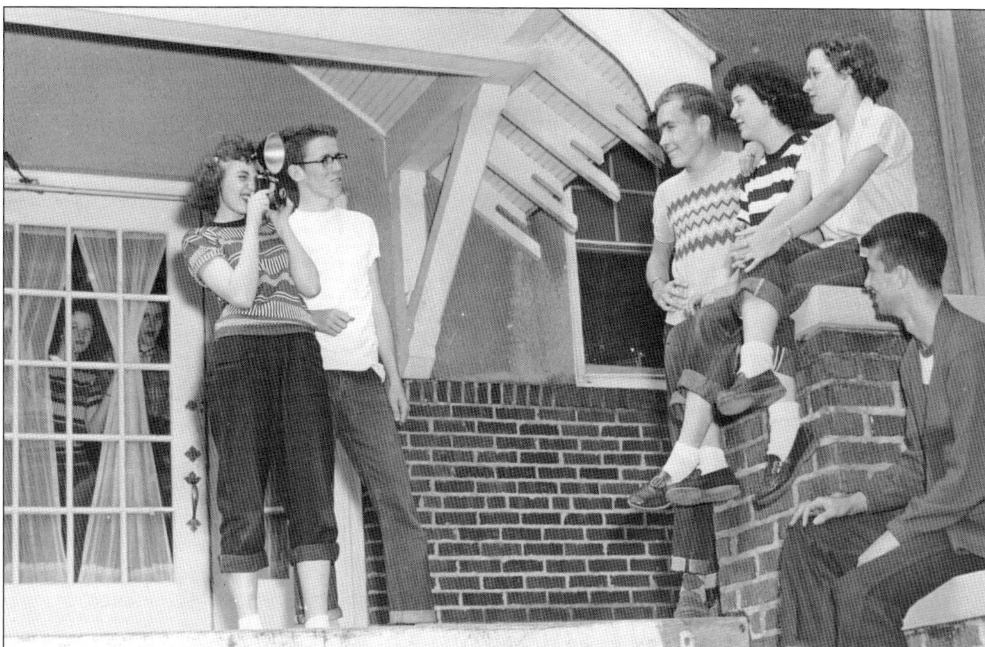

Peacetime has returned. Boys and girls gather to enjoy a spring afternoon on the front porch of Smith Hall. The young lady at left uses a new flash camera to record the occasion. Note the two curious girls peeking out from the door.

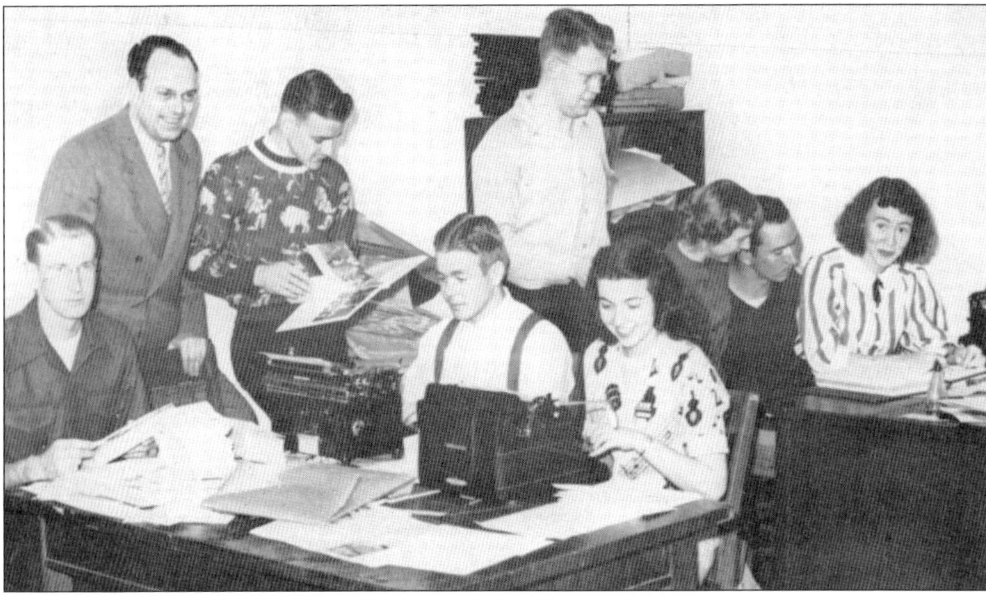

The *Moundbuilder* staff work on the 1949 publication. Shown here are, from left to right, Stanley Able, Earl W. Shaffer (advisor), William Scott, Sherman Edmondson, George Weber, Ruth Ellen Craig, Elma Dannenfelser, Robert Lloyd, and Joan Fennema.

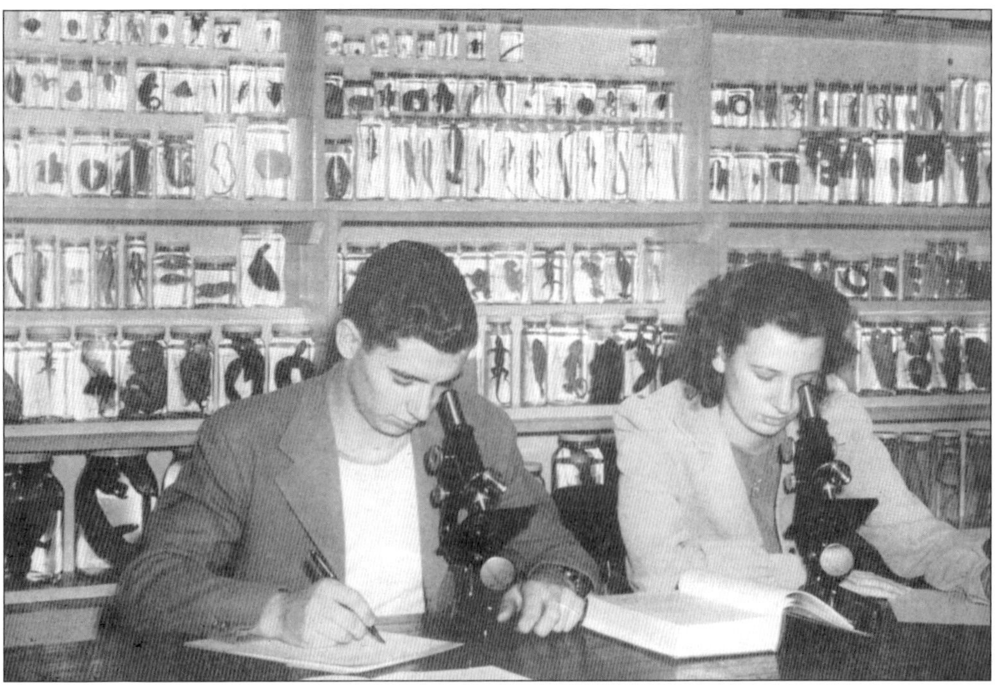

Southwestern College's science department had long received high praise. These young science students peer into microscopes. Note the well-stocked shelves of specimens behind them.

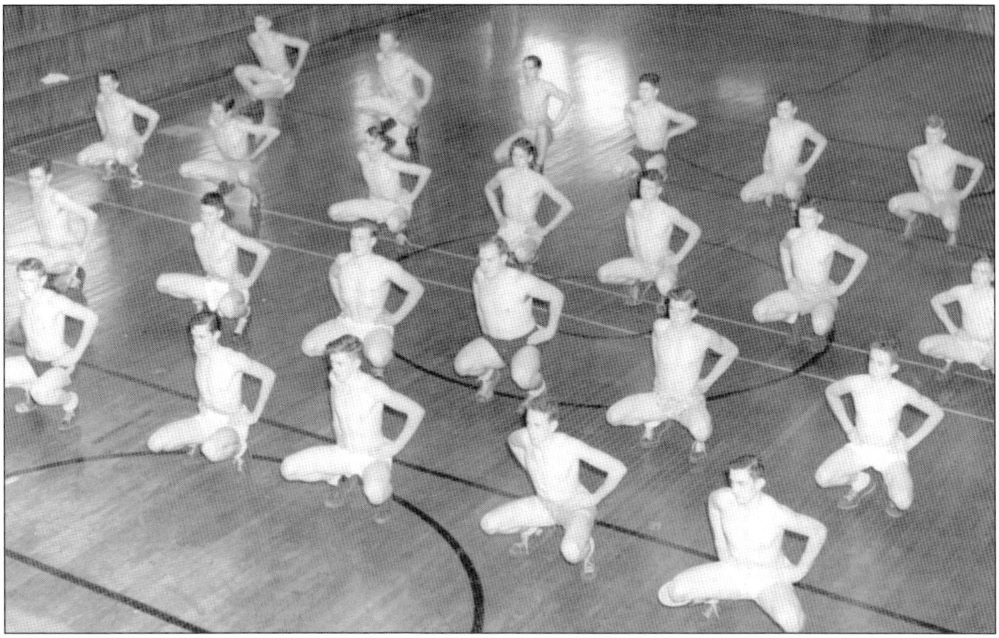

Southwestern did not have a physical education program until the construction of its first gym, the "Prexy's Barn," in early 1908. Fred H. Clapp (class of 1911) had charge of the first physical education classes, which were available for both men and women. One hour's credit was given. Here, men work out in the field house.

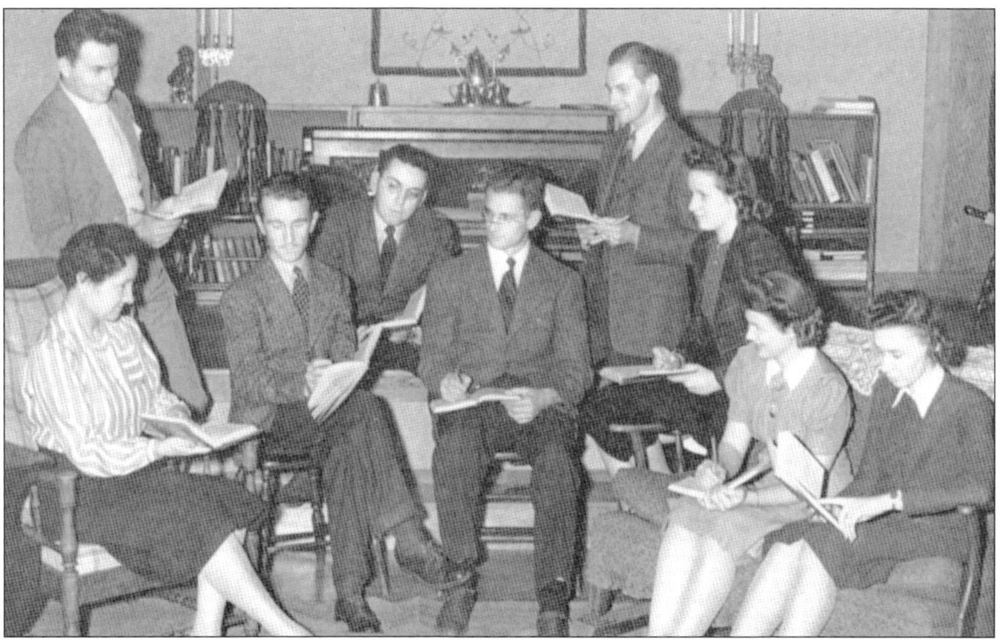

Helen Graham (class of 1919), who had taught drama at the school since the 1920s, is seen at far left with the campus players. They appear to be looking over the script of a new play. The actors had long been noted for their fine repertoire and outstanding performances. The 1948 homecoming play was *Thunder Rock*, a three-act mystic drama, and the 1949 commencement play was *Claudia*, a three-act comedy-drama.

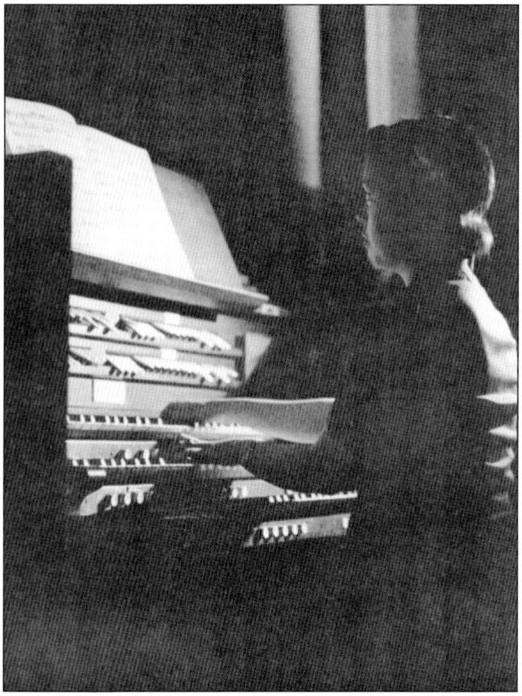

The Kibbe three-manual pipe organ was a gift of H.E. Kibbe to the college in 1938. A distinct addition to the college, it was installed in the auditorium of Richardson Hall. Over the years, students of the organ, like this young lady, were privileged to practice and give concerts on this fine instrument. The Southwestern Organ Club was formed around it.

The war is over, men are back on campus, and the weekend is near. Here, male students gather around their rooming house phone to line up dates. This Moundbuilder photograph is captioned, "Everybody helps Sam get a date."

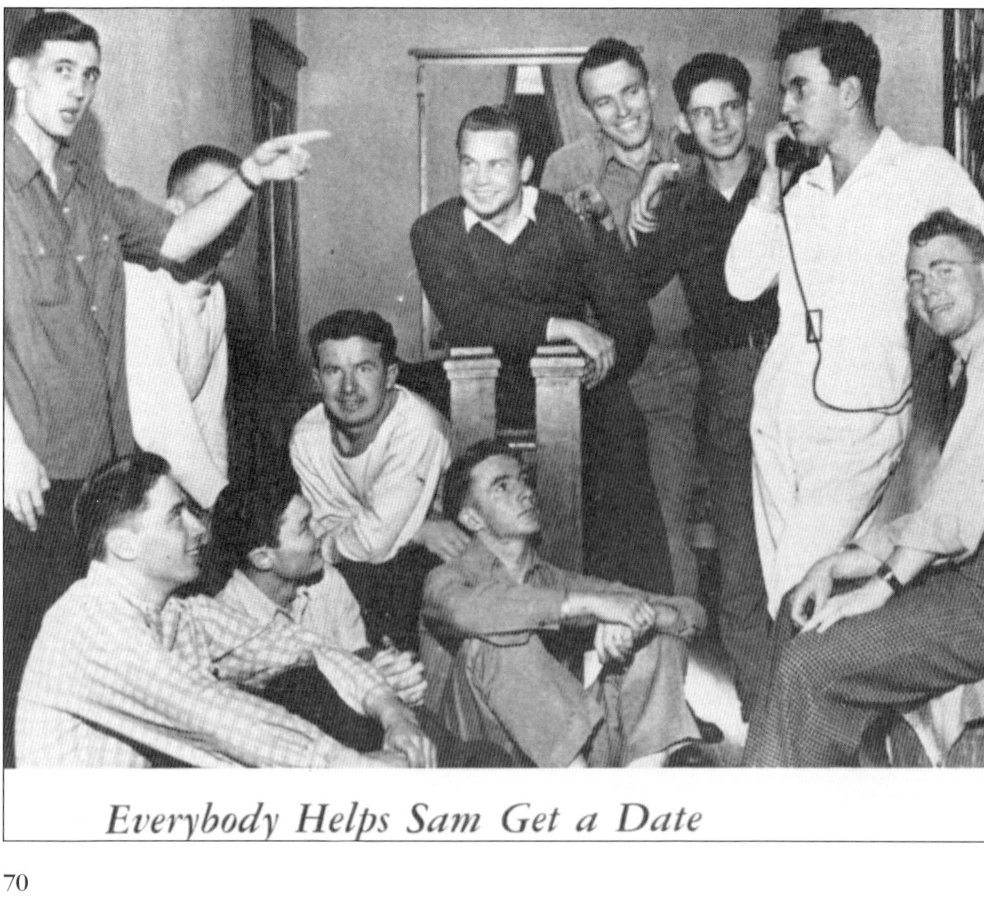

Everybody Helps Sam Get a Date

Four

FIRE'S DESOLATION 1950–1953

In the early hours of Sunday, April 15–16, 1950, Richardson Hall burned down, its flames lighting the sky for miles around. For 40 years, Richardson had provided administrative offices, classrooms, and an auditorium. The domed building at the crest of the hill was the symbol of Southwestern College and a Winfield landmark. Now, only its blackened walls remained; everything else had turned to ashes, except for the vital scholastic records in its fireproof vault.

Many of those gathered at the bottom of the 77 Steps that night thought the college was finished. Richardson was a burned-out shell, North Hall was being demolished, and there was ongoing debate about eliminating Southwestern by merging it into another institution.

Pres. Alvin White Murray, a great motivator and organizer, was determined to save the college. Indeed, as he prophetically proclaimed, this was "the dawn of a new day" for Southwestern. At once, he moved into action, inspiring confidence. He found temporary classroom space for several hundred students. Classes met Tuesday afternoon, thus only a half-day was lost to the fire.

The college was fortunate that Presidents Schofield and Culver had already started planning for a modern campus. Some funds had been raised for what would become Mossman Hall and a new Memorial Library. Dr. Murray pushed ahead with these plans, "making the dirt fly." He also started construction on a new administration building using Richardson's still-standing walls. Luckily, the old building had been well insured.

Dr. Murray's greatest challenge came on June 29, 1950, at a special session of the Central Kansas Methodist Conference in Hutchison. The delegates had to decide whether to go forward with Murray's "Million Dollar Building Program," or another option. Surrounded by Southwestern students and supporters shouting, "On Southwestern!" Murray delivered a persuasive, extemporaneous speech on behalf of the school. The delegates voted overwhelmingly to rebuild the college. Southwestern would live!

Afterwards, Dr. Murray raised funds for and oversaw the rebuilding program: Mossman was opened in September 1951, Memorial Library followed in November, and the new administration building opened in July 1952, although it required further work.

In June 1953, following a disagreement with the trustees, President Murray resigned, effective July 1. He departed knowing that the foundation was laid for a new and greater Southwestern College.

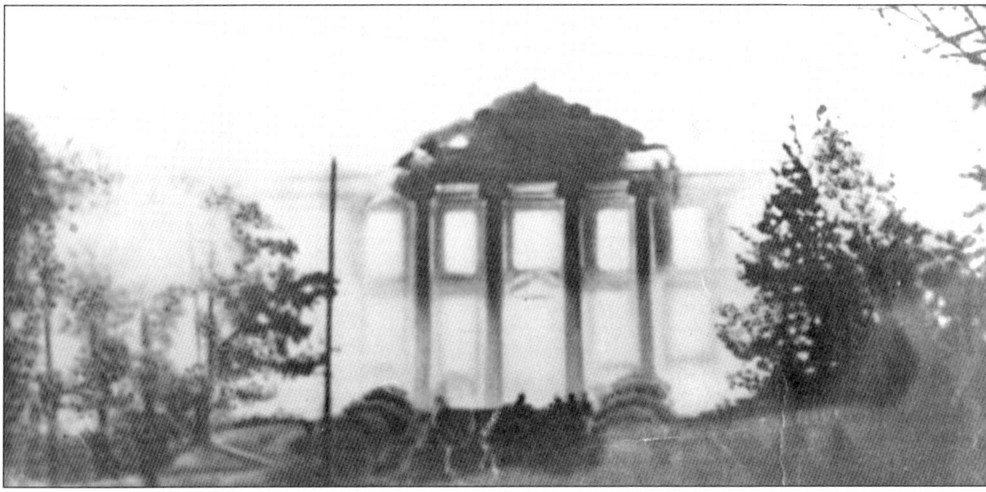

An inferno engulfs Richardson Hall. The symbol of the college and the center of its operations and activities went up in smoke, along with most of its valuable and irreplaceable holdings. Pulvis et Umbra (Dust and Shadows)!

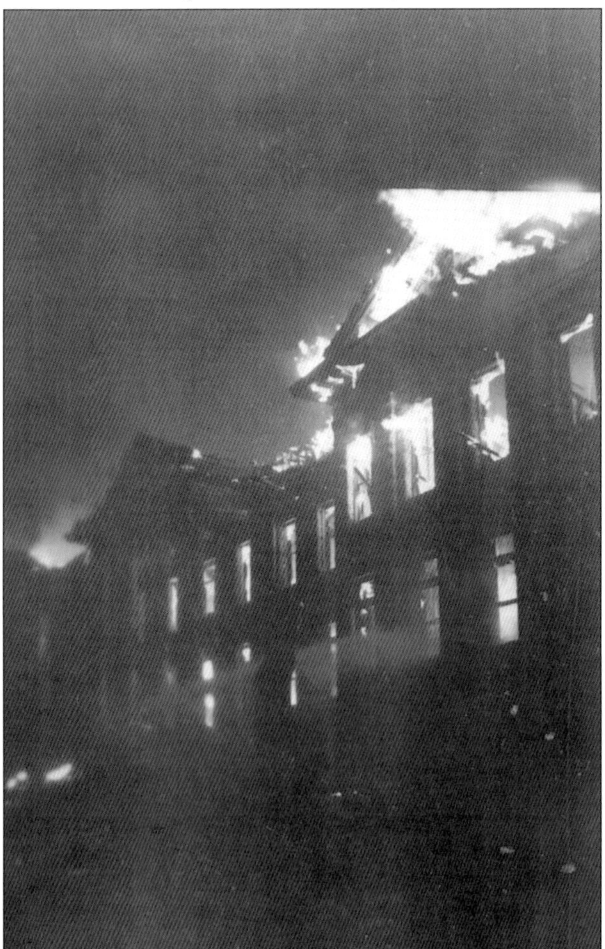

The Richardson Hall fire, speculation has it, started by spontaneous combustion in the basement as Saturday turned into Sunday, April 16, 1950. The fire spread rapidly down oak-finished corridors and through wooden doors and walls of plaster. The fire was discovered by two students, who called in the alarm, received at the firehouse at 12:19 a.m. The blaze worked its way up the rotunda's walls and through the dome above, transforming the rotunda into a giant flue.

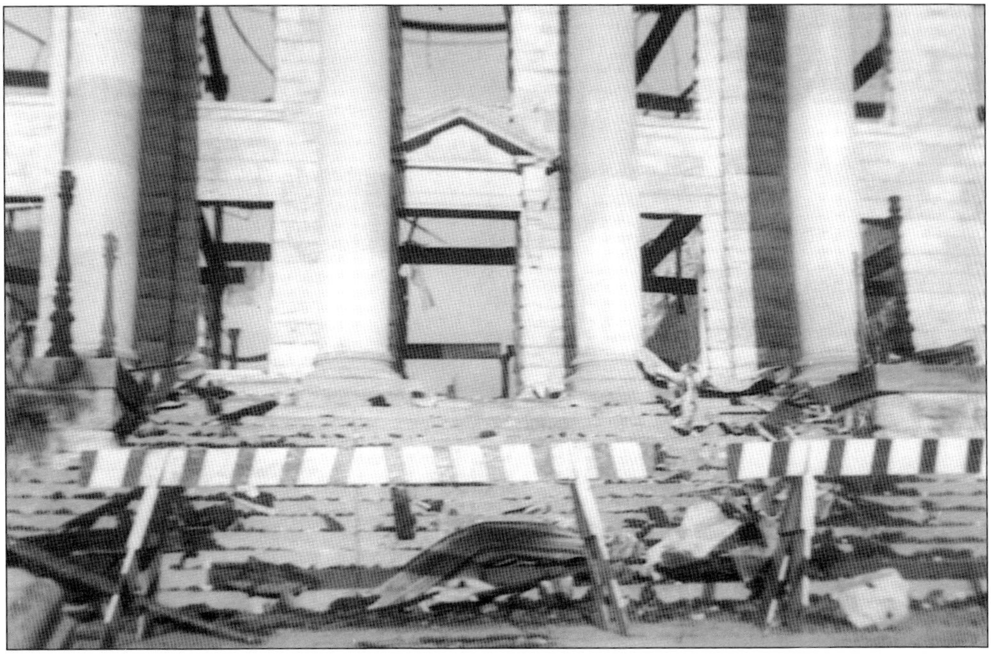

Local firemen and equipment were soon at the site, and more soon arrived from neighboring towns. The fire, moving quickly through the wooden interior, was by then out of control. The firemen worked to protect the vault containing important scholastic records. By the time firefighters finally subdued the flames at around 5:00 a.m., 300,000 gallons of water had been poured on the conflagration.

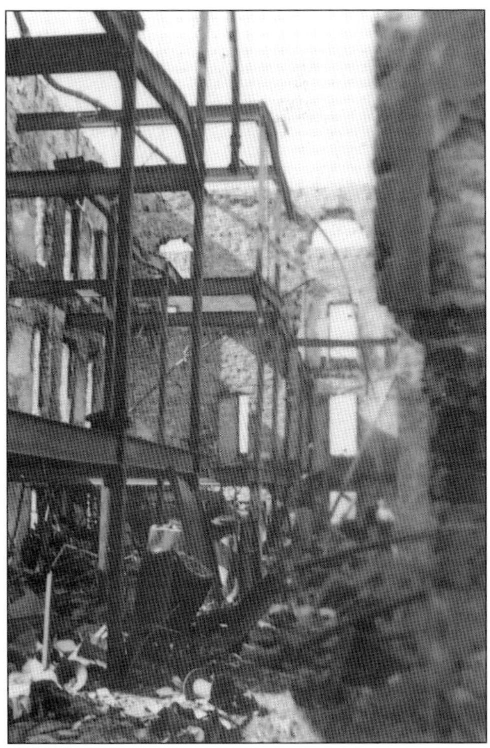

All that remained were darkened walls, windows looking out into empty space, and doors to nowhere. There had been no time to save the contents of Richardson Hall. Everything burned, other than certain vital records protected in a fireproof vault. Among the materials lost were professors' notes, lesson plans, books, diplomas, and personal effects; administrative and historical records; and memorabilia, such as trophies, photographs, paintings, and artifacts. On display in the rotunda were ceramic pieces by students, as well as the annotated Bible of pioneer preacher Peter Cartwright.

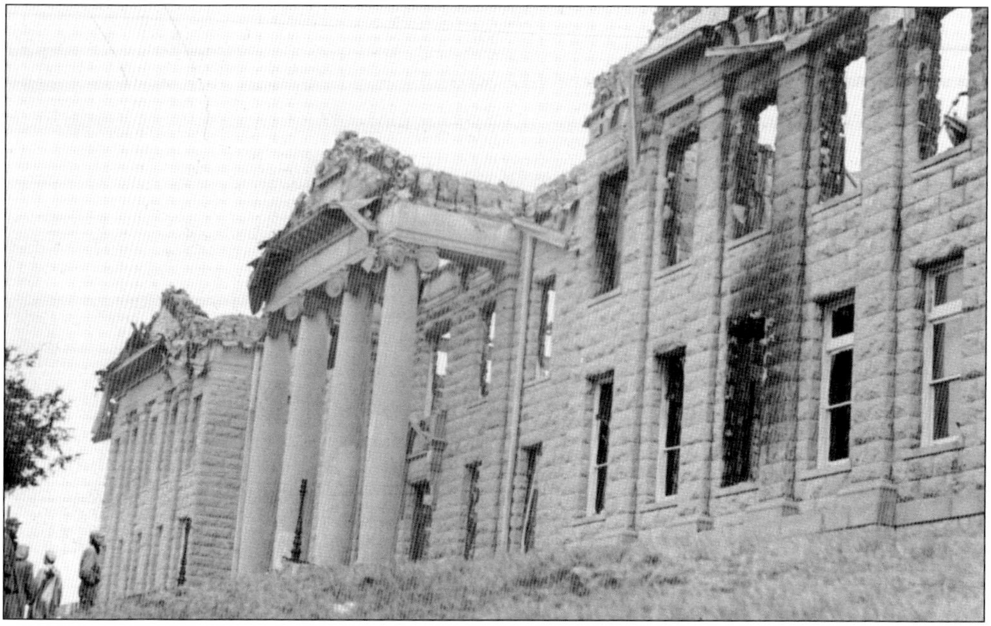

As written the *Moundbuilder*, "Although ravaged by fire, Richardson Hall will rise again." Following the disaster, this sentiment resonated among the college's students, faculty, and staff, as well as with the greater Winfield community and many in the Central Kansas Methodist Conference. In a rallying speech to a student assembly two days after the fire, President Murray said, "I know now [the fire] was not a midnight experience, but rather the dawn of a new day."

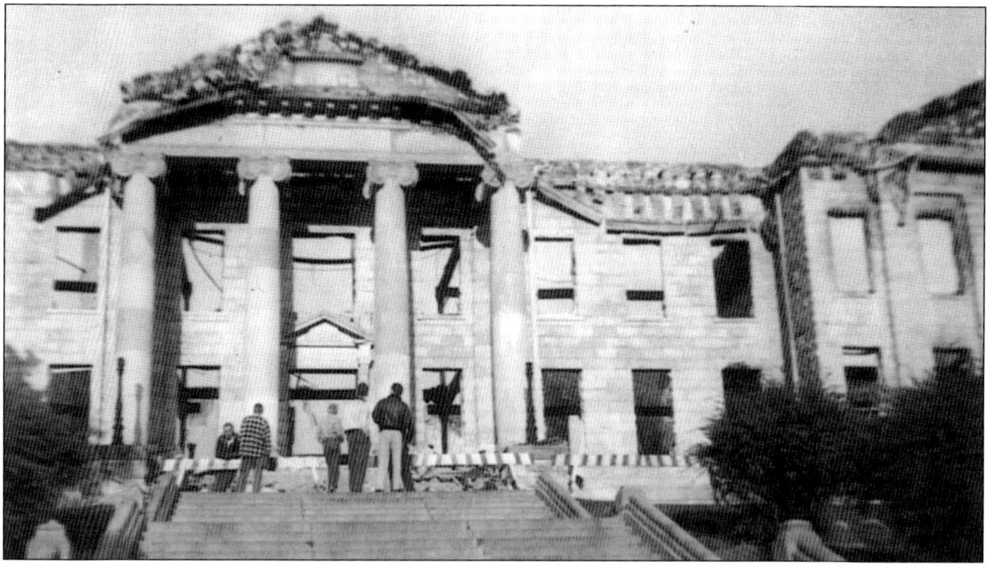

The day after the fire, students gather at the top of the 77 Steps to view the burned-out skeleton of the building—a sad, depressing sight. One of the great concerns following the fire was the fate of the students' academic transcripts. Fortunately, the transcripts, along with other vital scholastic and administrative records, were housed in the school's fireproof vault and survived intact. Dean William Monypeny advised students, "Environment is not essential to our education, but rather the mental attitude."

At the beginning of the school year in 1949, the state fire marshal had found North Hall unsafe and condemned it. The structure had served the college since 1886 and had long before seen its best days. In recent years, the building had been home to the science, art, and home economics departments. The building, while condemned, continued in use until the Christmas holidays, when its contents were moved to the basement of Richardson Hall. The demolition of the structure had begun six days before the Richardson fire. The loss of North Hall's classrooms added greatly to the disaster. Its demolition would be completed in July 1950. Mossman Hall would be located near where North Hall had stood for almost 65 years. These photographs show North Hall in its last days before demolition (right) and at the end, with the removal of its nameplate (below).

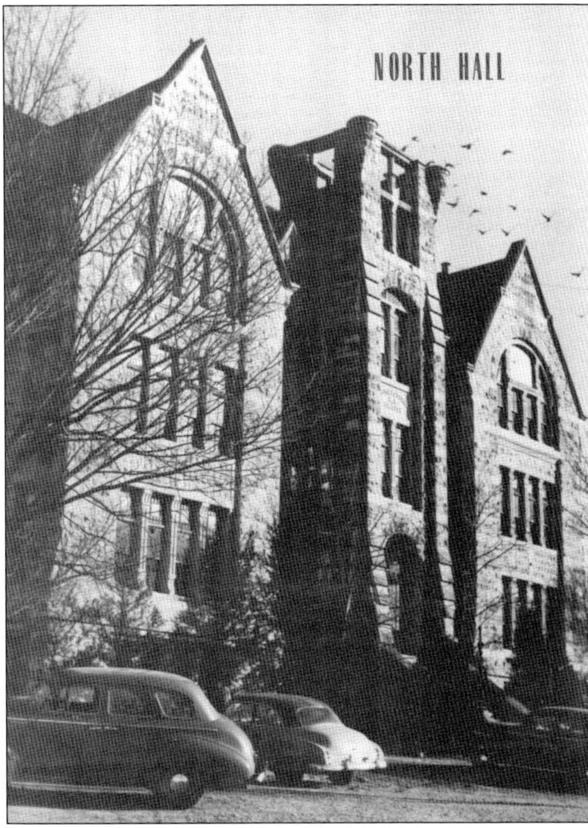

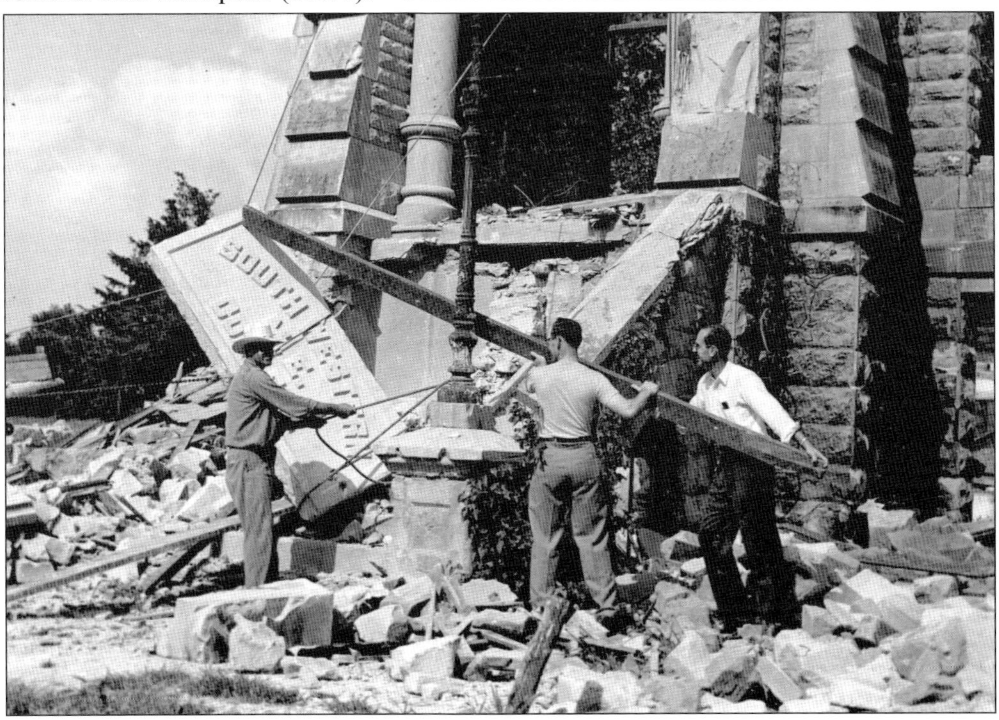

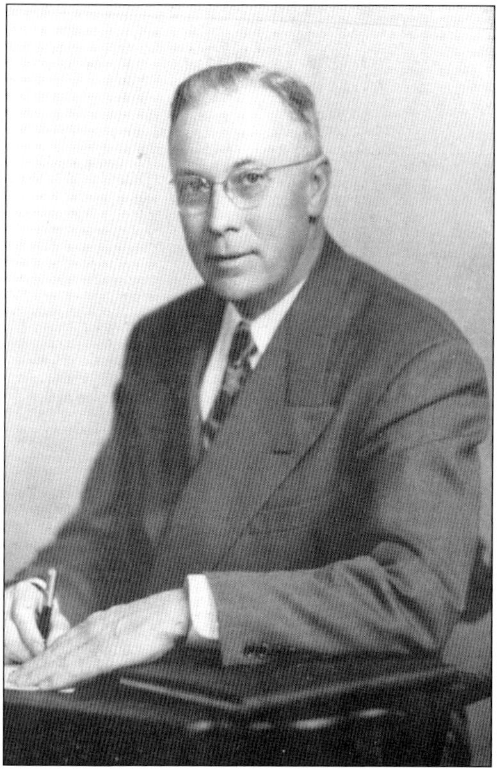

Alvin W. Murray became Southwestern College's twelfth president of on October 17, 1949, five months before the fire and ensuing crisis. He was a 1924 Southwestern graduate who had gone into the Methodist ministry. In the 1930s, he had served at Grace Methodist Church and taught at Southwestern. Murray, a forceful leader, met the crisis decisively: continuing operations, funding and starting a rebuilding program, and leading the fight to preserve the school. To him goes the credit for having saved Southwestern College.

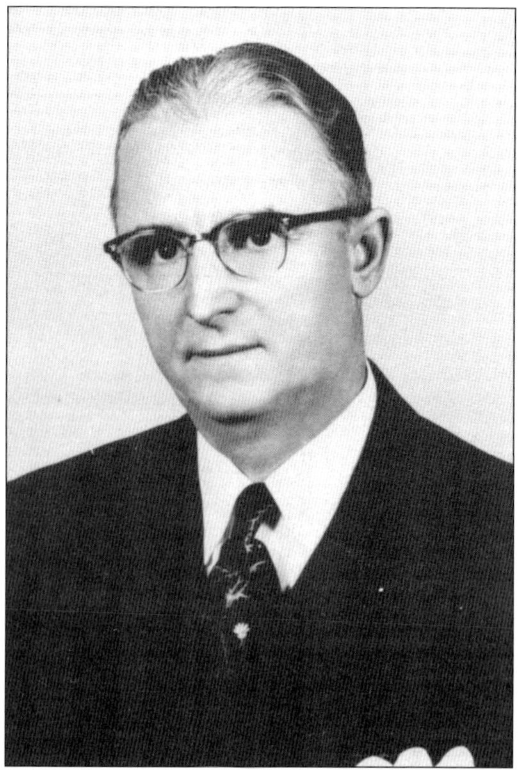

Raymond E. Dewey was superintendent of the Winfield District of the Central Kansas Methodist Conference and a member of Southwestern's board of trustees. He worked tirelessly, side-by-side with President Murray, in the fight to save the school. He would later give a compelling speech in favor of preserving Southwestern College at the special session in Hutchison.

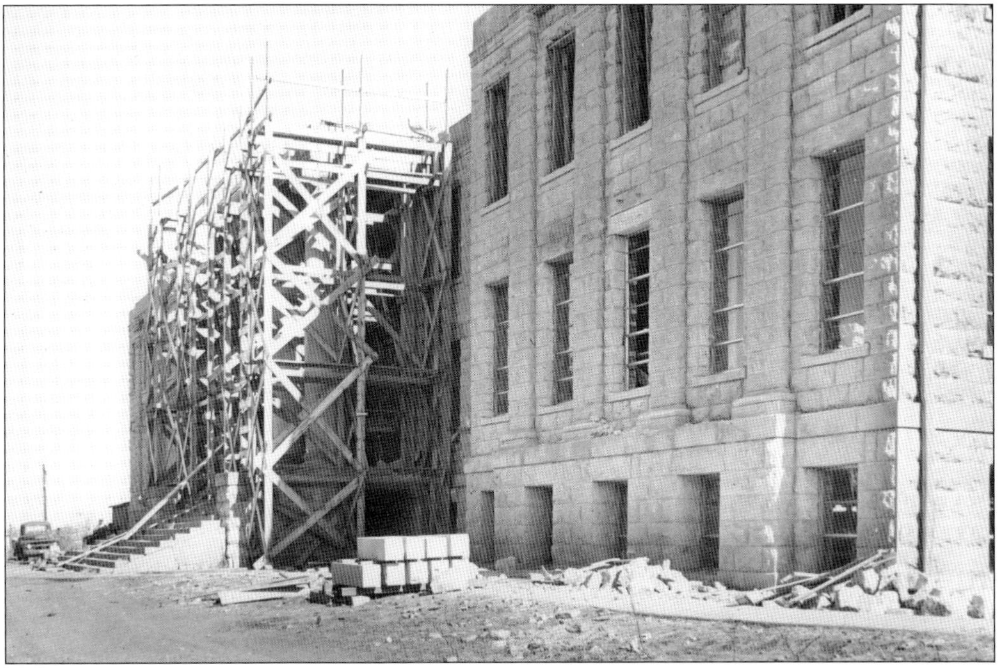

Plans for replacing Richardson Hall were completed around November 1950. The contract for the building was signed on February 2, 1951. The plans called for a modern, fireproof building. One major change was an eastward expansion of the auditorium. Work progressed at a steady pace, and the structure, then known simply as the Administration Building, was opened on July 18, 1952. The basement was still unfinished, and other areas still needed further work.

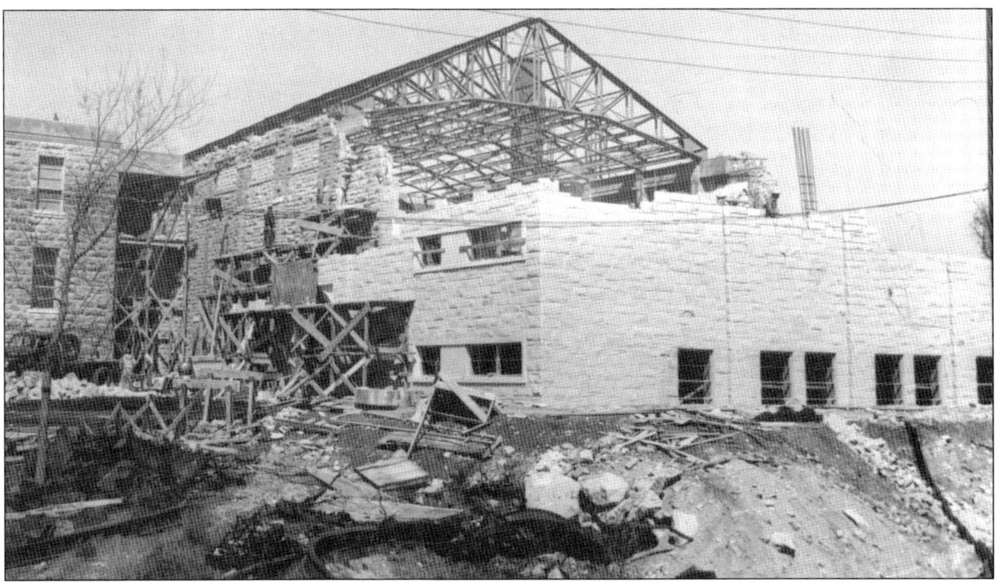

Besides not having a dome, the new administration building had one other major change. The rear of the structure, which was to house the auditorium, was extended 30 feet during the reconstruction. The extension required bringing in fill dirt to expand the back area. The new meeting space would later be given the name Richardson Auditorium.

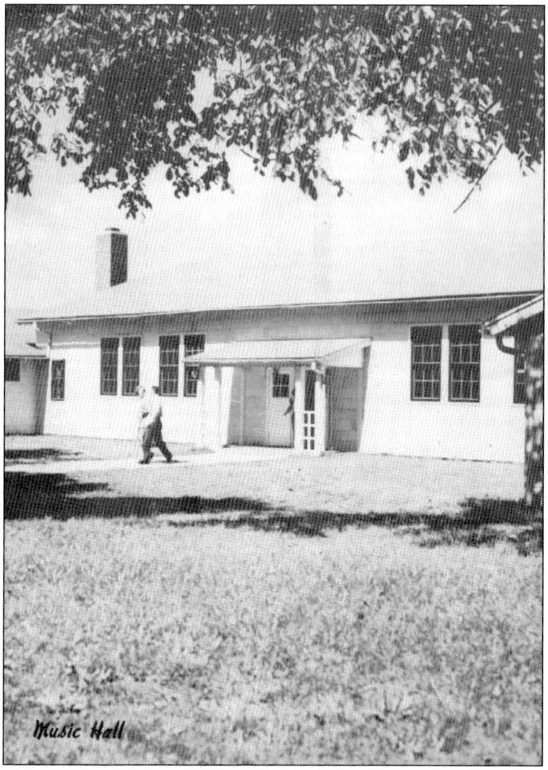

The Hall of Music was built from old barracks obtained from Strother Field. The building was dedicated in January 1948. Following the fire, the hall contained the only formal classroom space remaining on campus.

For the citizens of Winfield, the loss of Richardson Hall, along with the possible loss of the college, came as a great shock. Their ancestors had secured the college for the city. Over the years, Winfielders had been very active in their support, appreciating the $750,000 the school annually brought into the county. With the chamber of commerce leading the fight, citizens came together to save the college and help with its rebuilding, raising about $300,000. (Courtesy of the CCHS.)

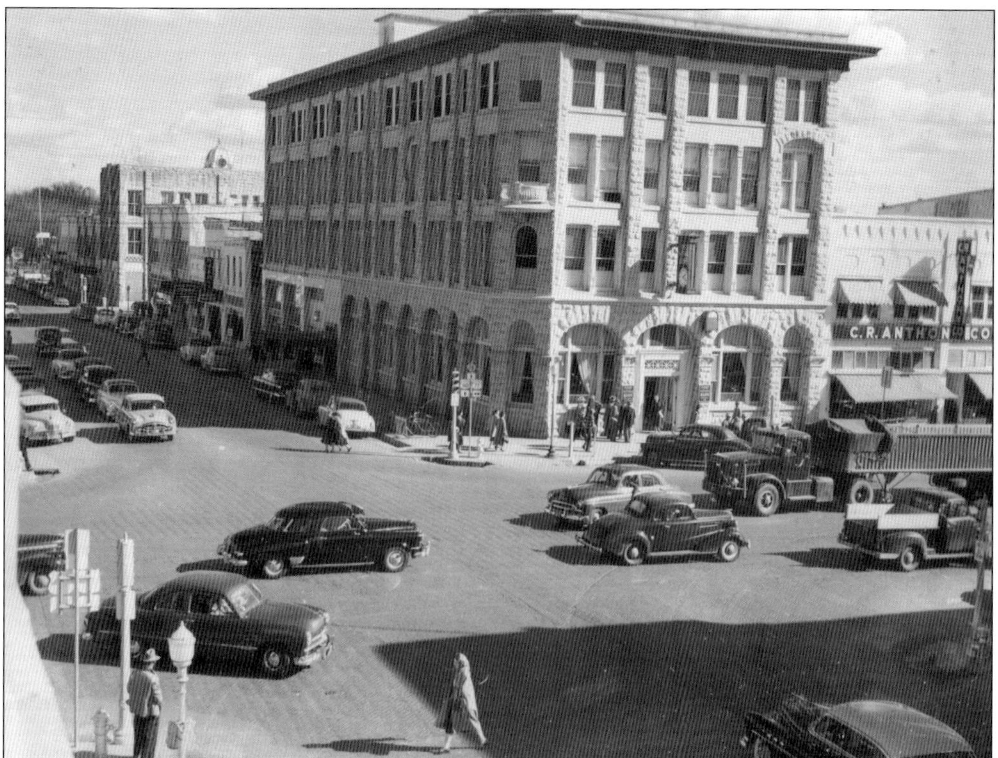

After the fire, Stewart Field House performed multiple duty as a sports arena, an assembly hall, and class space. Helen Graham's Campus Players even used the court area to stage its production of *Two Blind Mice*. Fortunately, the college library was located on the first floor of the building and was thus spared destruction by the fire.

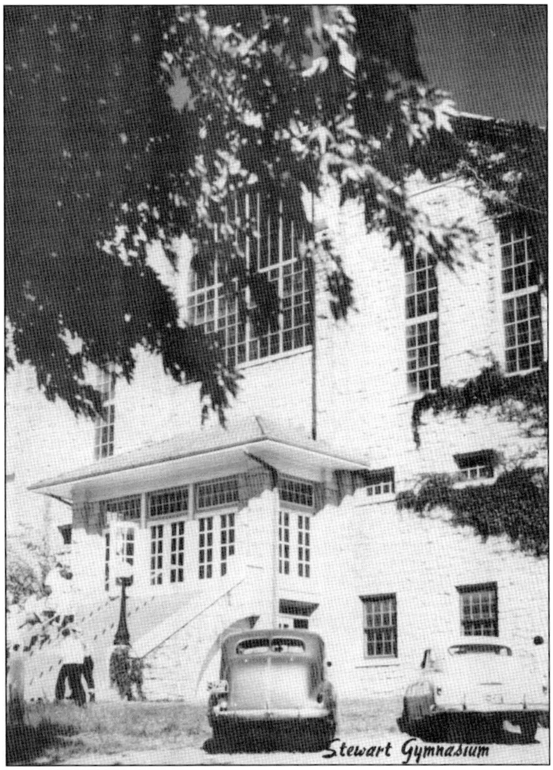

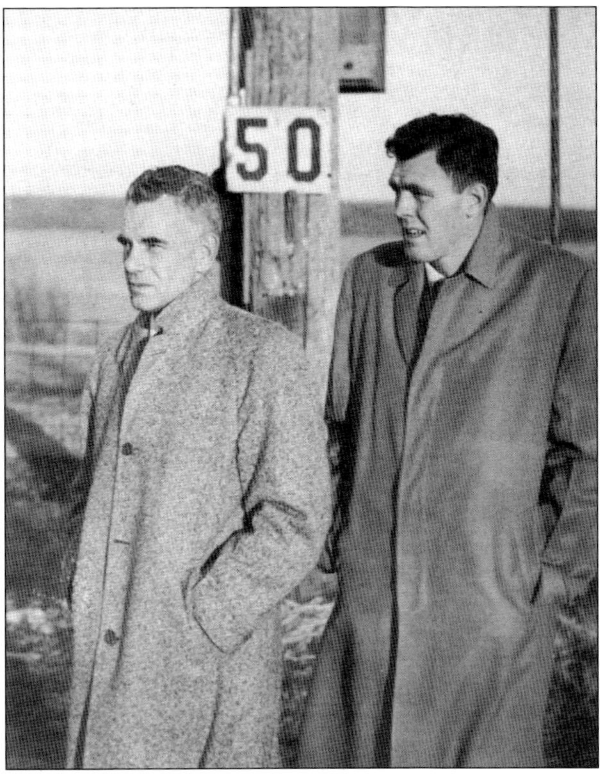

Pictured here are Southwestern coach Harold Hunter (left) and assistant coach William Corroll. Hunter gained favorable publicity for himself and the college by refusing one of his team's touchdowns, which was achieved illegally—the player had stepped out of bounds. The touchdown would have meant victory for his team. Hunter was named "Football's Man of the Year" by *This Week* magazine.

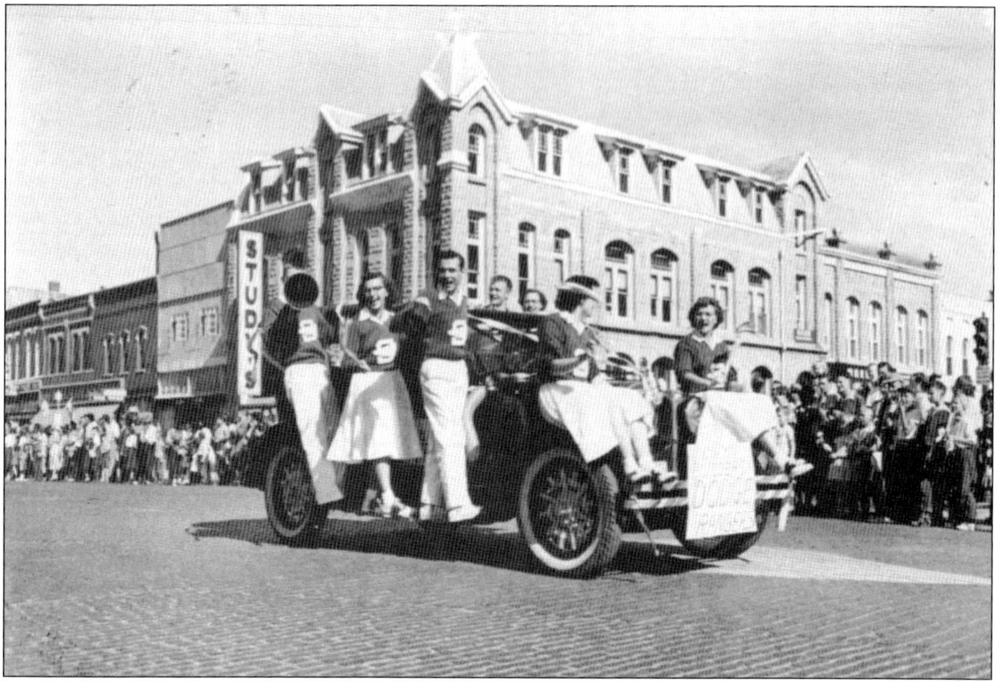

The 1951 Southwestern homecoming parade makes its way down Main Street. The cheerleaders are in action, and a large crowd of enthusiastic Winfielders have gathered to watch the festivities. That year, Southwestern junior Martha Bridge was crowned homecoming queen.

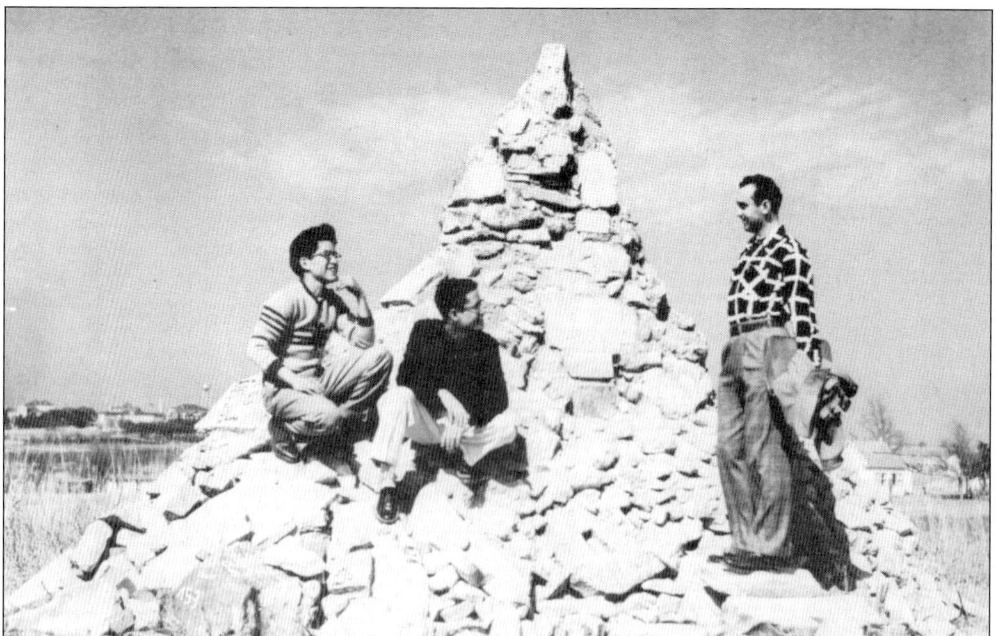

Under a bright Kansas sky, three students gather at the Mound. At the time, the Mound was located at the north end of the burned Richardson Hall and would remain there for several years after its reconstruction. The state hospital can be seen in the background. The area to the north and east of the college was still quite rustic.

Plans for the Memorial Library, now known as the Harold and Mary Ellen Deets Library, were finalized on August 22, 1950, and its building contract was signed the following month. Construction was slowed by shortages resulting from the Korean conflict, with shelving particularly hard to obtain. Nevertheless, the library was opened on November 28, 1951, about one year from the cornerstone laying and 19 months after the fire. The new structure was formally dedicated on May 17, 1953.

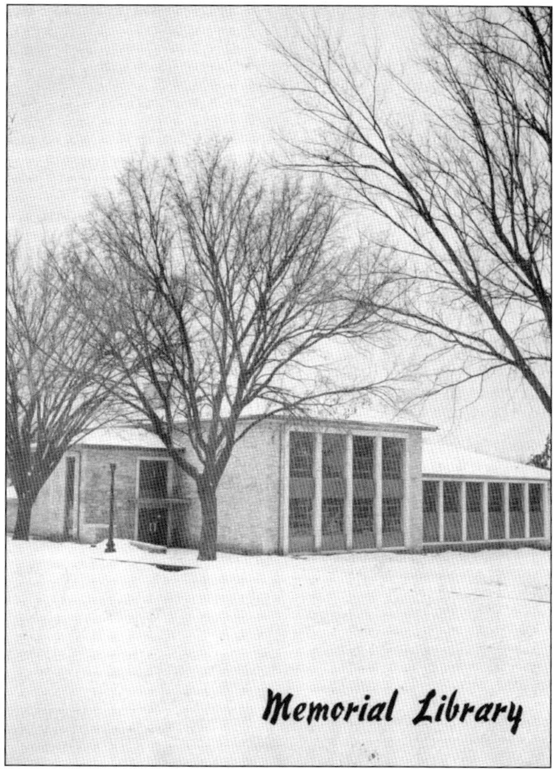

During a one-day holiday, students helped move books from the old library on the lower level of Steward Field House to the new Memorial Library, located in the center of campus. These students are Connie Kerr (left) and George Craig. The woman at center is unidentified.

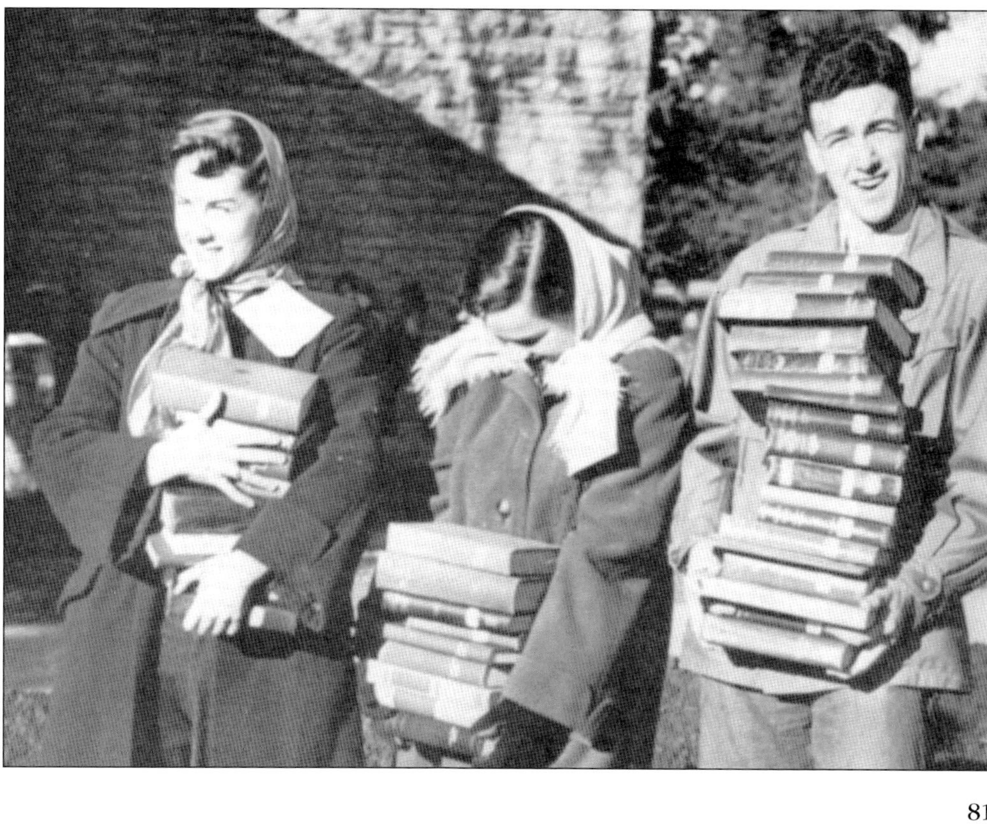

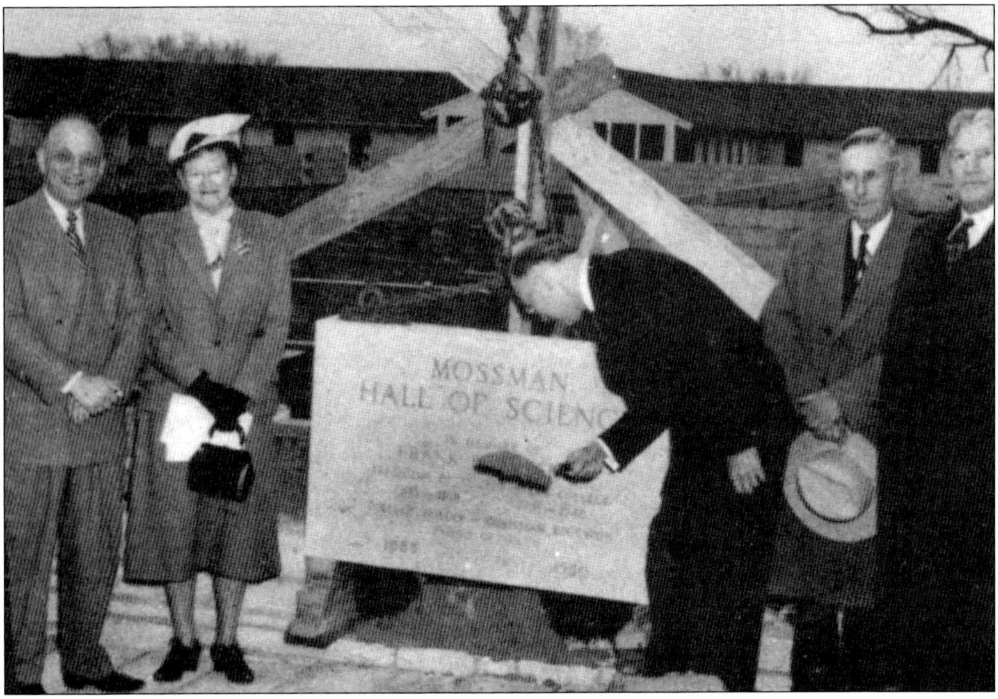

Pres. Alvin Murray lays the cornerstone for the Mossman Hall of Science on November 21, 1950. The building was named in honor of former president Frank E. Mossman, who had died on June 12, 1945. Shown here are, from left to right, an unidentified man, Frank's wife Zoa Mossman, Murray, trustee Allen C. Felt, and past president Albert E. Kirk. In the background are former military barracks converted to dormitories and apartments.

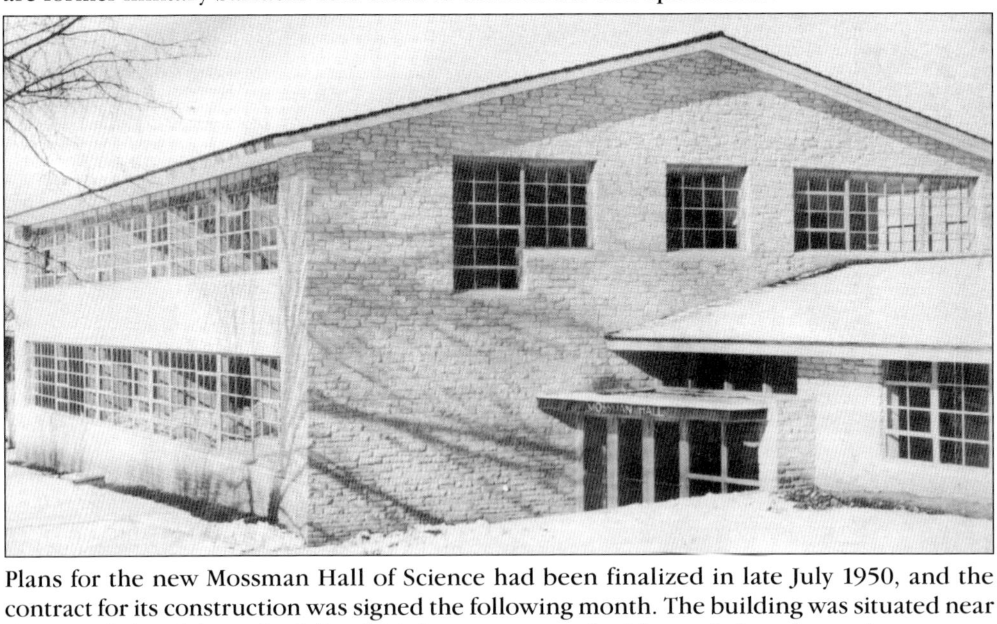

Plans for the new Mossman Hall of Science had been finalized in late July 1950, and the contract for its construction was signed the following month. The building was situated near the site of the Old North Hall, which for many years had housed the science department. Mossman Hall was opened on September 25, 1951, seventeen months after the fire. Its formal dedication took place on March 22, 1952.

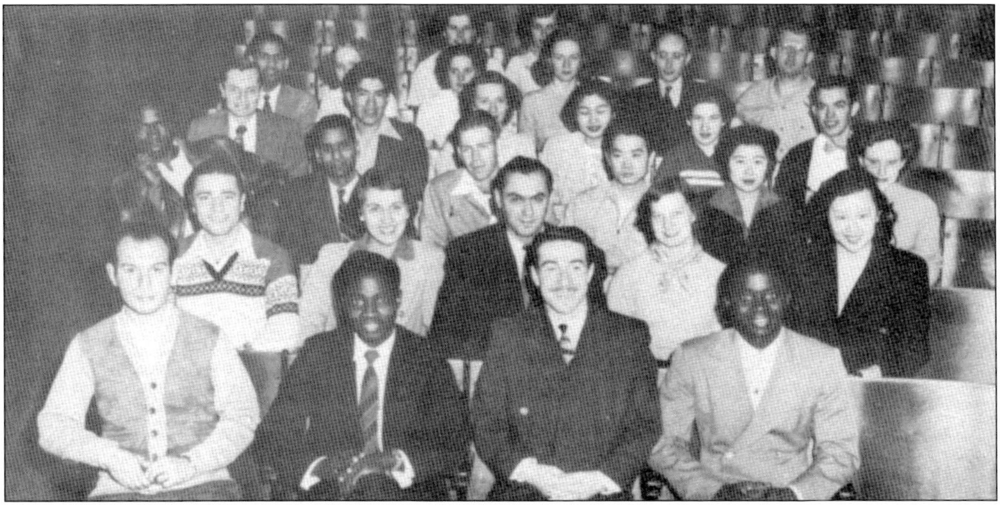

From its earliest day, Southwestern has welcomed foreign students. The first international student in the late 1890s was Pablo del Rio, "a polished gentleman" from Mexico, as described in *The Story of Southwestern.* Here are members of the Cosmopolitan Club, which comprised all Southwestern students from foreign lands and an equal number of American students. Its motto was "Humanity is above all nations."

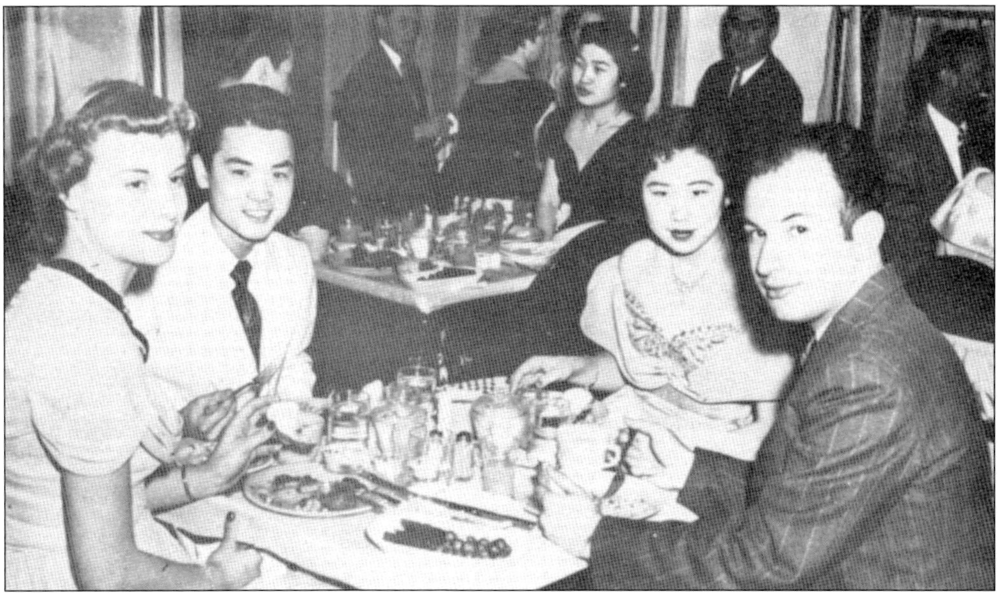

The Cosmopolitan Club staged an annual dinner and dance. The seated students seen here in 1950 are, from left to right, Phyllis Bunker, Thomas Tanaka, Nola Tang, and Mario Canedo. Lucy Gray Wright (class of 1928) had organized the Cosmopolitan Club in the fall of 1927. Originally, its membership was made up of all foreign, African American, and Native American students attending the college. The first president of the group was Harold Cottom.

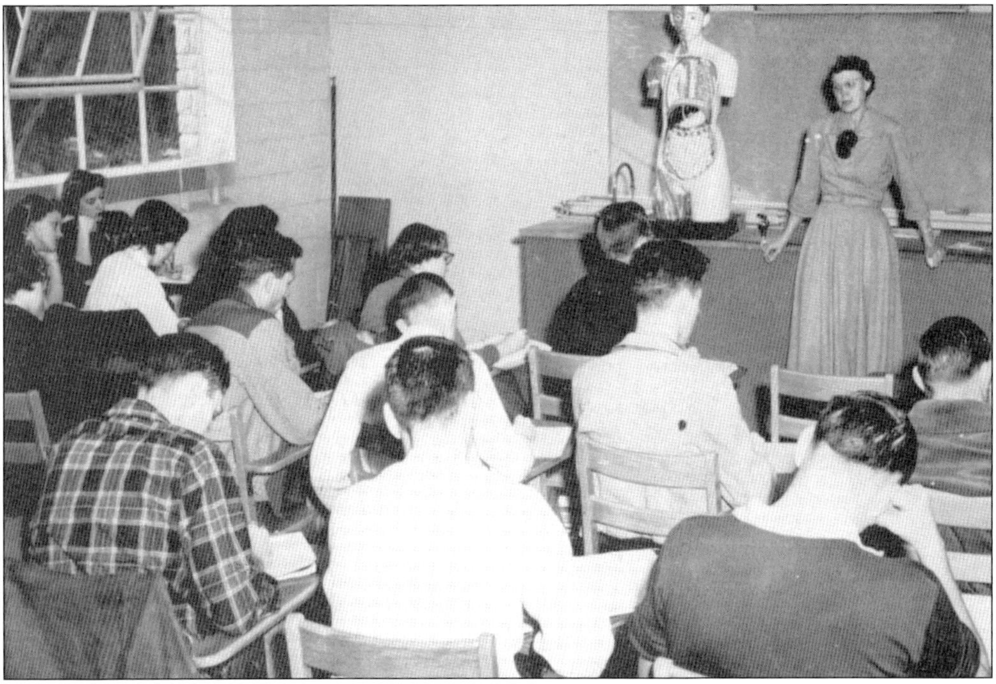

Lillian Cloud, a Southwestern graduate and longtime teacher, is shown teaching a health education class. The anatomical figure on the desk was known as "Bessie." Cloud also taught women's athletics and was responsible for staging the May Fete program.

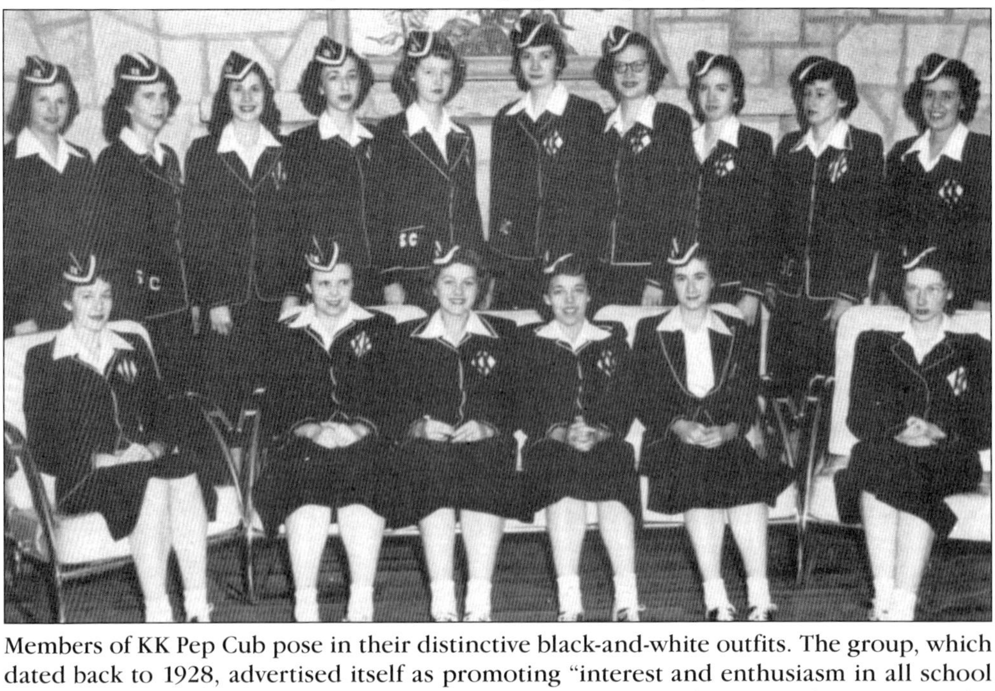

Members of KK Pep Cub pose in their distinctive black-and-white outfits. The group, which dated back to 1928, advertised itself as promoting "interest and enthusiasm in all school activities" and providing "opportunity for social development" for its members. Among the group's activities, it staged an assembly program, built a float for homecoming, promoted dances, and held "an annual picnic and paddle dance."

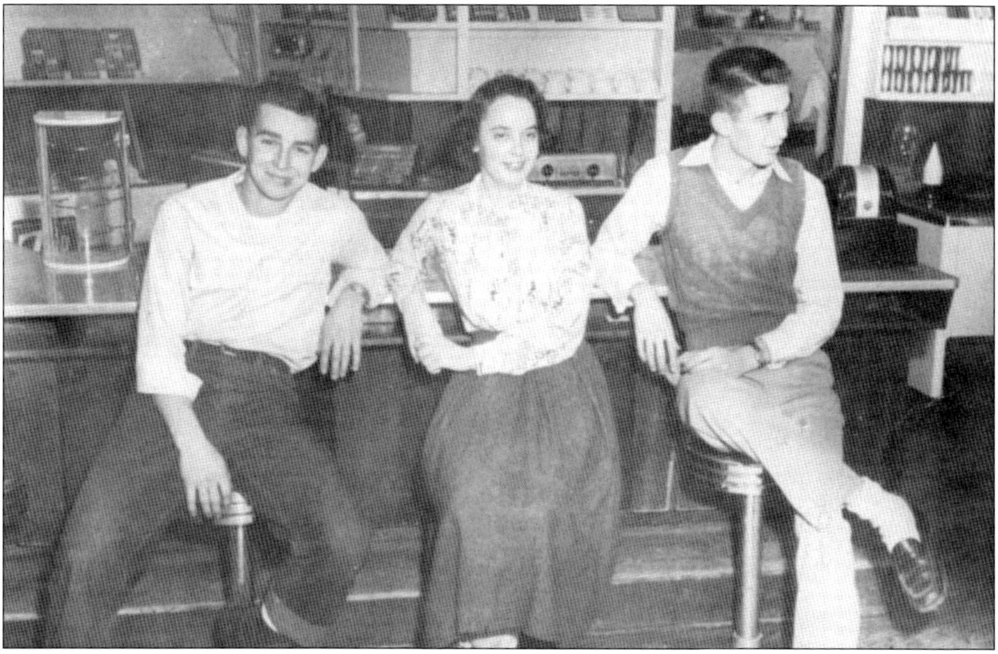

In the early 1950s, three students have stopped by the Student Union to enjoy refreshments. The Student Union was a favorite spot with students, who liked to drop by between classes, perhaps to have a piece of pie and a cup of coffee while listening to the jukebox. In addition, students could play a game of ping-pong, a very popular activity among students of the day.

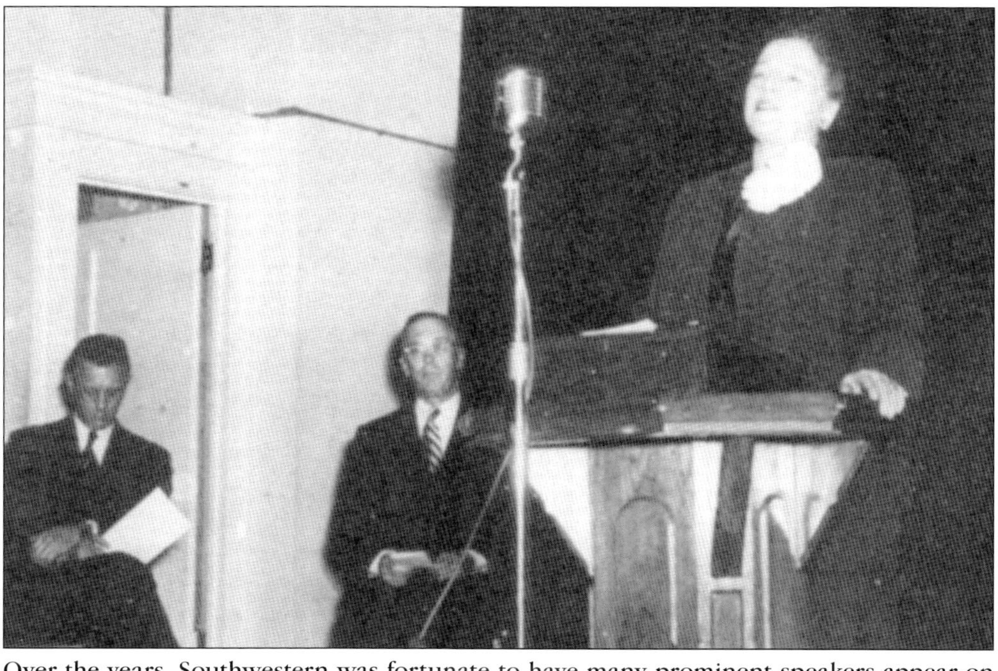

Over the years, Southwestern was fortunate to have many prominent speakers appear on campus, such as Pearl Buck, distinguished author of *The Good Earth,* shown here giving a talk concerning mentally challenged children in 1951. Other important speakers on campus included Alf Landon, Eleanor Roosevelt, and Ralph Nader.

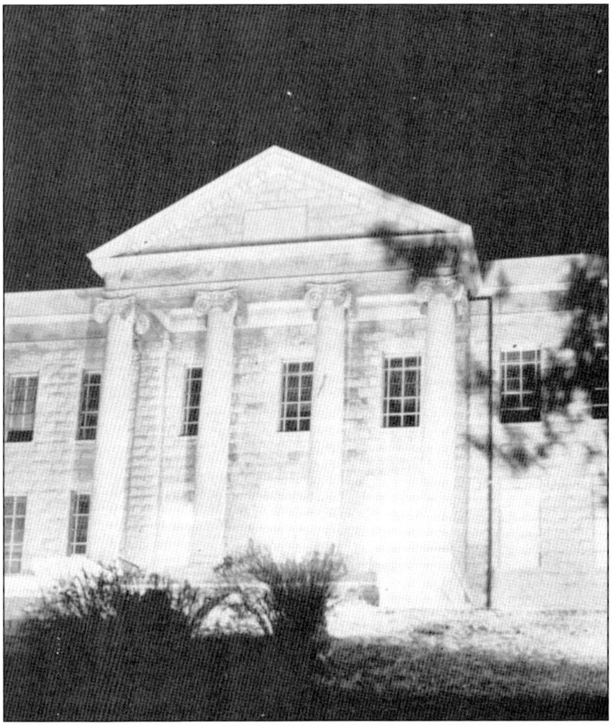

At the time of the dedication of Richardson Hall in the spring of 1910, Bishop William Alfred Quayle, known as "the Skylark of Methodism," exclaimed, while standing atop the 77 Steps, "Doubtless, God could have made a more beautiful scene, than this, but He never did." When it came time to officially rename the restored administration building—which had been delayed until March 13, 1956, when the impressive structure was dedicated—it became the Christy Administration Building. It was named in honor of R.B. Christy, a generous donor to the college endowment.

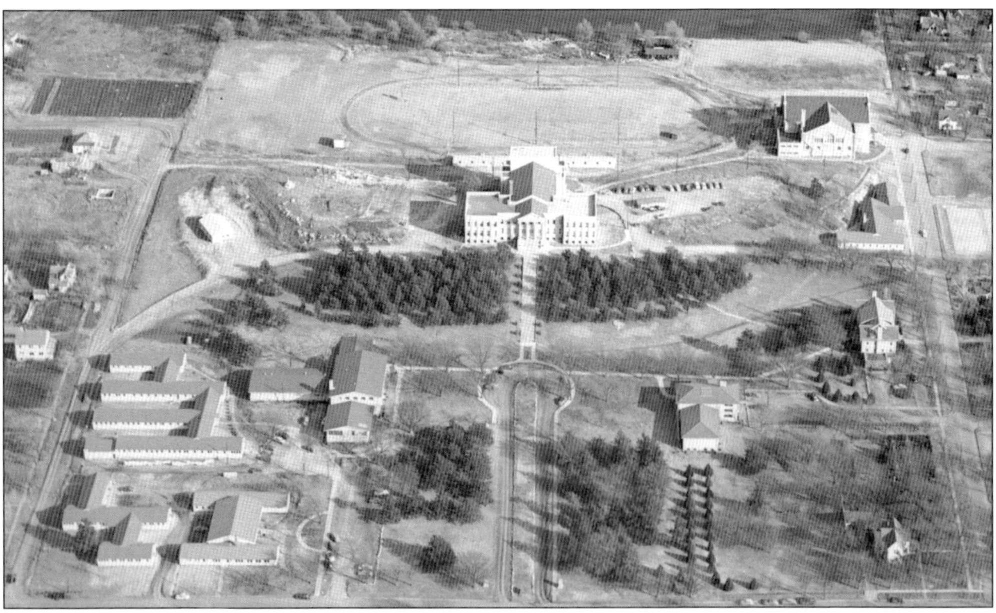

This aerial photograph shows the campus not long after Dr. Murray's departure. The almost-completed administration building, with its distinctive red roof, is at center. Behind it is Sonner Stadium. Mossman Hall of Science is at lower left, and Memorial Library is at lower right. Below Mossman is the Hall of Music, which was constructed from military barracks, like the dorms and apartments to the north of it. Other buildings seen here are the Field House (upper right), the Student Union below it (also built from barracks), and Smith Hall. In the extreme right lower corner is the President's House.

Five

Rebuilding and Revival 1954–1972

On December 31, 1953, as the day faded, Alvah Graham passed away at his Winfield home. He was the last surviving member of Southwestern's first graduating class in 1889 and had maintained a lifelong interest in his alma mater. An era had ended. The next day, January 1, 1954, C. Orville Strohl walked up the 77 Steps and assumed his duties as the 13th president of the college. With him came a new day.

Reverend Strohl, a member of the class of 1931, was an unassuming man. He had about him the look of Main Street, perhaps that of a small-town pastor—but he was far more than that. A man of strong faith, he came to Southwestern College a proven executive, organizer, and fundraiser with a deep interested in young people and in helping them to be the best they could be. He was a Builder in the full sense of the word. As president, his goal was to make Southwestern into an outstanding private educational institution, and he had the ability, the enthusiasm, and the vision, coupled with common sense, to make this goal a reality.

Over the next 18 and a half years, Dr. Strohl would remake the college into a first-rate institution. He assembled an outstanding faculty, expanded and improved the school's curriculum, and grew the student body. During his tenure, the following buildings would arise on campus: Darbeth Hall, Roy L. Smith Student Center, Wallingford Hall, Reid Hall, Sutton Hall, Broadhurst Hall, Shriwise Apartments, Honor Apartments, White Physical Education, and an addition to the Memorial Library. Most important for the long-term survival of the school, he grew its endowment until it became the largest of any private college in Kansas at that time. His work done, Dr. Strohl retired from the presidency at the end of June 1972. He left behind a strong and vital institution.

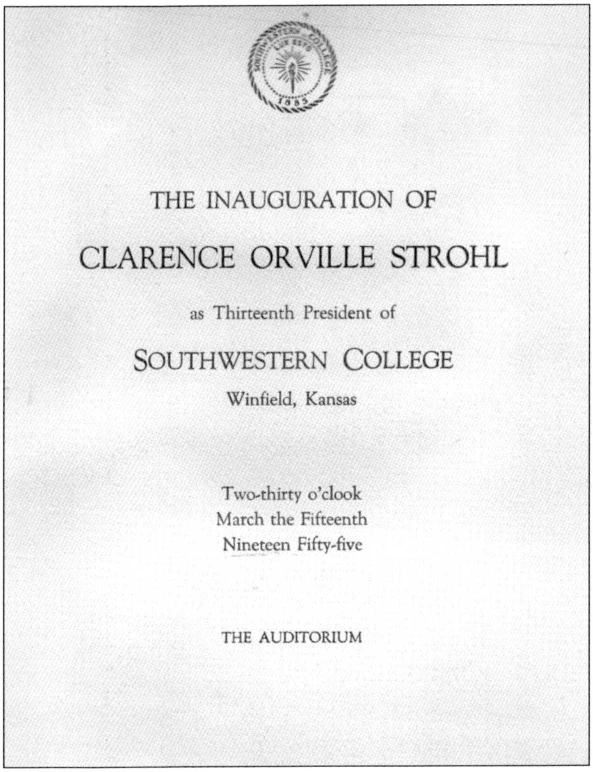

THE INAUGURATION OF

CLARENCE ORVILLE STROHL

as Thirteenth President of

SOUTHWESTERN COLLEGE

Winfield, Kansas

Two-thirty o'clock
March the Fifteenth
Nineteen Fifty-five

THE AUDITORIUM

In 1954, Dr. C. Orville Strohl returned to serve his alma mater as president. He would become the college's second-longest-serving president, after Mossman. During his undergraduate years at Southwestern, Strohl was a keen observer, a thinker, and a goal-oriented achiever. He came back to campus after a productive stint in Iowa as a Methodist minister and educator. Strohl deliberately delayed his inauguration as president for over a year, so as to be able to mention in his inaugural speech concrete accomplishments, rather than just cite a list of proposals. Besides adding many new contemporary buildings and campus sculptures, Strohl was also responsible for significantly building up the endowment, which he increased from $500,000 to $5 million, and implementing a strong liberal arts program.

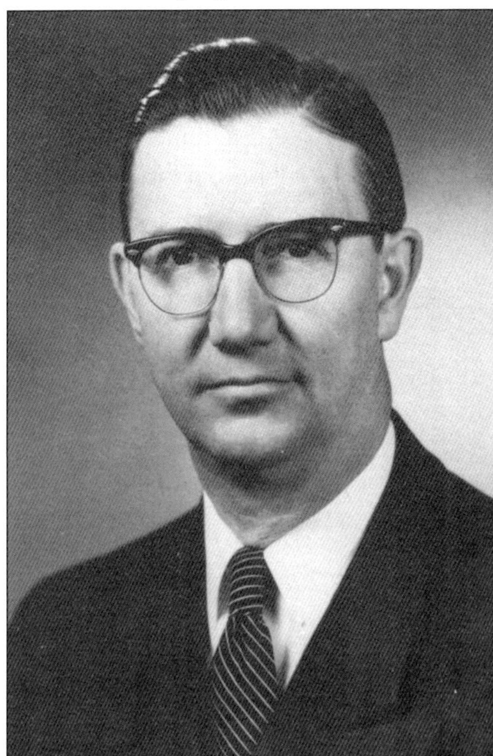

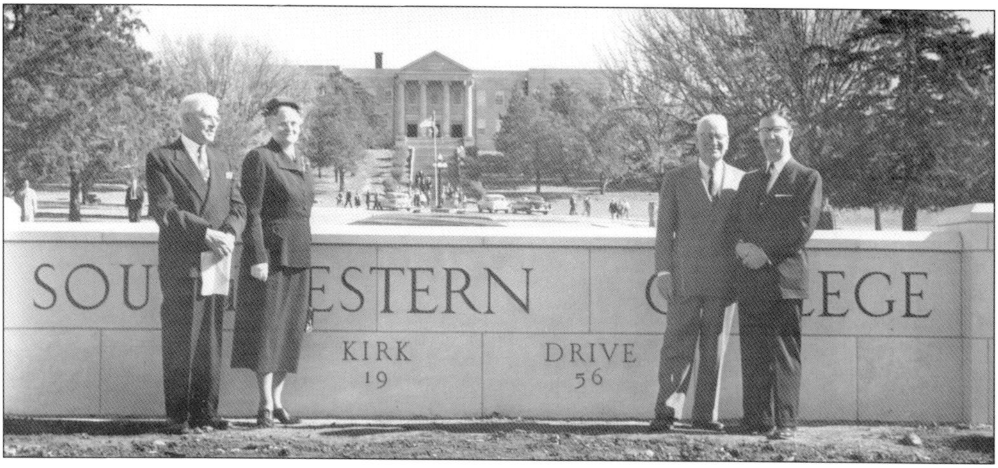

Dr. C. Orville Strohl (far right) stands with Sam Wallingford and Mr. and Mrs. Kirk before the newly dedicated Kirk Drive campus entrance in 1956. The long, horseshoe-shaped drive—which was periodically adorned with flower beds, Christmas trees, commemorative rocks, and international flags—was named after Kirk to honor his stewardship of the college in the 1920s.

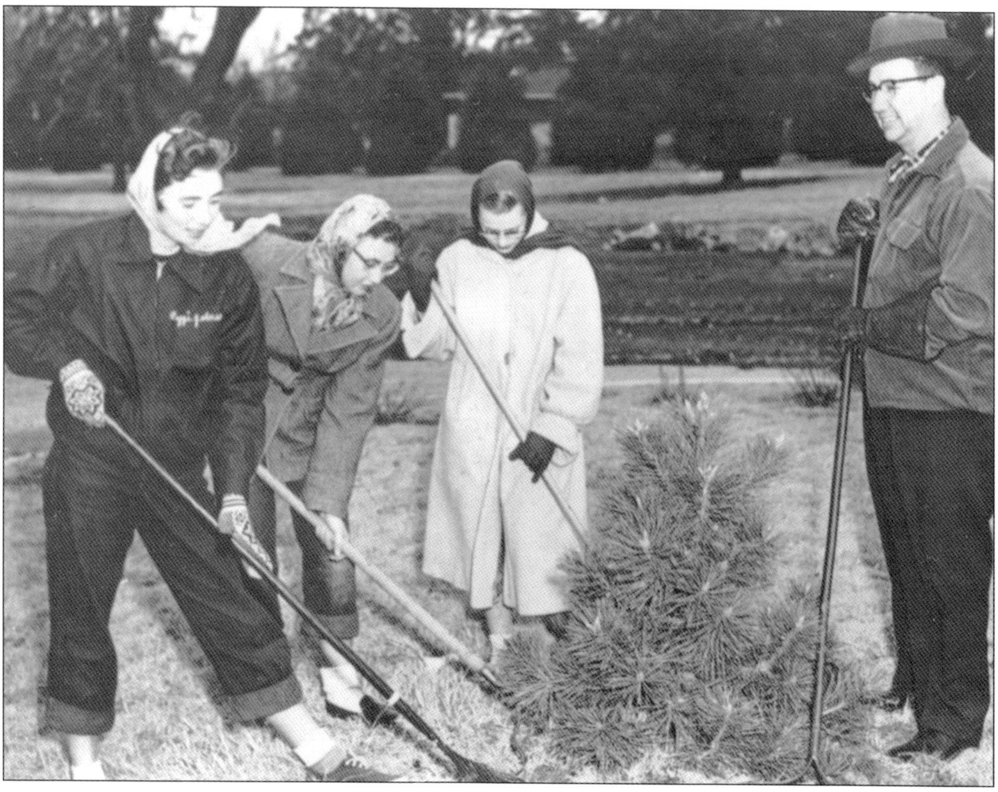

Here, Dr. Strohl and three students help to plant a tree in the yard of the new president's house, which was built in 1956 and later named after him. Strohl was proud of the fact that, during his long tenure, several buildings were erected, including Darbeth Hall, Roy L. Smith Student Center, Wallingford Hall, Reid Hall, Sutton Hall, Broadhurst Hall, Shriwise Apartments, Honor Apartments, and White Physical Education, as well as the addition to the library.

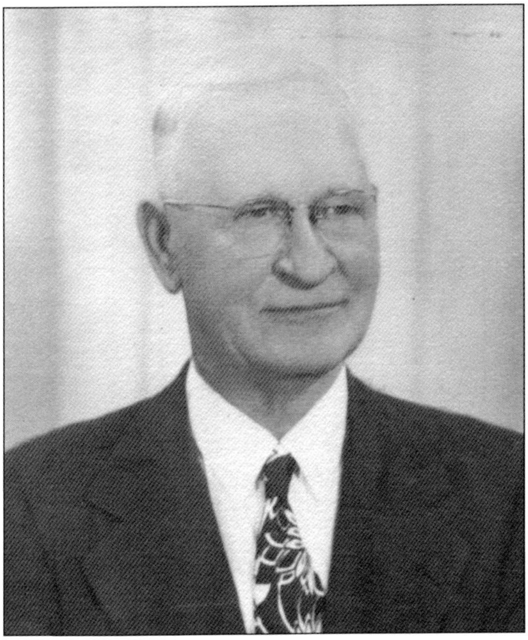

"The biggest day in Southwestern's financial history came on Monday, Oct. 31, 1955," wrote President Strohl in his personal papers. Following the regular meeting of the board of trustees, President Strohl announced to the students, faculty, and staff that R.B. Christy of Scott City, Kansas, had given Southwestern $500,000 in endowment. Christy (left) had attended Southwestern for three years early in the century. The students made him an honorary member of the class of 1956. Also announced was a second anonymous gift of $100,000 and a third, also anonymous, of $30,000. On this one day, Southwestern added $630,000 in new funds.

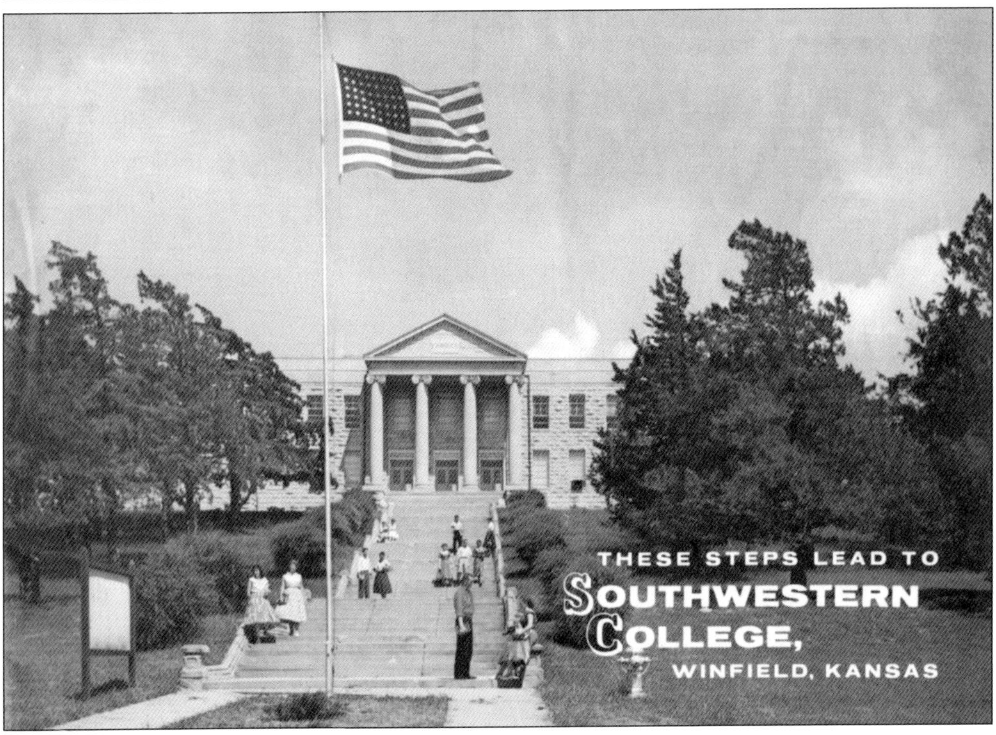

This rather serene and patriotic view looking up the 77 Steps has proven inspirational for many, including Southwestern alma mater composer Florence M. Cate, who composed the school song using 77 words. The song, which is sung to the Cornell University traditional tune, begins: "High above the Walnut Valley / On a lofty height / Stands our noble alma mater / Bathed in golden light." Cate was an instructor in French and Latin at Southwestern College for 12 years.

In March 1954, Olive Ann Beech, president of Beech Aircraft Co. in Wichita, and William Broadhurst, a Tulsa oil man and philanthropist, were awarded honorary degrees. Beech became renowned among journalists and aerospace enthusiasts as the "first lady" and "queen" of American aviation. She received aviation's highest honor in 1981, when she was awarded the Wright Brothers Memorial Trophy from the National Aeronautical Association in Washington, DC. Beech, who never learned to fly, was the first woman to receive that award. She served as chairwoman of the SC Committee on Endowment and Investment and was a longtime member of the board of trustees. (Courtesy of the Kansas State Historical Society.)

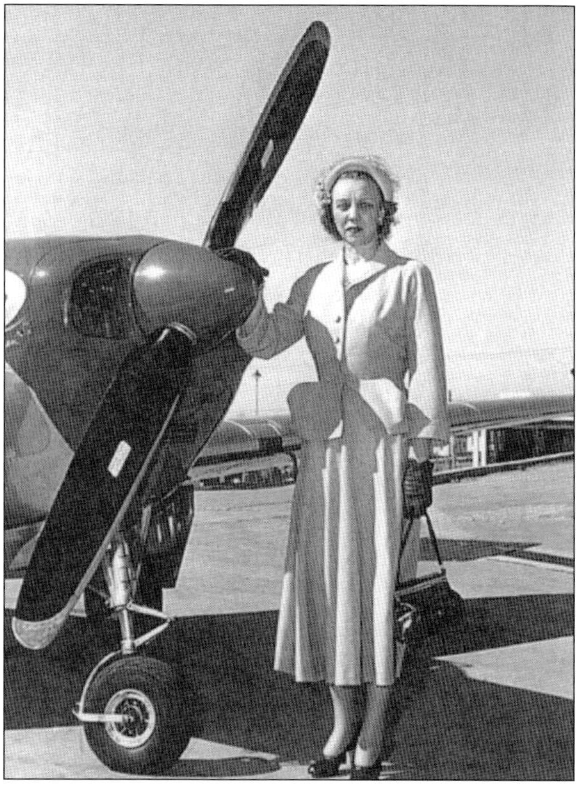

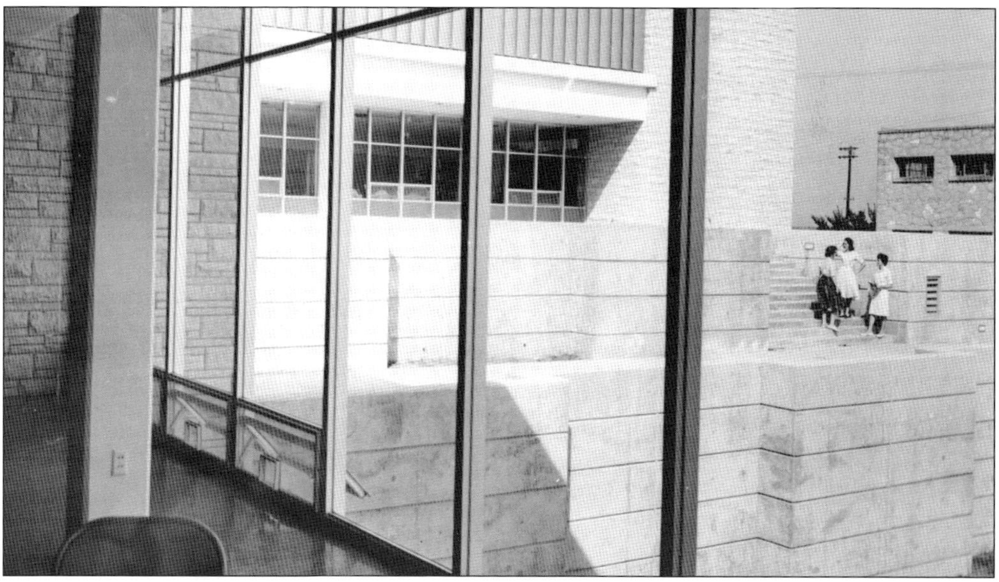

The need for a campus social hub was solved in 1960 with the completion of a new student union building. The Student Life Center was named for Dr. Roy L. Smith, a 1908 graduate whose name would also be attached to the Smith-Wilson Lectureship series. Smith was widely known as a journalist, editor, author, and world traveler. The Student Life Center housed a snack bar, television and smoking lounges, the cafeteria, ping-pong tables, and a jukebox, along with mailboxes and a bookstore.

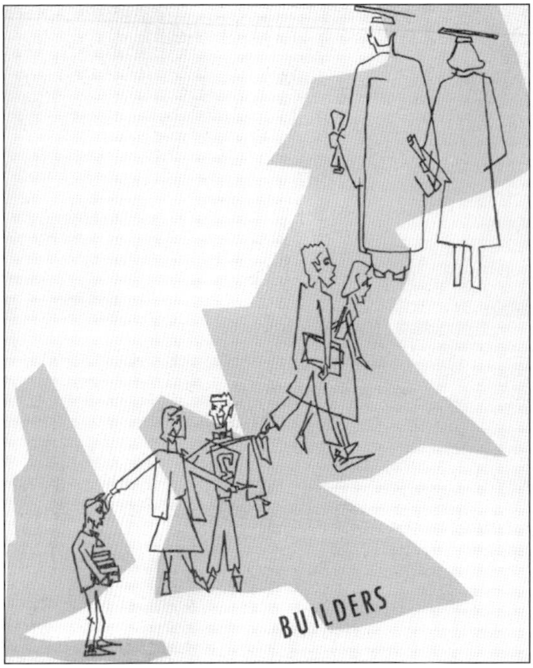

This graphic design depicting the progression from freshman to graduate visually illustrates the Builder story. The term "Builder" is explained in an article from a 1919 *Collegian*: "As one lives under the constant influence of an institution, he unconsciously adopts the characteristics and ideals which that institution holds paramount. The highest claim of superiority any college can hold is that it builds a noble type of manhood and womanhood. And that is the claim Southwestern holds. She builds a true, noble type of character. To any student who will allow the true spirit of Southwestern to permeate his life, she holds forth a promise of future usefulness which few are able to attain."

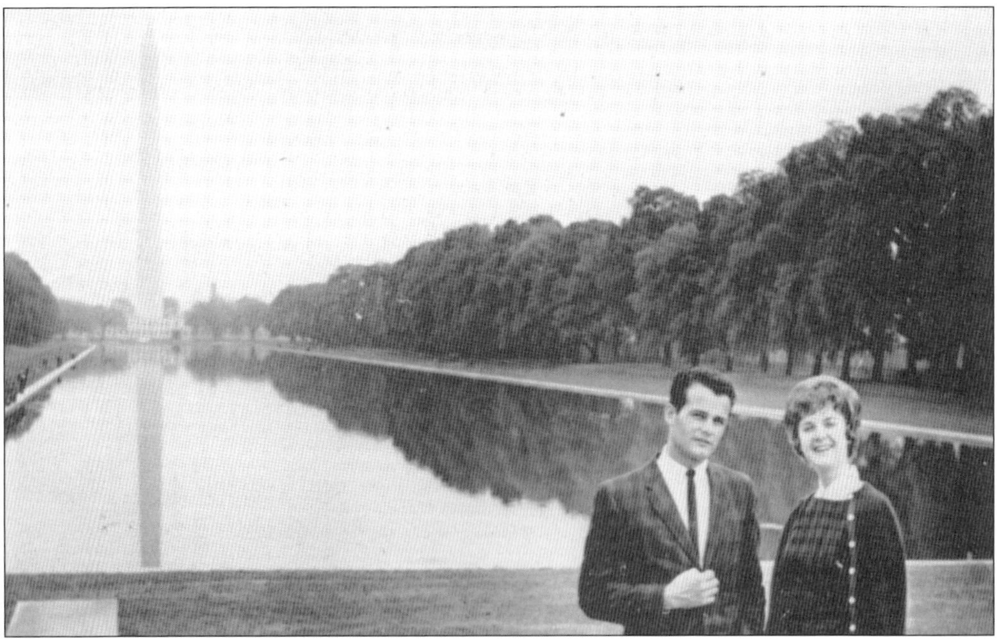

There were many student organizations in the 1950s through the 1970s on the Builder campus, including Jinx Janes, KK Pep Club, S Club, Pi Epsilon Pi, Kappa Rho, Student Council, and Campus Christian Council. Some students, however, truly wanted an off-campus experience. The Washington Term was a popular semester-long option for students interested in studying American government. Students were chosen based on their scholarship, academic achievement, interest in American history, and leadership activity. Here, Russell Vail and Jane Glotfelty pose at the reflecting pool between the Washington Monument and Lincoln Memorial in 1963.

The 1954 *Moundbuilder* was dedicated to Lillian Cloud, a SC graduate who returned to her alma mater to be director of physical training for women, then associate professor of health and physical education. After 1942, she was director of social and recreational life. While William Monypeny was in the Kansas Office of Veterans' Affairs, she carried on his task of writing to all Southwestern students in the military. "Lillian Cloud is known to every one at Southwestern for her friendliness, her warm personality and her ceaseless efforts for us all," said C. Orville Strohl.

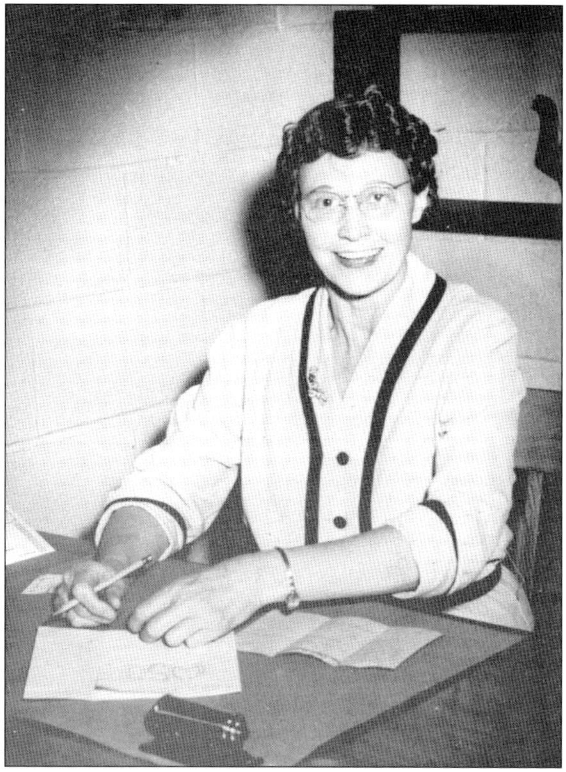

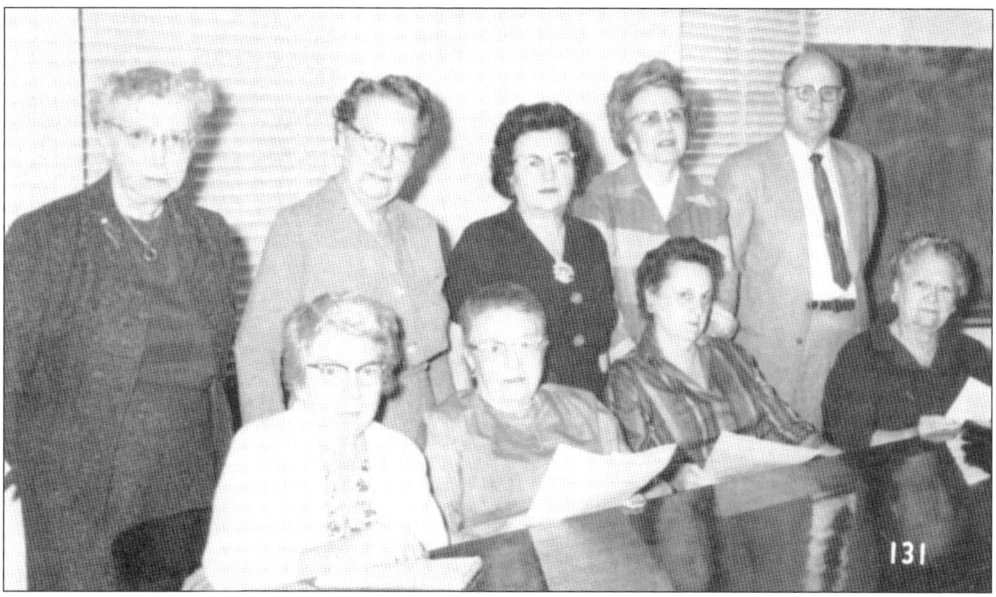

During the first half of the 20th century, housemothers ruled the roost in the dormitories. They acted as the predominant authority figure for students, many of whom were away from home for the first time in their lives. This group of housemothers—and one housefather—exerted control, order, respect and cleanliness over Fisher Hall, Wallingford Hall, Broadhurst Hall, Holland Hall, Smith Hall and New Hall for Men. Today, only freshmen are required to live on campus.

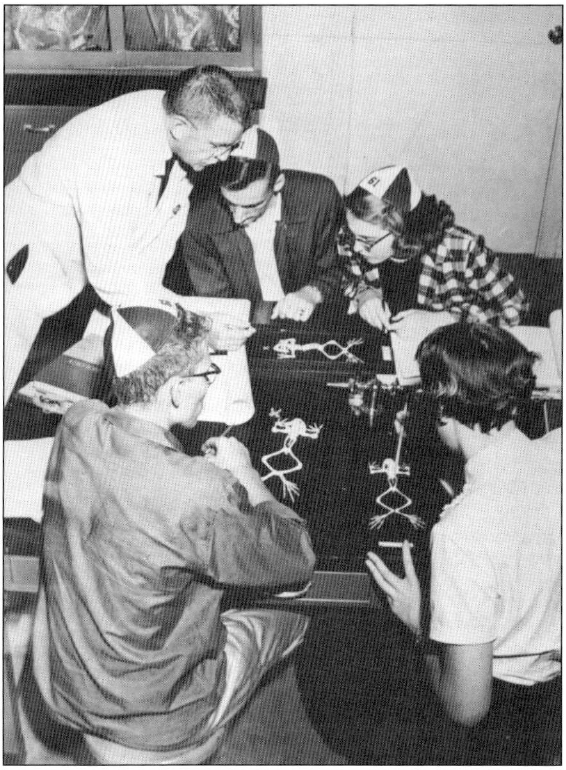

Much of the typical college day in this era was spent in the classrooms, studying all sorts of subjects, including English literature, secretarial science, home economics, forensics, speech and theater, mathematics, chemistry, physics, botany, history, education, business, economics, Bible, psychology, and physical education. These biology students learn the anatomy of a frog in 1961. The beanies were given to the "lowly" freshmen to prove they could coexist with their "lofty" upper classmates.

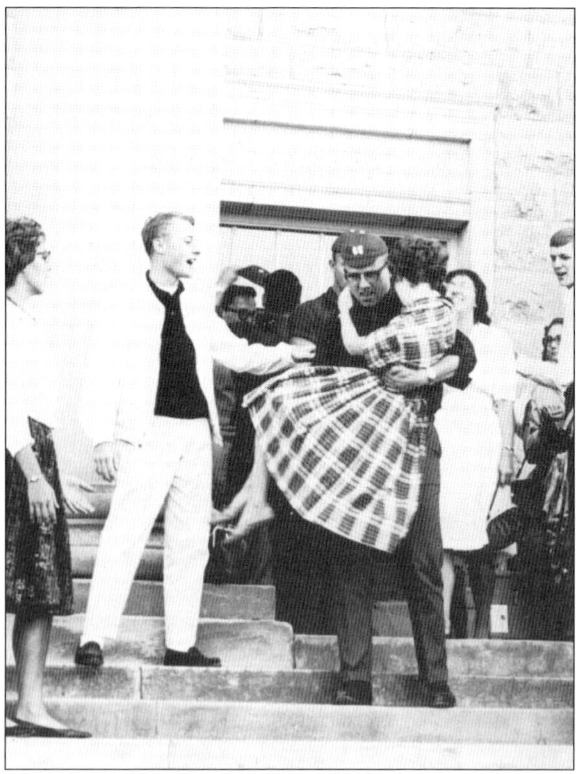

Chivalry is not dead, especially for the beanie-wearing freshmen, shown here at the top of the 77 Steps in 1962. For many Builders, the iconic 77 Steps, built in 1910, was the site of many a first kiss, first fight, or marriage proposal. The top level, named for President Murray, has hosted chapel services, a Volkswagen bug, rock and gospel concerts, anniversary celebrations, and even small wedding ceremonies, as well as countless private moments of significance.

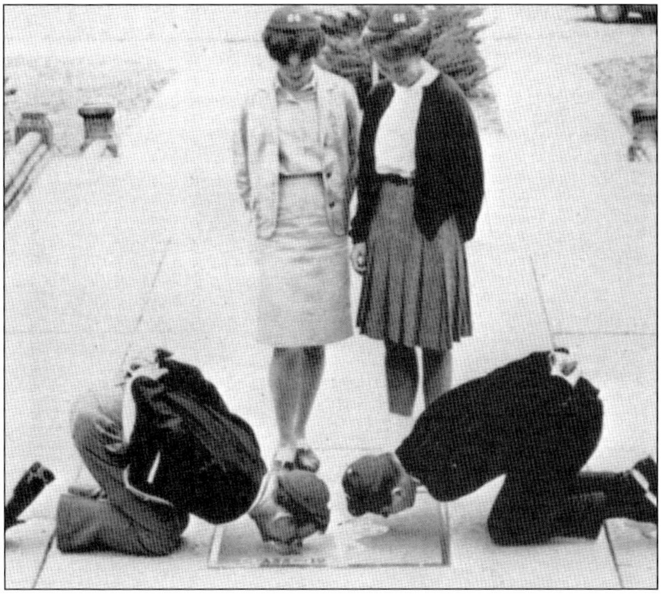

In 1963, proudly sporting their freshmen beanies and following Southwestern tradition, Joan Anderson (left) and Margaret Harp watch Mike Shelor (left) and Mike Case kiss the Jinx on the 77 Steps. Tradition dictates that anyone who steps on the Jinx has to get down on the ground and kiss the slab.

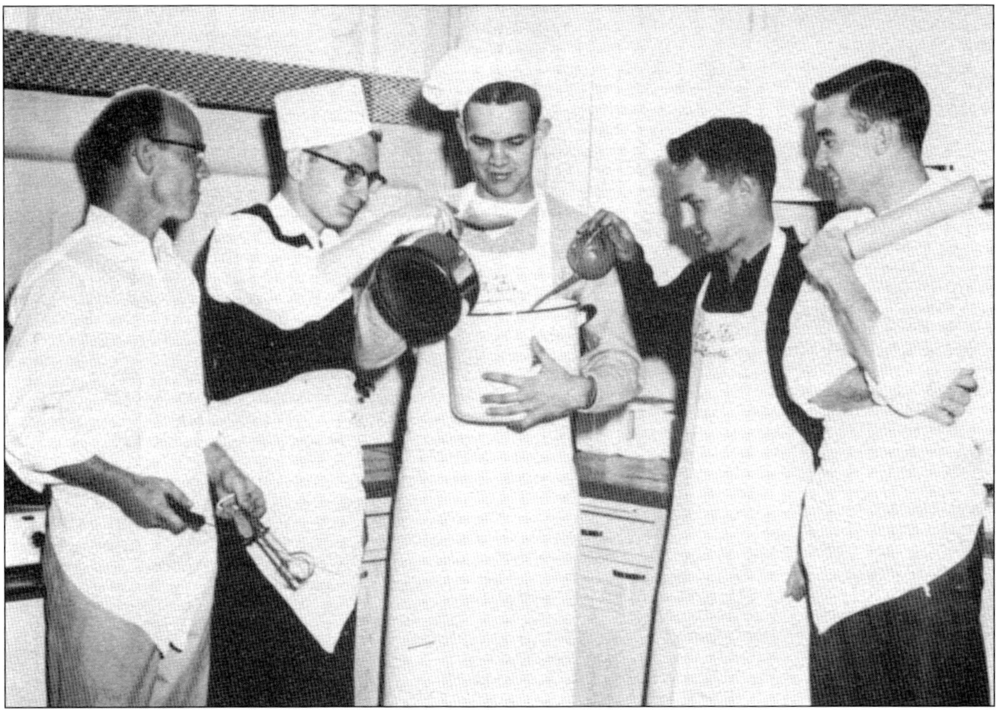

The tradition of the Spice King began in 1956 with the selection of Jack Focht (class of 1957) as the first king. It continued well into the 1980s. Each year, Gamma Omicron sponsored a Spice King dance, allowing the women to ask the men for a date. The women also voted for the king. Candidates were "judged by their proper grooming, personalities, participation in activities, and their interest in the promotion of home economics on the campus." Of course, the ultimate selection was based on which candidate possessed the best qualities for becoming a husband. Here, the Spice King and his attendants whip up a delightful treat in the kitchen.

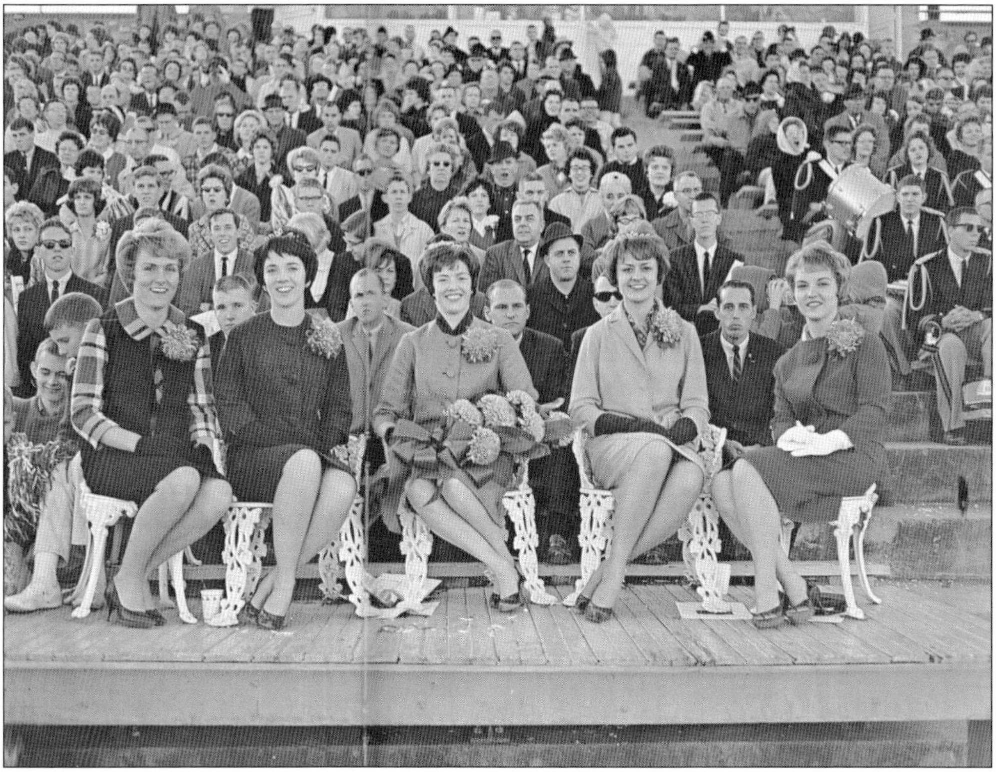

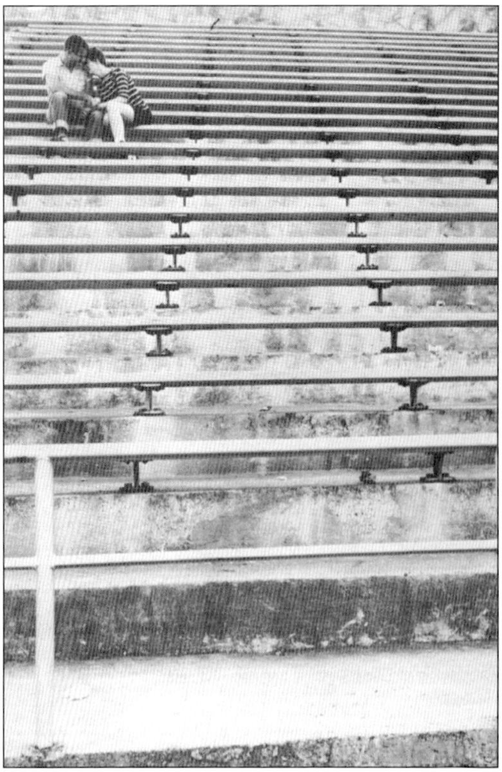

Homecoming weekend is about as big as it gets among the traditions at Southwestern College. There is the downtown parade, the big game, and the crowning. In this 1964 photograph, a panel of royalty sits in front of Builder football fans at Sonner Stadium. Homecoming queen Jan Anderson (center) is pictured here with her attendants. From left to right are Jackie Blackwell, Sherry Urban, Anderson, Shirley Herron, and Jan Wallrabenstein.

Sonner Stadium, dating from 1947, needed to modernize its dirt track. In 1960, SC track coach Bob Dvorak and his squad put down the forms, poured the cement, and worked the cinders down. The track was named for William W. Monypeny, a longtime coach and director of admissions and placement. The new track and Dvorak's coaching turned the SC track program around, resulting in a winning streak that dates back to Kansas Collegiate Athletic Conference victories in 1961, 1962, and 1963.

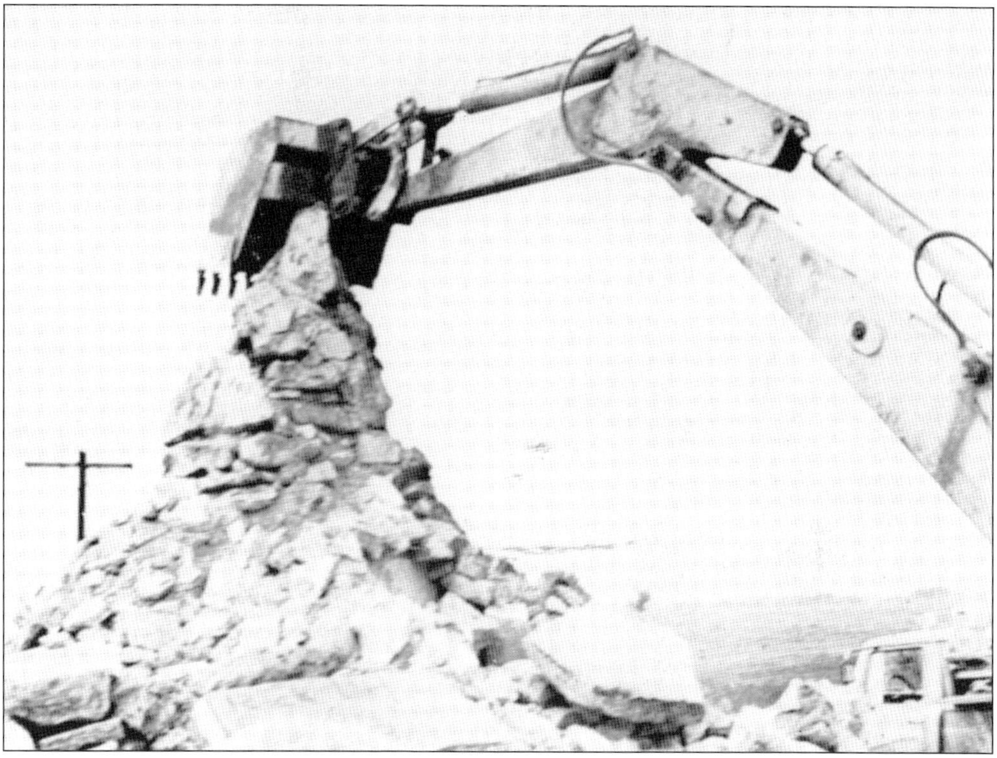

In 1962, the Mound, which had been located at the top of the hill north of Christy Administration Building, was moved to a new location at the bottom of the hill in front of Mossman Hall. The defining Moundbuilding tradition would live on, in a newly relocated spot at a more central place on campus. The spot would be transformed three decades later into a ceremonial platform named Cole Mound Plaza, recognizing thousands of Builder names through the generations.

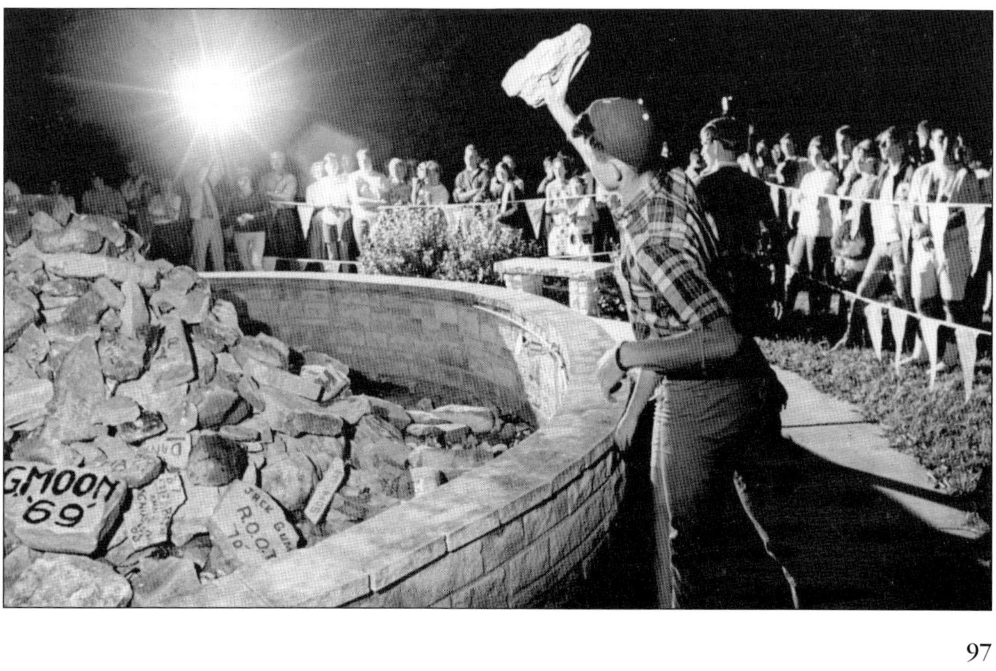

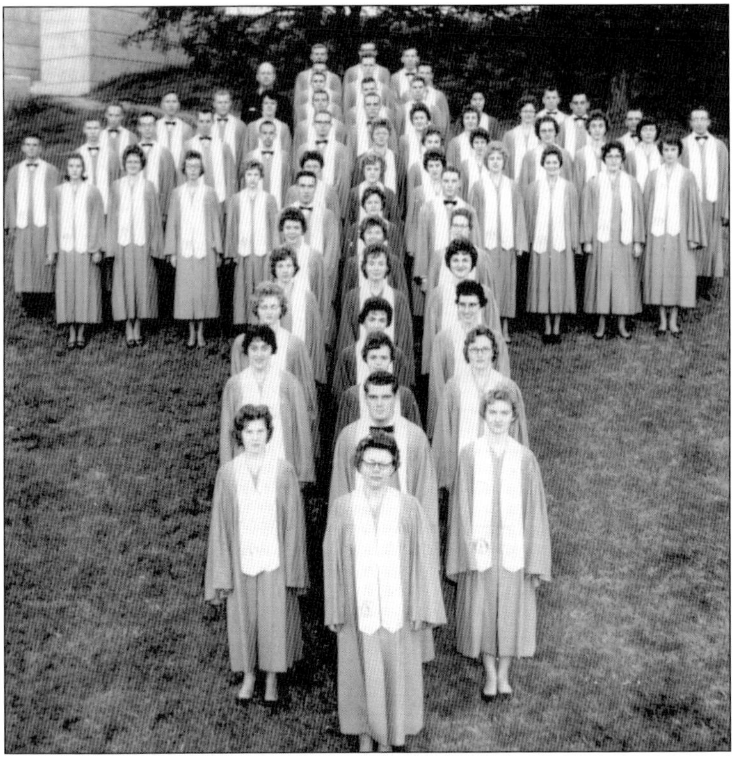

Throughout the college's history, music could be heard all around campus. After 1965, most of the melodic sounds originated from the newly built Darbeth Fine Arts Center. Musically inclined students flocked to join the many singing and orchestral groups, including the Purple Robed Choir, the Southwestern Symphony Orchestra, and the Southwestern College Band.

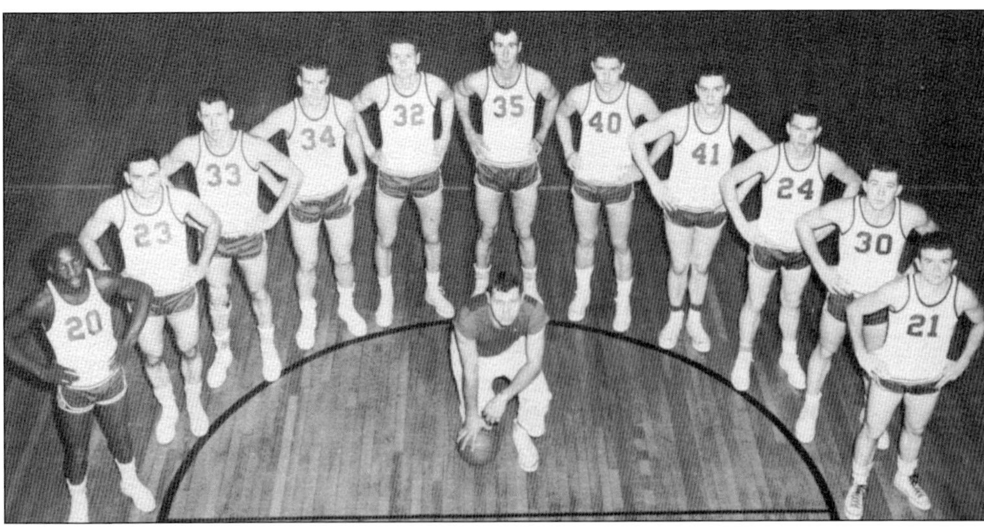

In 1955, the Southwestern men's basketball team won the CIC championship and advanced to the NAIA tournament for the first time in 12 years. At the tournament, held in Kansas City, the team won the first NAIA game against Loyola, but were defeated in the second game, against Eastern Texas State Teachers College. It was a hard-fought defeat, but a proud finish to the season, nevertheless.

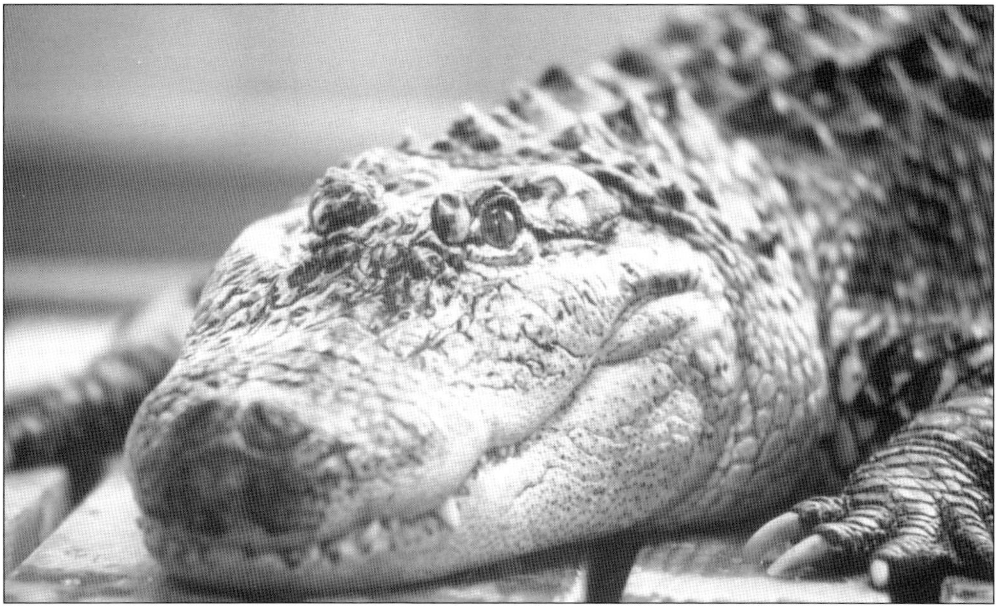

In 1961, Alvin arrived on campus as a gift to Pi Epsilon Pi fraternity members from their brothers in Florida. The baby alligator become a beloved mascot for the college. The science department treasured its "celebrity," who was later moved from a bathtub to a special Mossman Hall suite with a pool. Alvin lived until 2000 and is immortalized today with a commemorative slab on the 77 Steps.

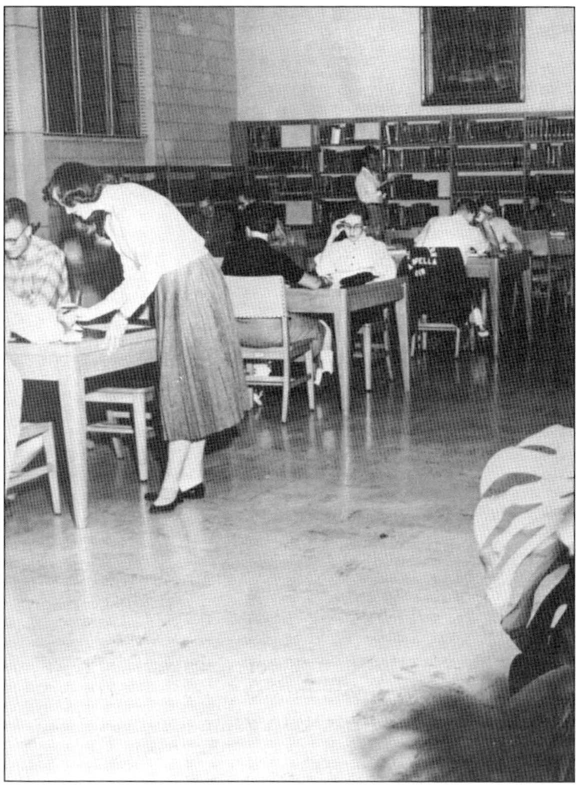

Founders Day 1967 celebrated the dedication of a new addition to the Southwestern Library, named the Frank A. White Library Addition, and the Throckmorton Educational Center, named for Adel Throckmorton, former state superintendent of schools and a 1920 graduate. Also, ground was broken for a new women's gymnasium east of Stewart Field House. Construction of the Ruth Warren Abbott Laboratories, including the campus greenhouse, was completed in 1971–1972. It featured new labs for classes in floriculture and botany.

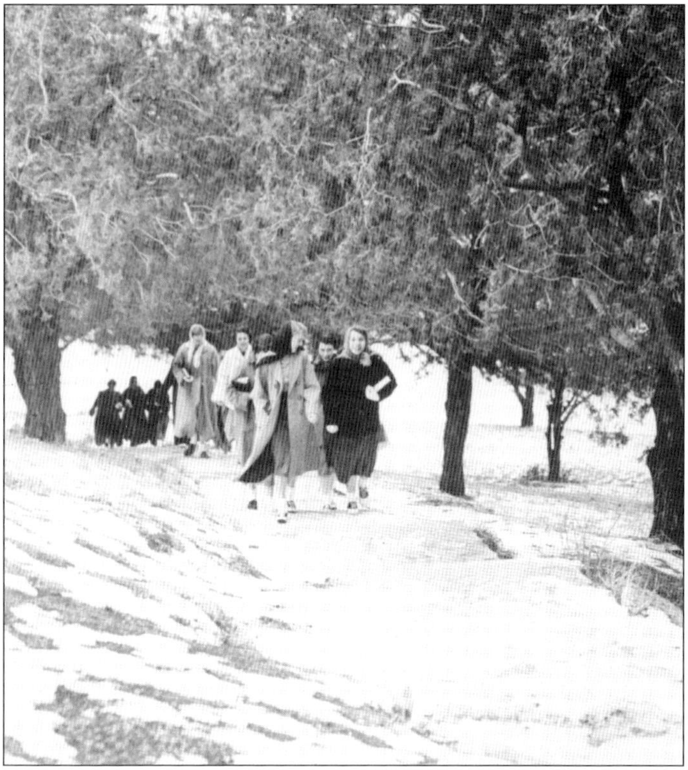

Getting to class meant trekking across Southwestern's 80 acres, whether in bobby socks and saddle shoes, like these students, or in flip-flops, like today's men and women. But, no matter the year, trudging up the sides of College Hill was not for the faint of heart. Here, students in the mid-1950s climb the snow-covered walk from the south end of campus to Christy.

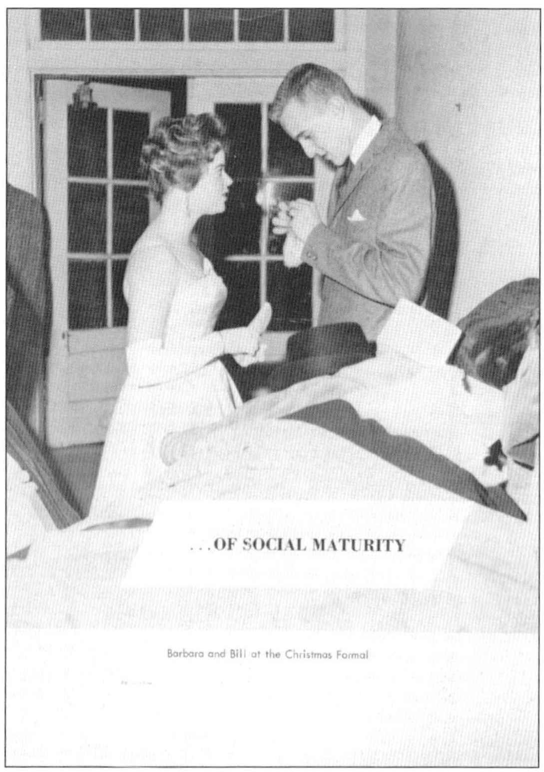

Christmas festivities and traditions at Southwestern usually included the annual presentation of *Eagerheart*, class parties, dorm gift exchanges, worship services, room decorations, and, of course, the elegant Christmas formal dance. The 1961 *Moundbuilder* includes this apt description: "The gayety of the holiday season was evident the evening of the Christmas Formal: music, talk and intermittent laughter created a memory-filled evening . . . an appropriate climax before Christmas vacation."

In 1957–1958, Southwestern began a weekly television program aired each Saturday during the noon hour. The 15-minute program, titled *This Is Southwestern*, was telecast for viewers of KARD-TV, channel 3, out of Wichita. Throughout the months, various departments on campus cooperate to make the show a lively and entertaining feature. During his stint in Iowa, Dr. Strohl was an early advocate of the new medium, using television as an educational tool in the church ministry.

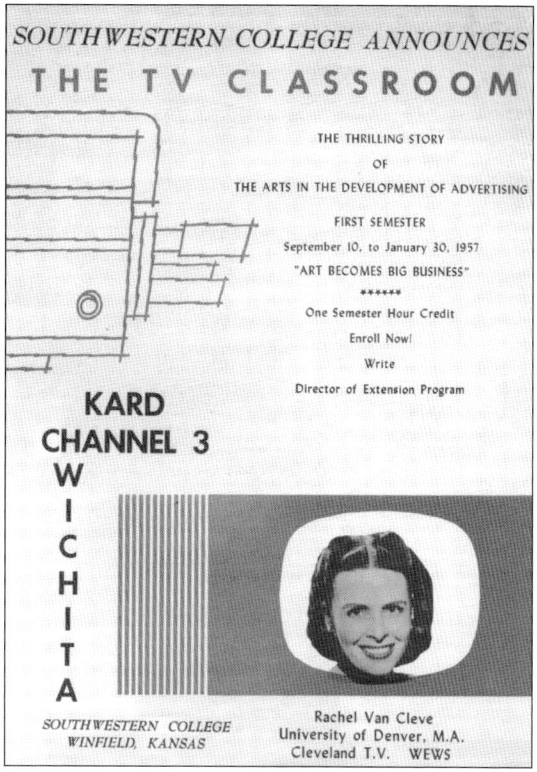

The new Darbeth Fine Arts Center, located where the original Mound once stood, was completed and ready for use by the fall of 1965. Major funding came from Dr. Beth Thompson Wells (class of 1922) and her husband, Darwin, who played an important role in the growth of Christian higher education in Kansas and Oklahoma. Both were awarded honorary doctorates by the college in 1966.

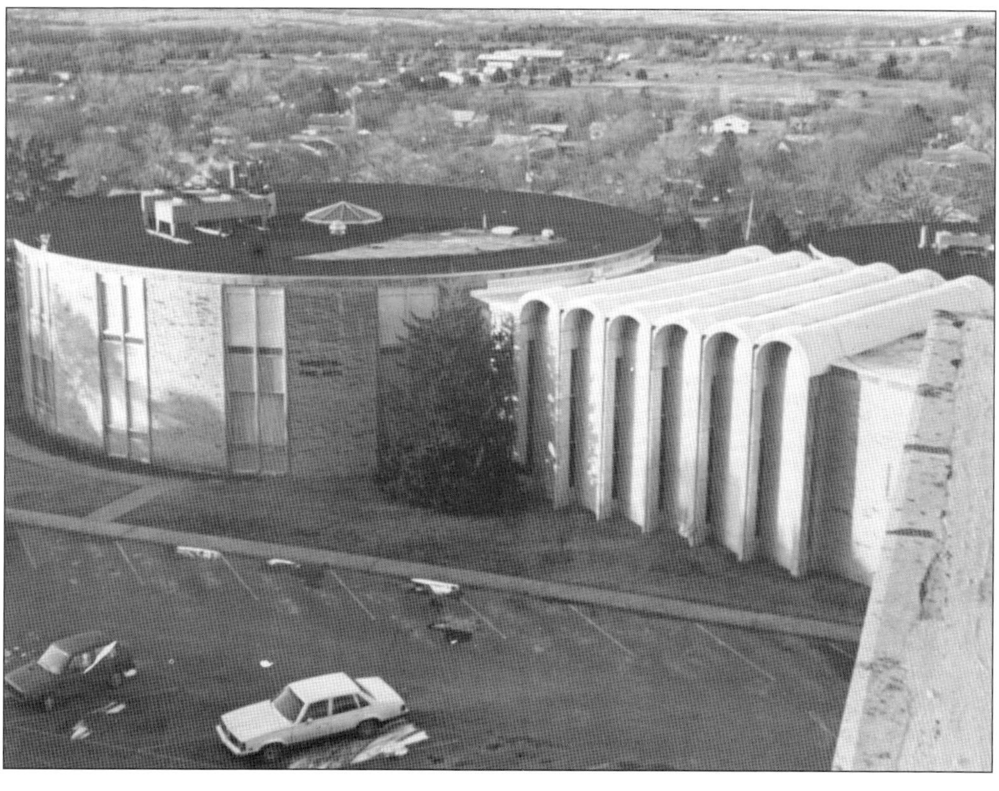

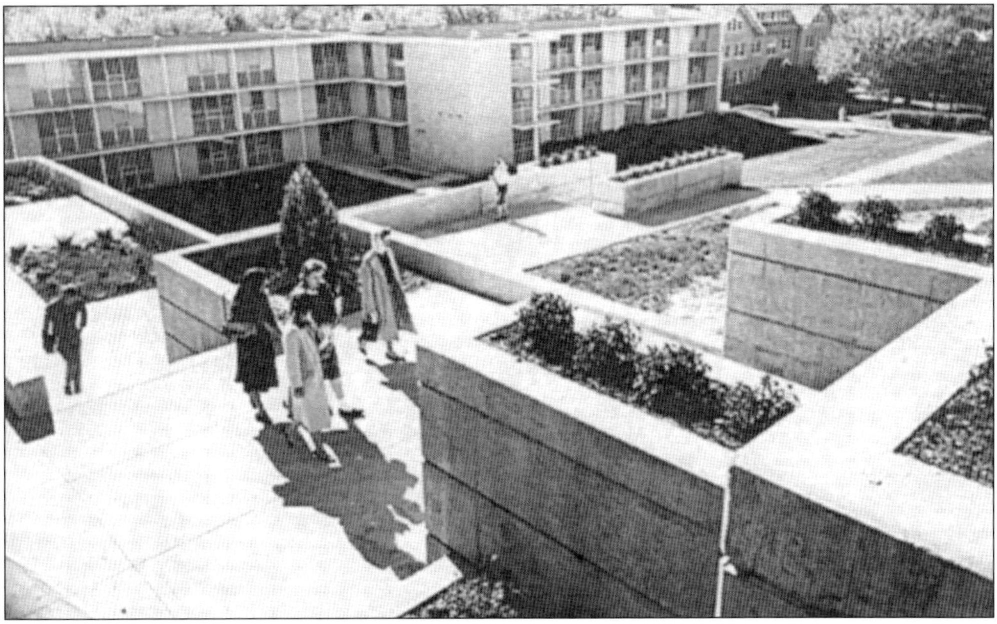

By the time President Strohl stepped down in 1972, Southwestern students were living on a modern, contemporary campus. One constant in the college history will always be the stunning views stretching out over the expansive Walnut Valley.

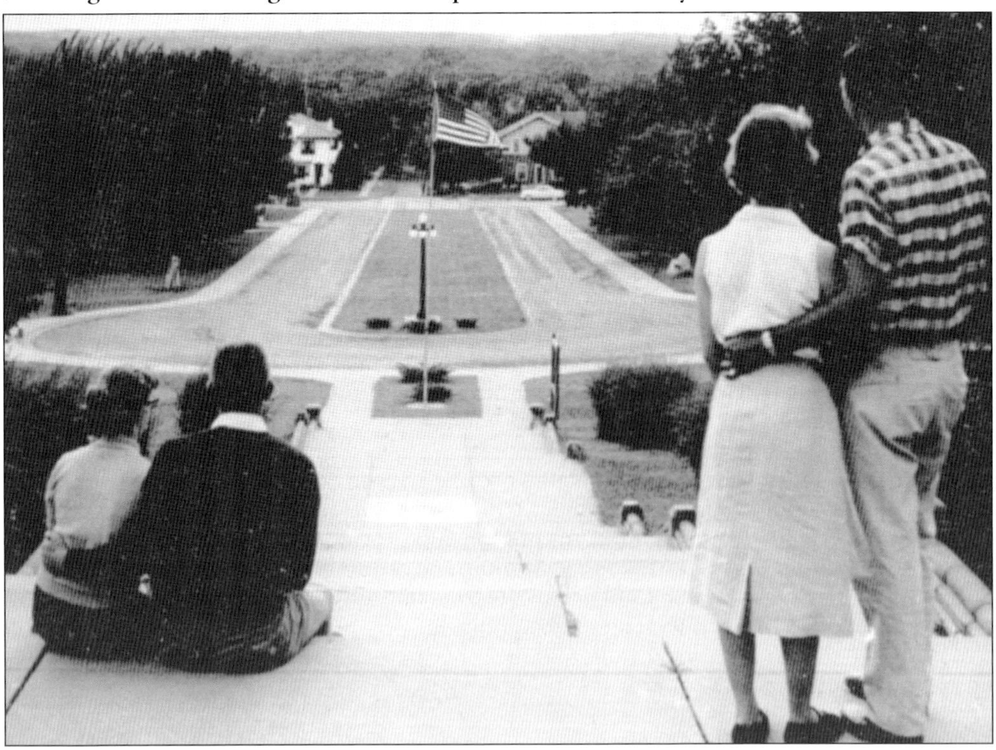

Looking out over Walnut Valley, two couples contemplate their futures. As stated often in the *Moundbuilder* when remarking on the changes at Southwestern, "The past is torn down . . . and replaced by the present . . . while we continually prepare for the future."

Six

Stability and Growth 1973–1998

A new era began at Southwestern when Donald B. Ruthenberg became the college's 14th president in 1972. He was fortunate, beginning his eight-year term with a 700-student enrollment, a complete physical plant, a debt-free balance sheet, and the largest endowment of any college in Kansas. Known for his many ideas and his guiding interests, which formed a vision for the college, Ruthenberg's more flamboyant style was a direct contrast to Strohl's. Like his predecessor and successors, Ruthenberg had to deal with a vocal and assertive student body, then influenced by the cultural changes of the 1960s and energized by concerns for racial justice and opposition to US military involvement in the world.

A quick succession of presidents followed Ruthenberg—first, Robert Paul Sessions (1981–1984), and then Bruce Blake (1984–1988), who left behind a record of positive achievements. After Blake came Southwestern graduate Carl Martin (class of 1960). He knew the college well, having previously been a faculty member, campus chaplain, and trustee.

Martin's mission during his decade-long tenure (1988–1998) was to ensure the college would not fade into "shabby oblivion." His two biggest challenges involved the "neglect of the pursuit of excellence" and physically deteriorating and outdated facilities. A "Builder" in the spirit of Orville Strohl, he would spend $15 million on campus improvements, upgrading facilities to their finest condition ever. Notably, he built the Beech Science Center and renovated Stewart Field House. He championed recruiting a diverse student body. He also established Professional Studies Centers in Winfield and Wichita, aimed at the fastest-growing segment of college students: the working adult.

Of particular note during this era, athletics became an even more prominent factor in school life. After joining the Kansas Collegiate Athletic Association (KCAC) in 1960, Builder sports teams continued to bring home KCAC championships, including those in men's basketball, men's cross country, men's and women's tennis, and men's golf. These victories led to the formation of the Southwestern College Athletic Hall of Fame in 1990, honoring outstanding players, coaches, administrators, and SC supporters.

But, by the dawn of the next millennium, it became clear that an inventive vision was necessary to move the school forward.

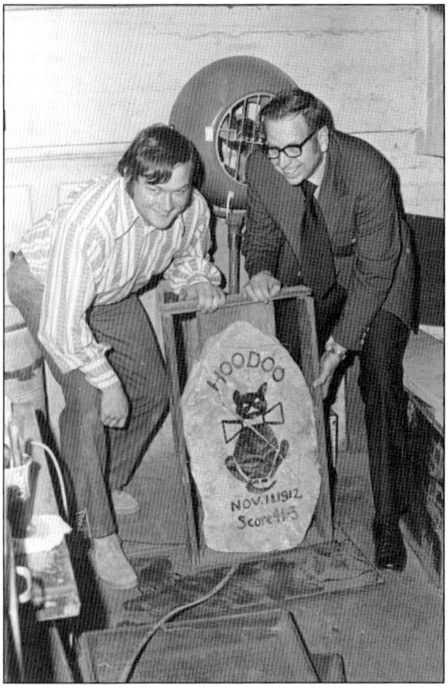

On July 1, 1972, Donald B. Ruthenberg assumed the presidency of Southwestern College. He served until 1980. Here, Ruthenberg (right) and SC student Bob Nation display the original Hoodoo Jinx tombstone, which was rediscovered in 1973 after being concealed in a crate behind a false wall in Stewart Field House for almost 60 years. In the early 1900s, a long-lasting tradition began at SC: whenever the college won a football game, Southwestern students would inscribe the name of the defeated school and the score on a tombstone and place it with other tombstones in a mock cemetery on the campus. One of these tombstones, with a drawing of a black cat (now the Jinx, mascot of Southwestern) and dated November 11, 1912, became the target of thievery by Fairmount College (now Wichita State University). It was stolen, re-stolen, and as legend has it, blown up.

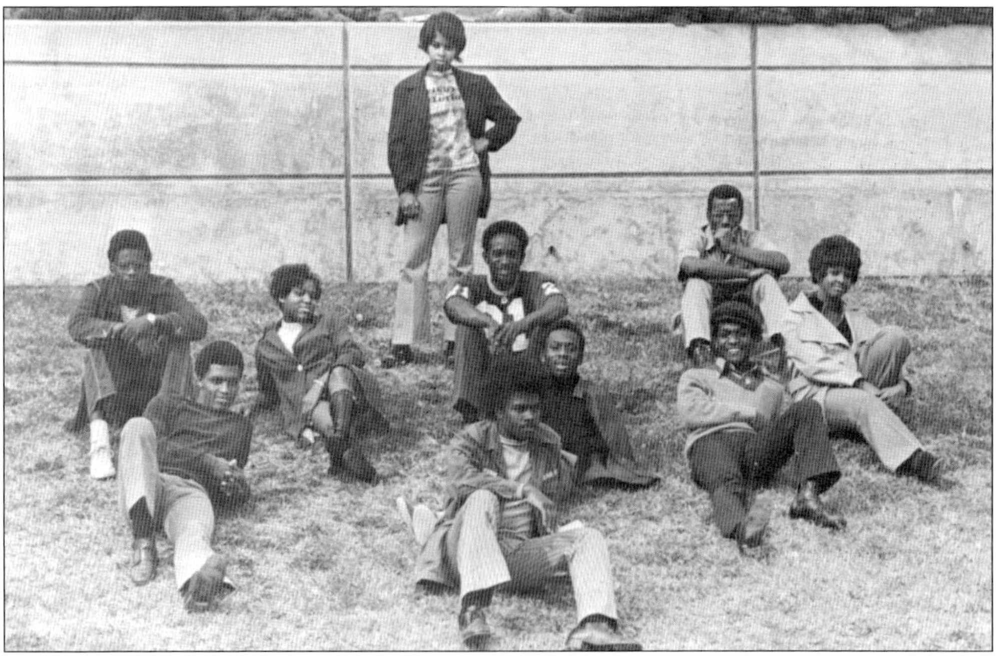

In 1969, a new organization arose on campus: the Black Student Union (BSU). The group reflected the interests and concerns of African American students, part of the national black awakening. The group's goals included the following: "To insure the equality of the Black students at Southwestern; to help reach a better understanding within the campus community of black culture; to provide a medium for the communication of black point of view in the area of curriculum, student recruitment and campus activity; to establish and maintain a healthy communication link between the Black Community of Winfield and the black students on campus." BSU members are shown here in 1972.

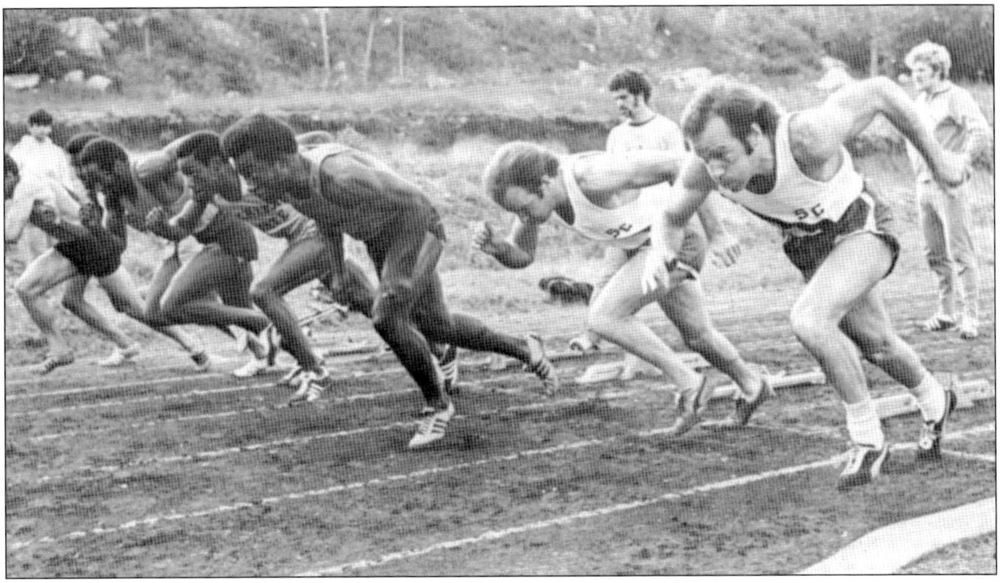

In the spring of 1972, the Southwestern track team captured the KCAC championship by overwhelming second-place McPherson, 198 to 128. This win completed a record-breaking season for the Builders, with records set by Tom Mundinger, Doug Hunter, Darnell Jones, Hal Hinson, Ken Nixon, Edreese Sherman, Dale Mills, Rory Hanson, and Mike Baldwin. Seen here, captains and brothers Angie (second from right) and Vinnie Benevento (far right) start the mile race.

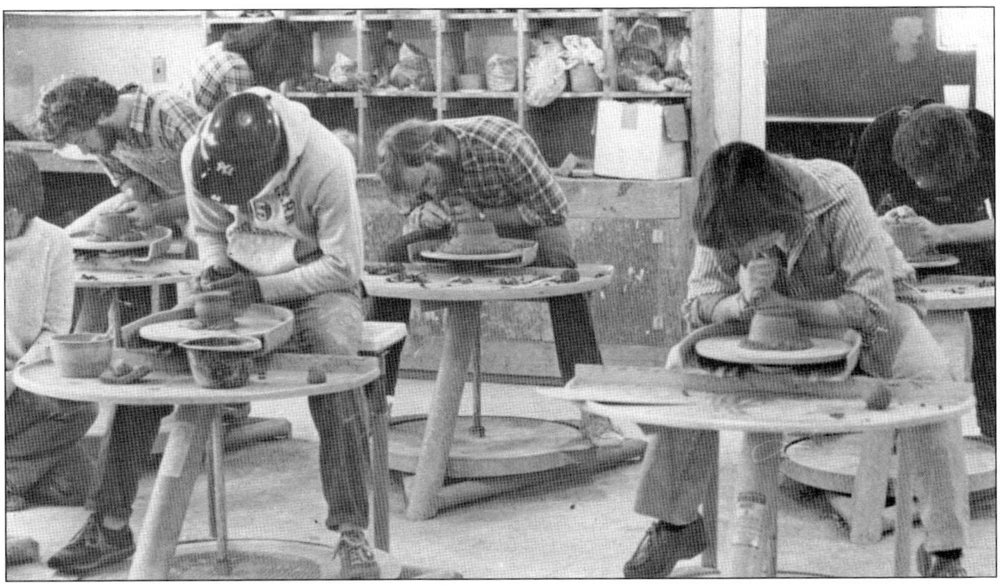

Begun in 1969, January Term brought about a profound change in the curriculum at Southwestern. Designed to open up opportunities for students for independent thinking, depth of study in a single field, problem-solving through individual research, and exploration of the unconventional, the four-week intensive period offered students the chance to remain in Kansas at another peer institution, or travel internationally or to a larger urban center. Non-letter grades were given to encourage students to explore unfamiliar areas. "Jan Term" continued into the early 1990s.

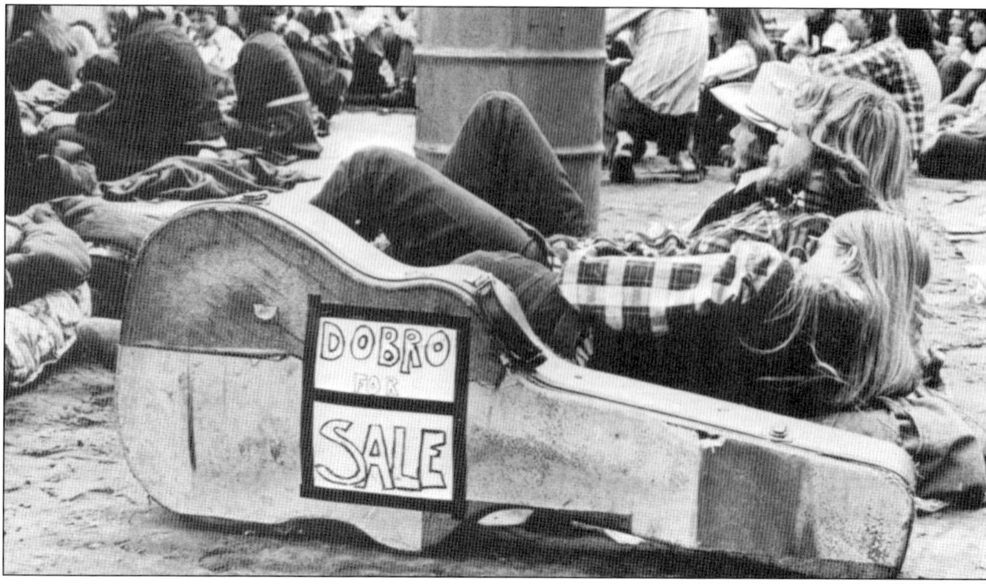

The Walnut Valley Folk Festival was born on Southwestern's campus in the fall of 1971. The Cultural Arts Board and Student Activity Association sponsored the festival, which was planned and organized by Ruth Huber, Mike Totty, and David McMullen in collaboration with Stuart Mossman. With afternoon workshops, concerts, and a fantastic display of "flat-pickin'," this was the perfect beginning for what would become the internationally known Walnut Valley Bluegrass Festival. In late September 1973, the bluegrass festival and the second-annual Flat-Picking Championship was held at the fairgrounds, attracting music lovers from across the United States. Today, the multiday festival continues to be Winfield's premiere attraction.

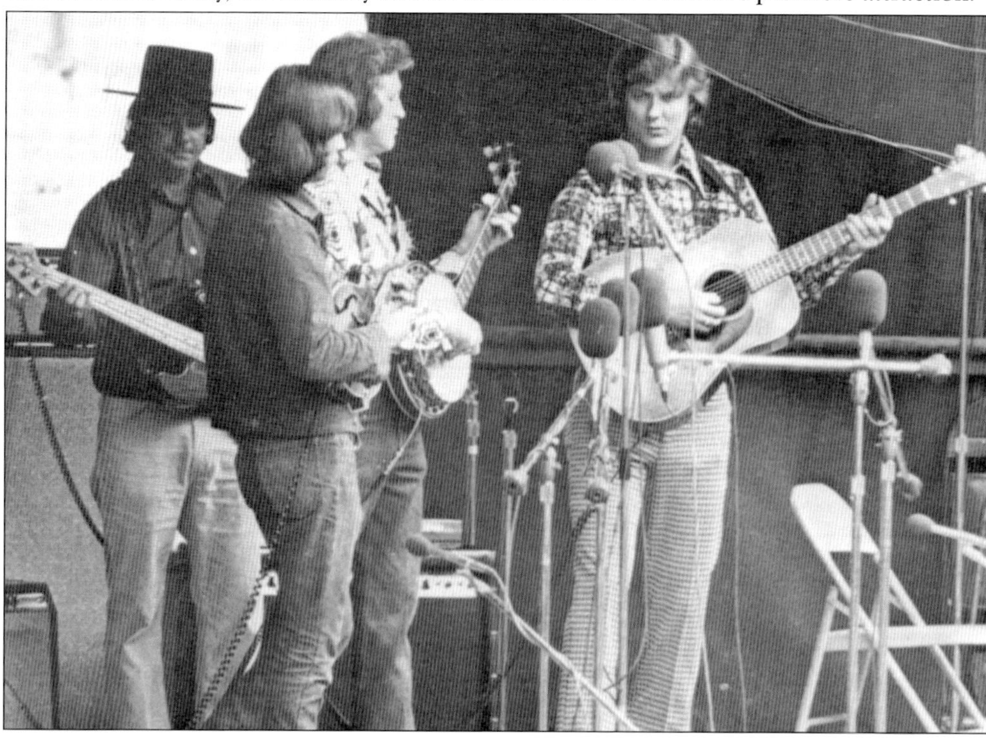

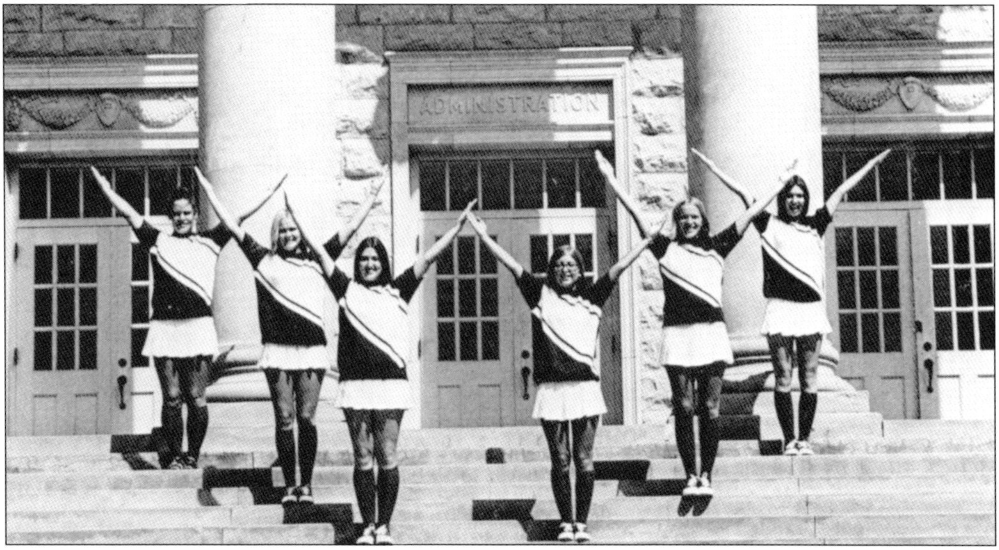

In 1974, varsity cheerleaders, from left to right, Laura Monson, Krista Goff, Susie Scheider, Terry Pulaski, Lynette Helmer, and Jo Lynn Skaggs attended a national spirit and sportsmanship workshop sponsored by the National Cheerleader Association. At the workshop, they learned new cheers. The squad placed third in the competition against 15 other colleges.

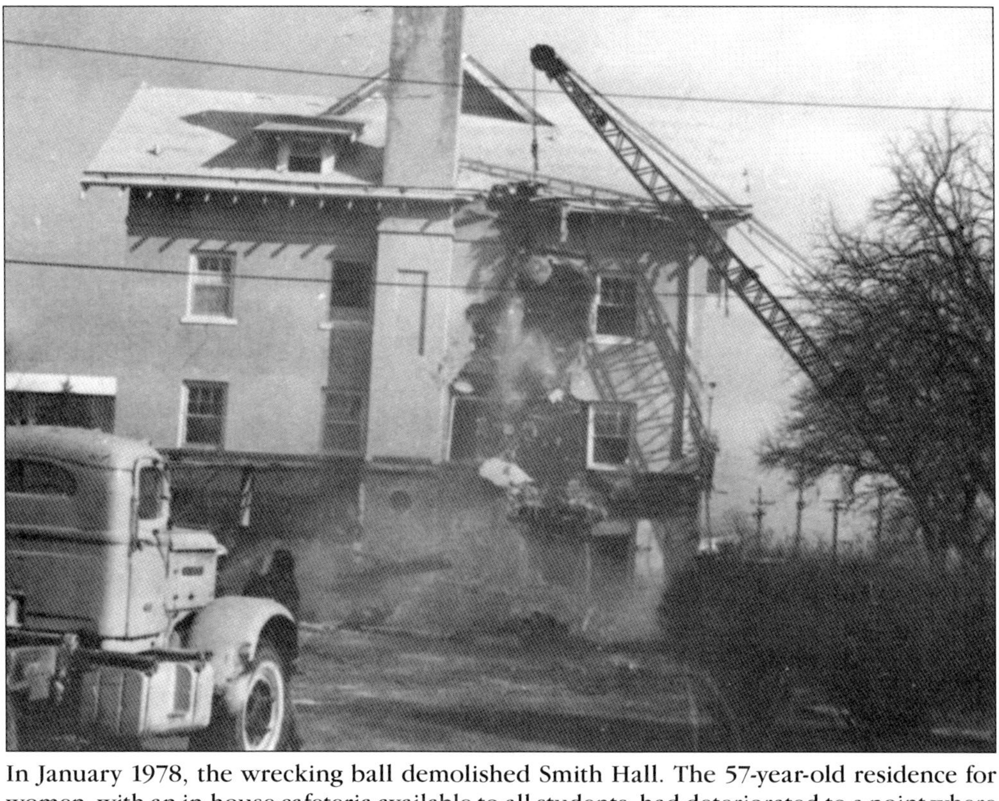

In January 1978, the wrecking ball demolished Smith Hall. The 57-year-old residence for women, with an in-house cafeteria available to all students, had deteriorated to a point where it was no longer usable, just like Holland Hall. With Smith gone, the other residence halls were Broadhurst, Reid, and Wallingford.

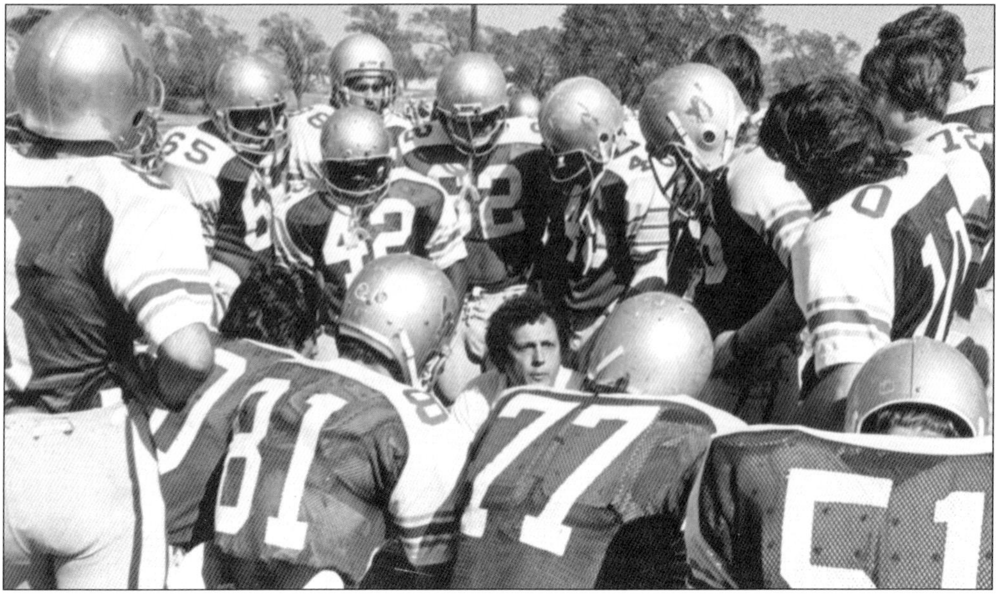

Builder football adopted a new game plan in 1977, when Phil Hower (class of 1964) took over as head coach. Hower ramped up player size, squad depth, and focused on quickly maturing the 35 new faces he added to the 27 returning players, in order to be strong enough to play highly competitive KCAC varsity ball. Phil Hower coached the Moundbuilders from 1977 until 1980. Phil is the son of former Moundbuilder coach Robert Hower. Both are now in the SC Hall of Fame.

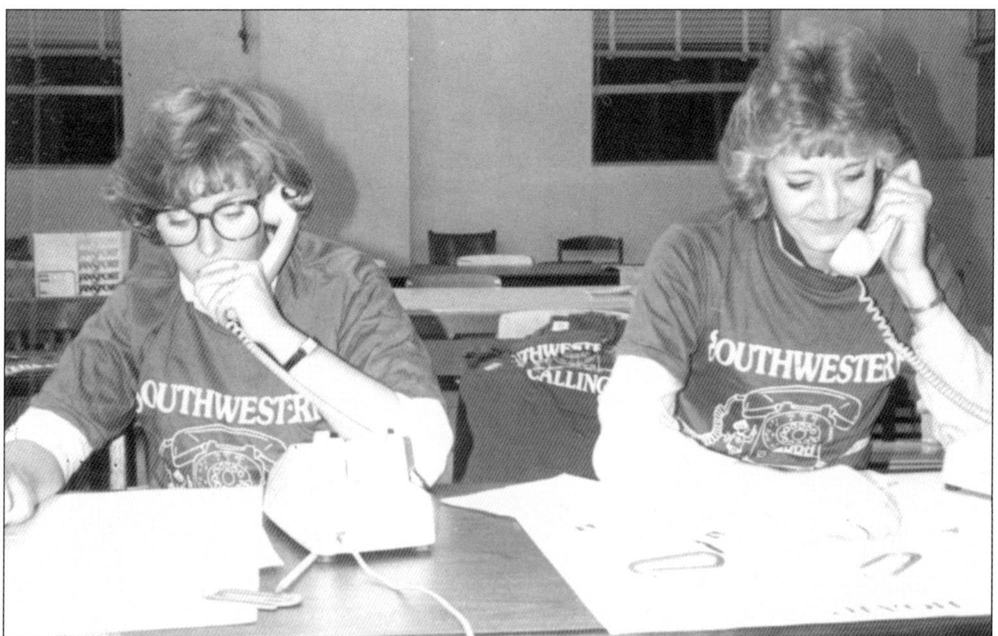

The annual 24-hour Phone-A-Thon became a college tradition beginning in the 1970s. Supported by scores of alumni volunteers and current students, the dialing for dollars originated from a calling center on campus, and it continued for many years. Much of the money raised each year would underwrite the 1976 Centennial Scholars.

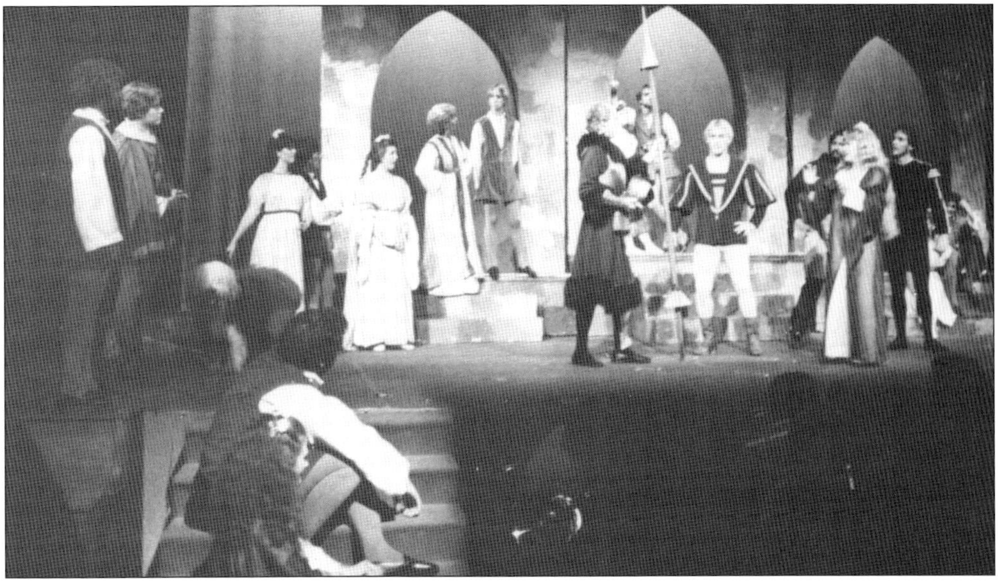

The classic musical *Camelot* was the highlight of the 1980 homecoming. The combined efforts of SC's drama department, St. John's drama department, and Winfield Community Theatre made possible the hiring of a New York director, Jack Eddleman, along with costume and set designers. Volunteers throughout the community of Winfield made over 200 costumes for the production. The play was a rousing success.

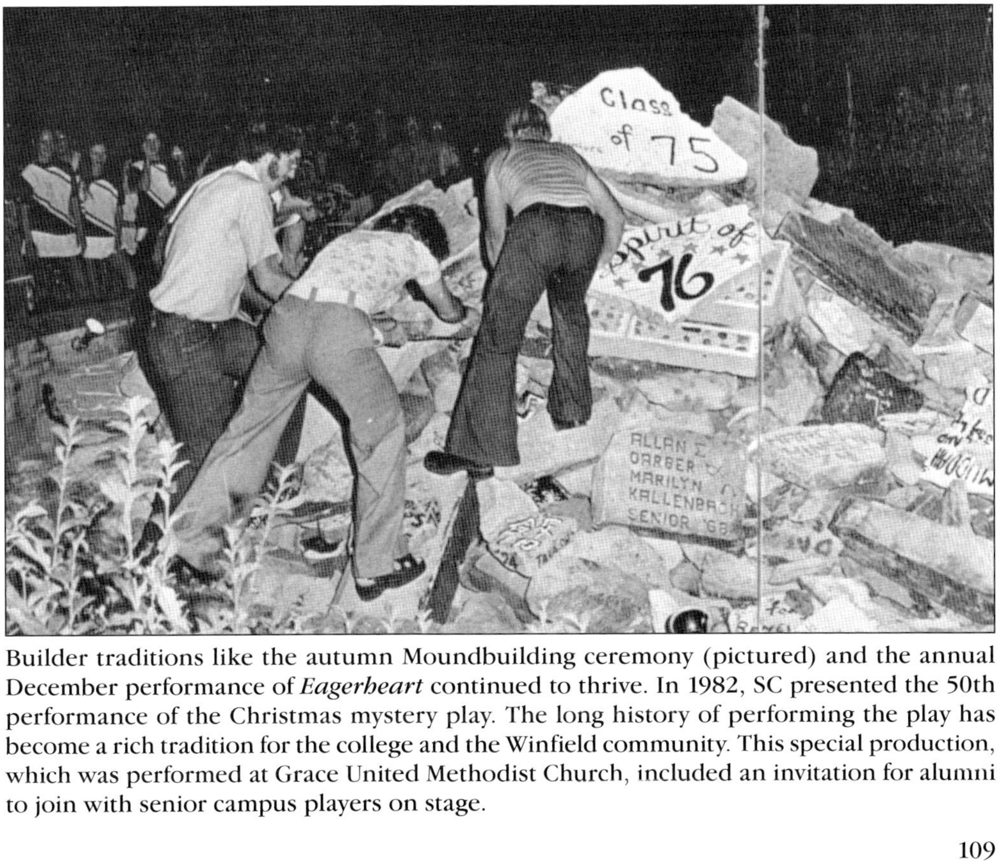

Builder traditions like the autumn Moundbuilding ceremony (pictured) and the annual December performance of *Eagerheart* continued to thrive. In 1982, SC presented the 50th performance of the Christmas mystery play. The long history of performing the play has become a rich tradition for the college and the Winfield community. This special production, which was performed at Grace United Methodist Church, included an invitation for alumni to join with senior campus players on stage.

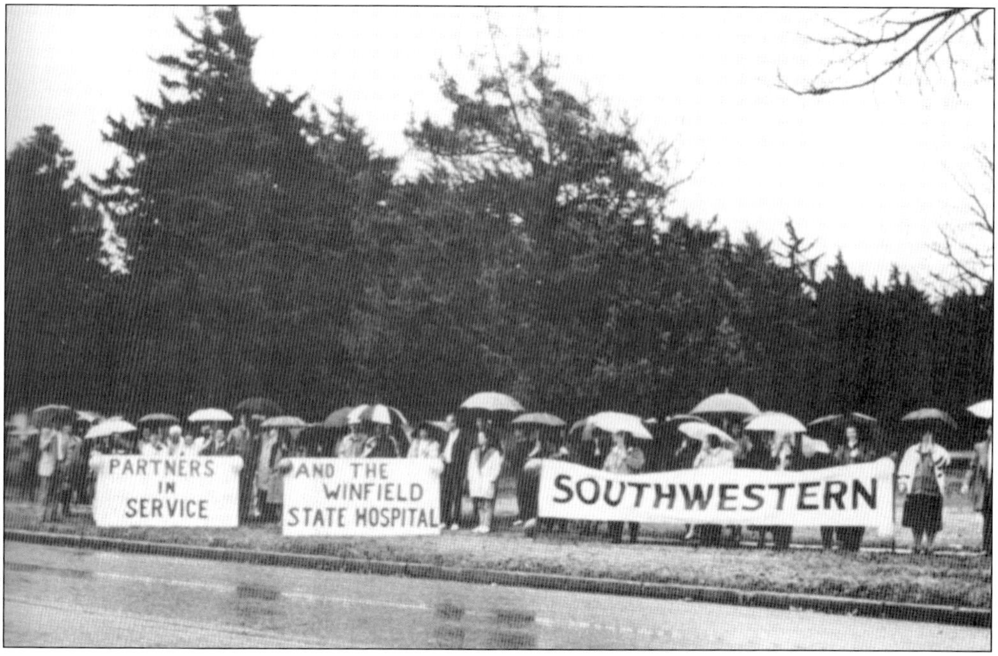

On a cold, rainy day in 1993, Southwestern students, faculty, and staff joined the city of Winfield to demonstrate their support for keeping the Winfield State Hospital open. The Kansas State Legislature threatened to close the longtime Winfield facility. The institution was eventually closed.

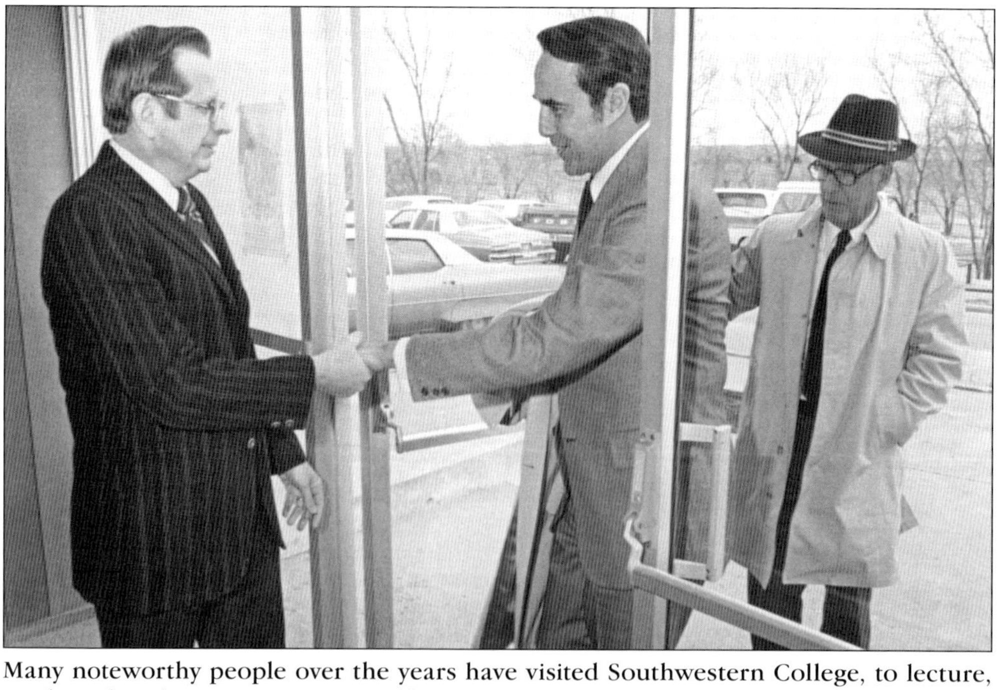

Many noteworthy people over the years have visited Southwestern College, to lecture, teach, and study. Kansas senator and longtime Republican majority leader and presidential contender Bob Dole visited the campus in the early 1980s. Here, Dole (center) is greeted at the door by President Ruthenberg.

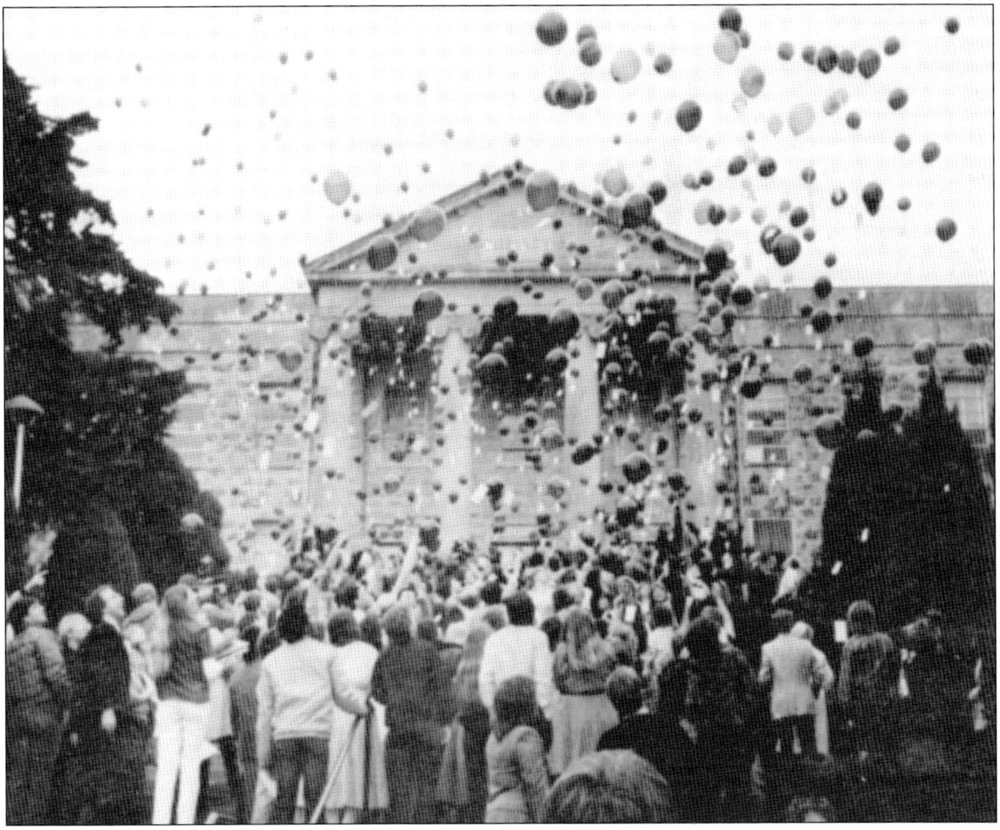

In April 1985, a big party consumed the campus of Southwestern College for the 100th birthday celebration. Highlights included a newly redecorated Christy lobby, balloons with messages attached launched from the 77 Steps, a Founders Day dinner, a massive birthday cake, and distribution of centennial medallions to those in attendance.

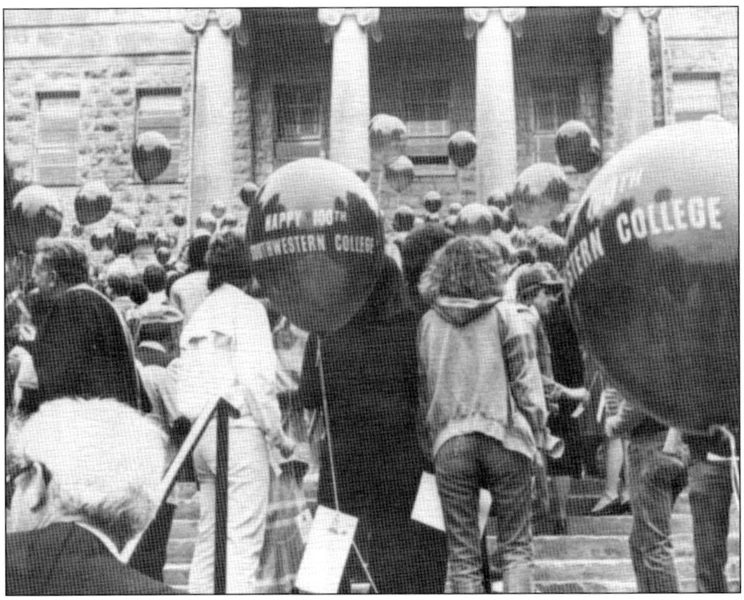

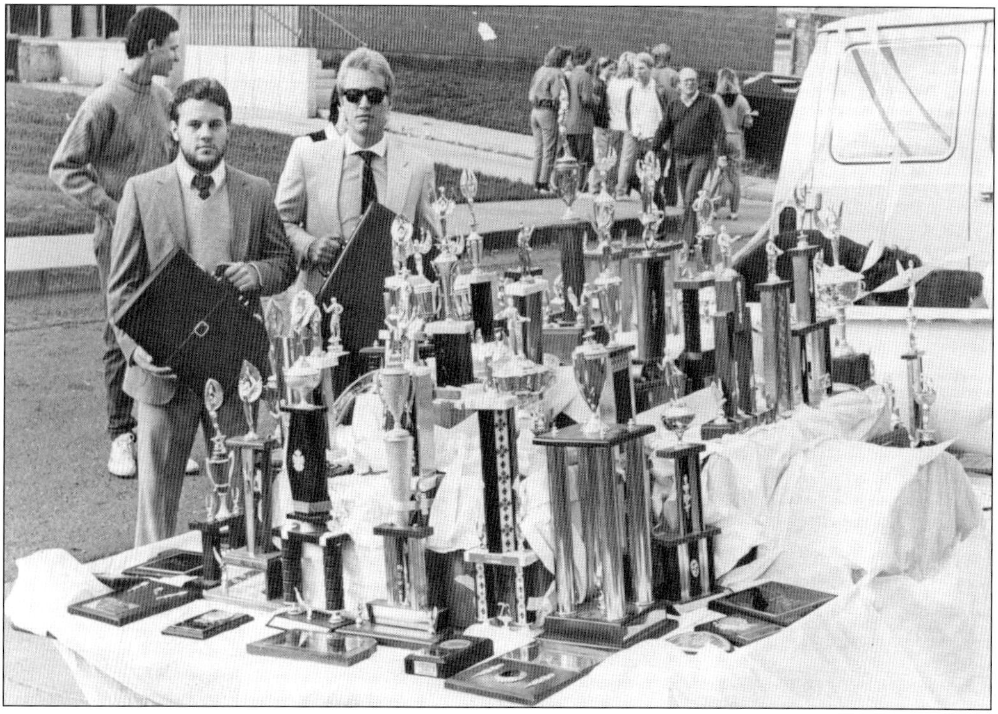

Southwestern debaters Paul McDonald (left) and Bill Sweeney stand at attention beside the 1986 homecoming float with a display of debate trophies. Their competitive team, consisting largely of freshmen, competed in four national tournaments and finished the year ranked among the top 30 out of 323 schools competing in cross-examination debate.

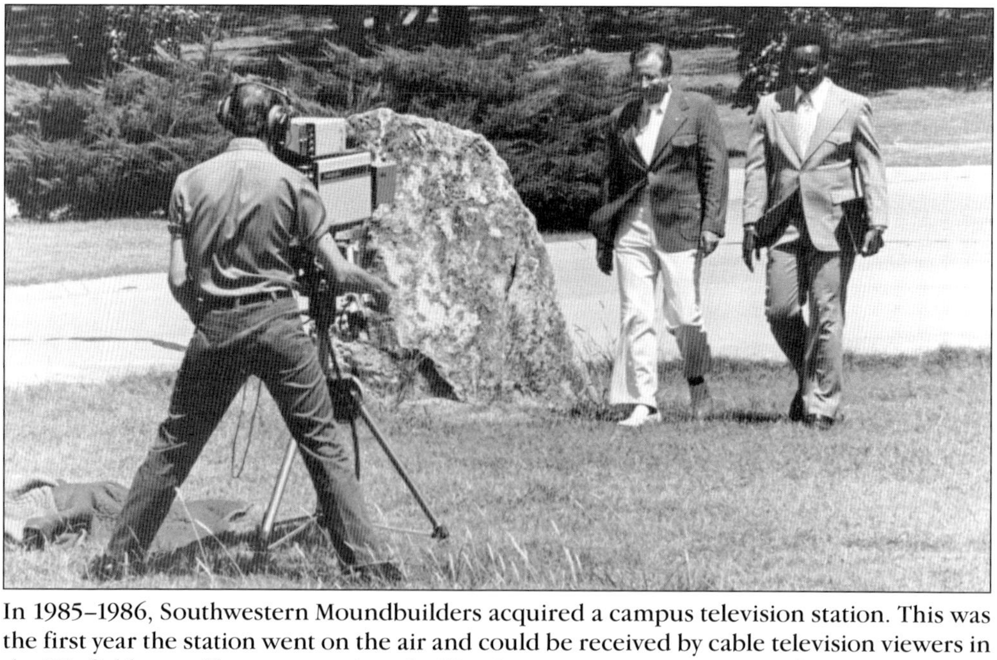

In 1985–1986, Southwestern Moundbuilders acquired a campus television station. This was the first year the station went on the air and could be received by cable television viewers in the Winfield area. The crew produced a 30-minute program consisting of campus-oriented activities, and station personnel interviewed administrators, faculty, and students.

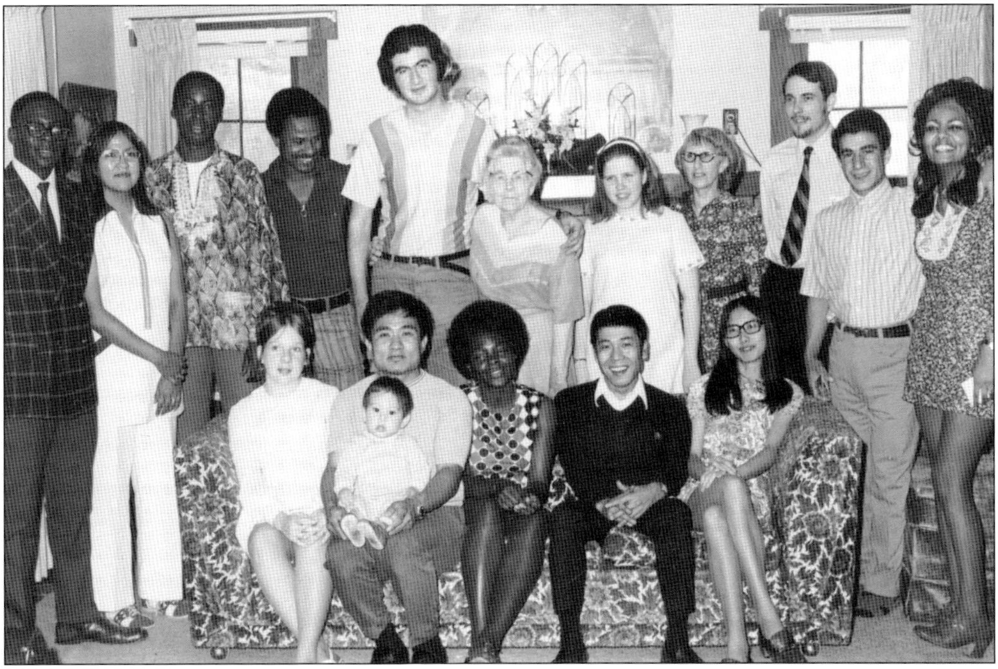

Once called the Commonwealth Club, now the International Club, this organization has for decades introduced foreign students and their home nations to the student body, as well as the Winfield community through a host-family program. By emphasizing the importance of cross-cultural experiences, the club also promotes community talks and an annual International Cuisine Night, featuring native dishes and authentic music from other parts of the globe.

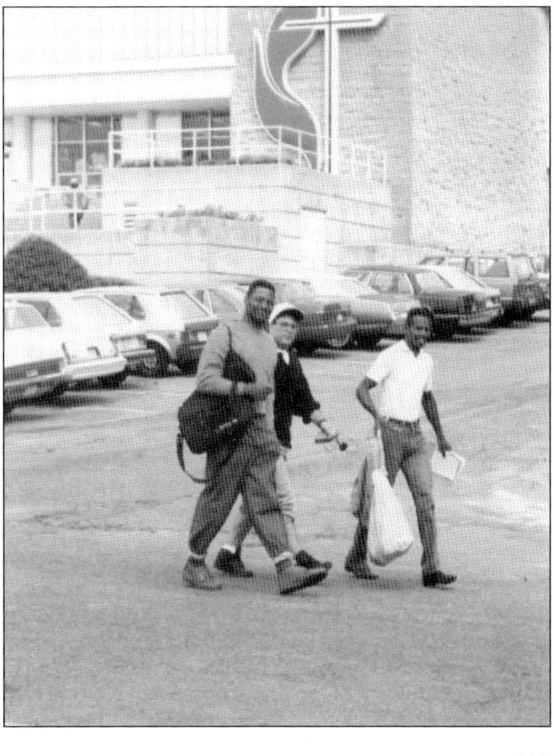

In 1987, the Methodist cross and flame logo made its appearance on the side of the Roy L. Smith Student Center, where it would remain for two decades. Although the logo was removed years ago, the shadow of its outline is still visible today, signifying the less-direct relationship between the school and the church.

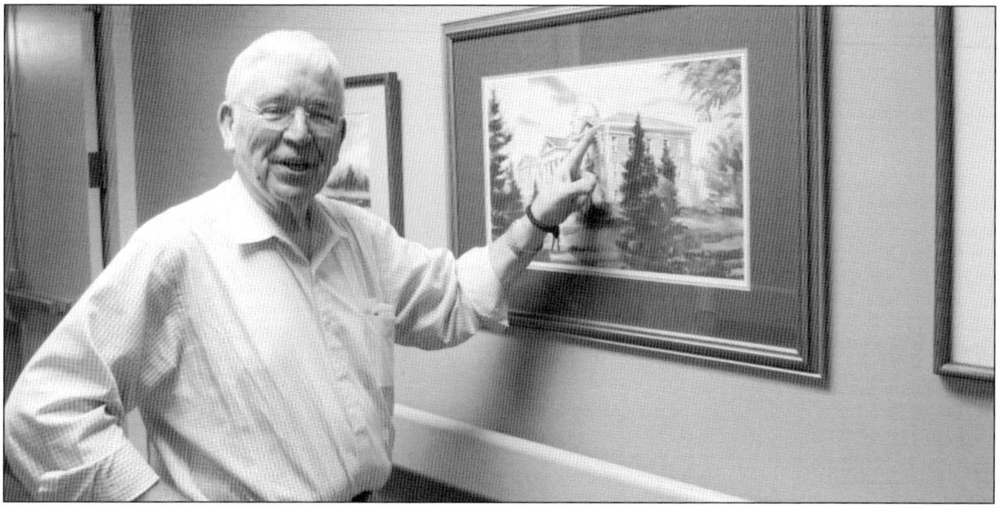

In September 1988, Carl E. Martin, an SC graduate (class of 1960) with a degree in history, speech, and political science, became president of Southwestern College. Martin had served his alma mater as chaplain and as a member of the faculty before taking the reigns as president for a decade. Here, Martin, now retired, points to the Richardson Hall dome in a favorite painting he owns.

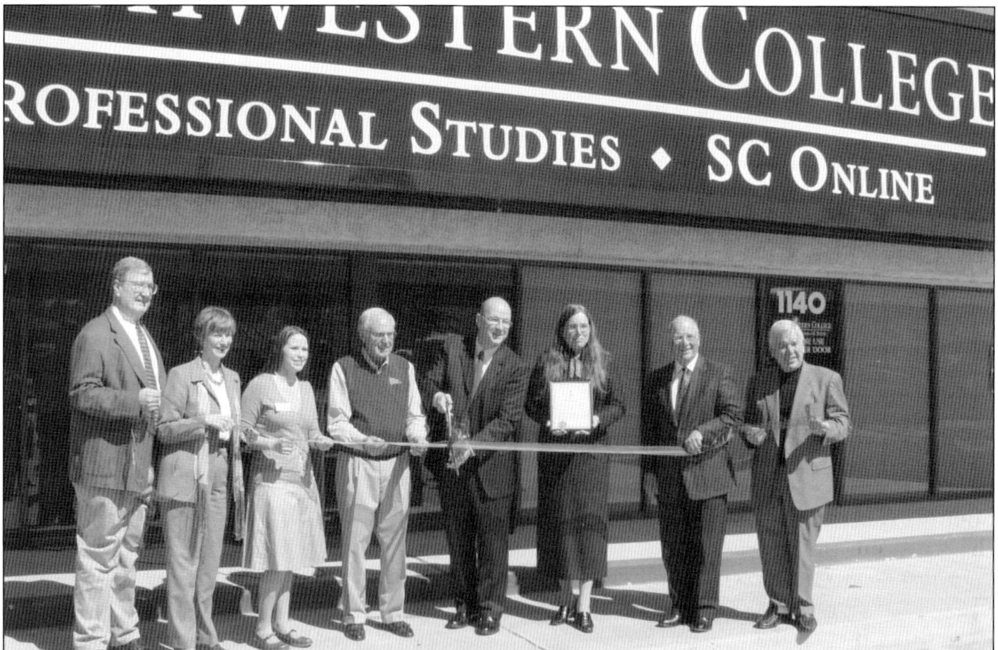

A significant event occurred on May 3, 1996, when Southwestern opened its doors to a larger and more diverse constituency that enrolled in SC's Wichita Professional Studies Center classes. The program for degree-oriented adult learners was received enthusiastically. By 2001, business administration and pastoral studies were added. The ribbon-cutting ceremony on March 10, 2005, included Pres. Dick Merriman (center with scissors) and to the right of him, from left to right, Karen Pedersen, Marvin Hafenstein, and SC president emeritus Carl Martin.

Seven

Moving into the 21st Century 1999–Present

Dr. William Richard Merriman Jr., son of a United Methodist minister, became Southwestern's 18th president in August 1998. He had the distinction of being the first lay president in almost a century. He brought his experience as a scholar, educator, administrator, and most importantly, a fruitful fundraiser to the college.

Southwestern required a new operational model if it was to survive and prosper in the 21st century. Simply put, more students, more programs, and more money were needed. The trustees charged Merriman with achieving these vital goals.

His predecessor, Carl Martin, had begun the process of transforming the college's finances with the establishment of the professional studies program and by encouraging popular courses in business, teacher education, and nursing. Merriman would build and expand upon on these initiatives. In doing so, he welcomed new technologies. Southwestern would be the first college in a multistate region to issue each incoming freshman a laptop computer. Then, thanks to the Internet, online learning was made available to students around the globe through the professional studies program.

In implementing his vision, Merriman formalized the college's transition from a liberal-arts institution into a comprehensive college, focusing on serving a wider range of students in terms of age, race, socioeconomic status, nationality, and variety of degrees. He did this by providing a wider range of pedagogies and means of delivering instruction. In all this, Southwestern was reaffirming what it had long done—providing quality education to meet the requirements of the day.

In May 2015, Dr. Merriman completed his tenure at Southwestern. On his watch, the number of undergraduates had doubled from 1998, and the number of graduate students had grown from three into the hundreds. Most important, he had put the school's finances on a sound basis. The endowment had increased to $30 million, up from $14 million. Annual giving to the college had more than doubled, from about $2 million to about $4.5 million. He also led two capital campaigns and several project-specific fund drives that raised more than $50 million for campus improvements, endowment, and other student services.

President Merriman shall always be remembered as an exceptional Builder, ranking in the tradition of its best presidents.

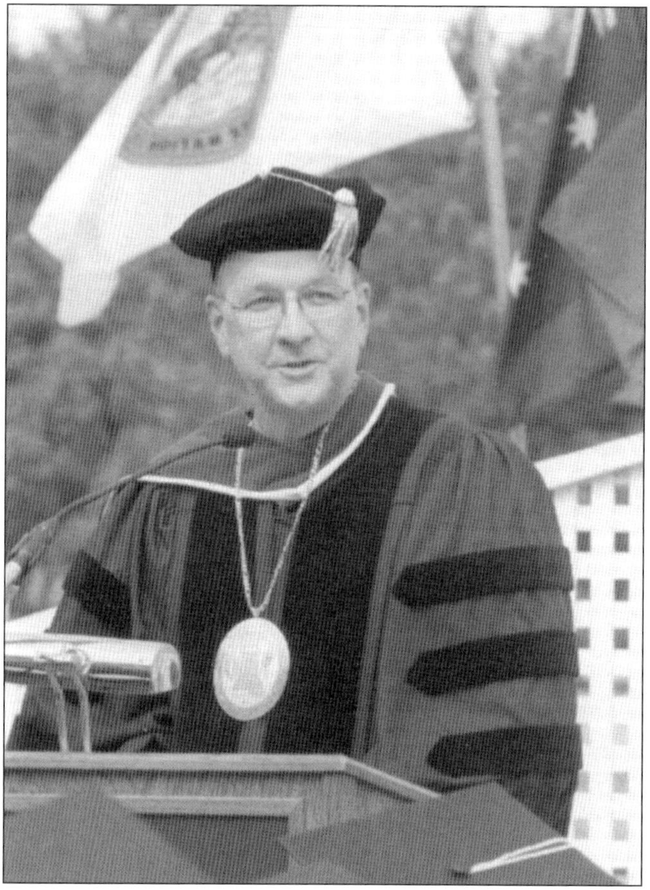

Pres. W. Richard Merriman presided over his 17th graduation ceremonies on May 10, 2015, before leaving for the University of Mount Union in Ohio. Merriman converted the college into a 21st-century institution offering a comprehensive educational program. In doing so, he focused on meeting the needs of students, making full use of modern technologies, and growing the professional studies program. Merriman took particular pride in the success of SC's adult learners upon their graduation.

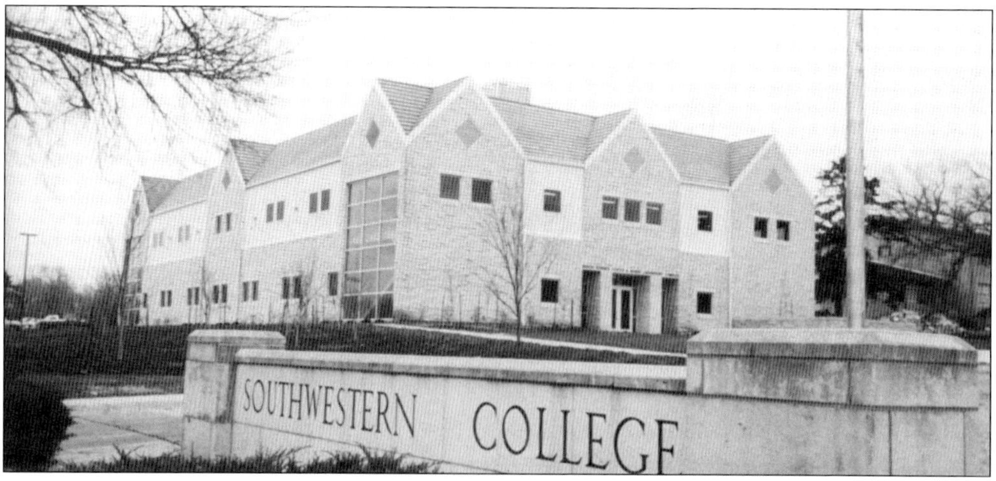

Situated on the northwest corner of campus, the impressive Beech Science Center and Mabee Laboratory Complex opened in 1998 with the most up-to-date science facilities located in the southern Kansas region. Inside the 35,600-square-foot building is the one-of-a-kind cadaver lab, where students receive close to a professional forensic experience. From the college's early days, science has played a prominent part in the curriculum. Both the program and its graduates have received much national acclaim.

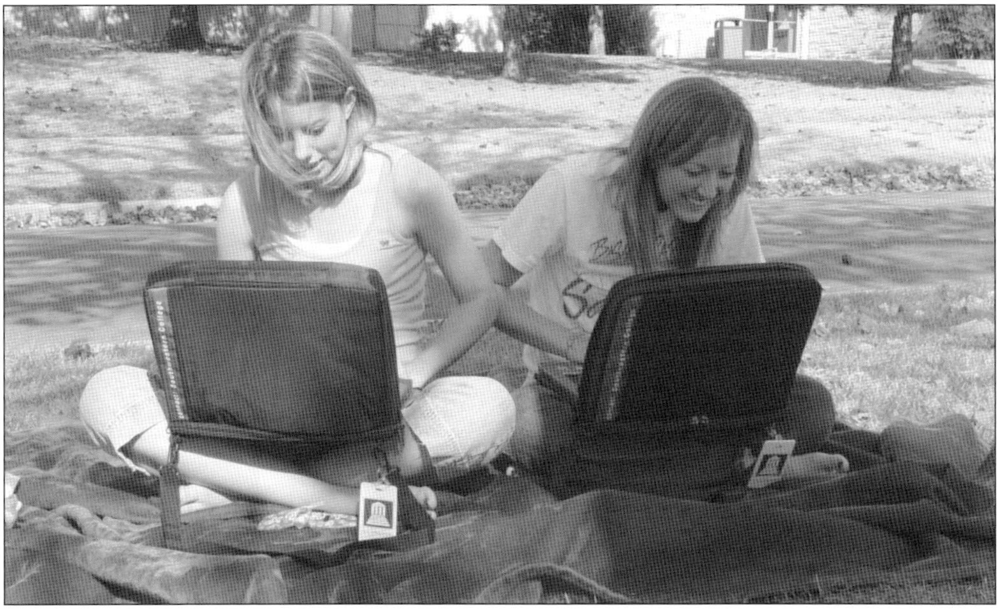

Southwestern fully entered the 21st century in 1999 when it became the first college or university in the region to issue laptops to all new students. It also became the first college in Kansas to go wireless, with access provided in all classroom and commons areas across the campus. From the lawns and cafeteria to the library and locker rooms, students were delighted to be digitally connected.

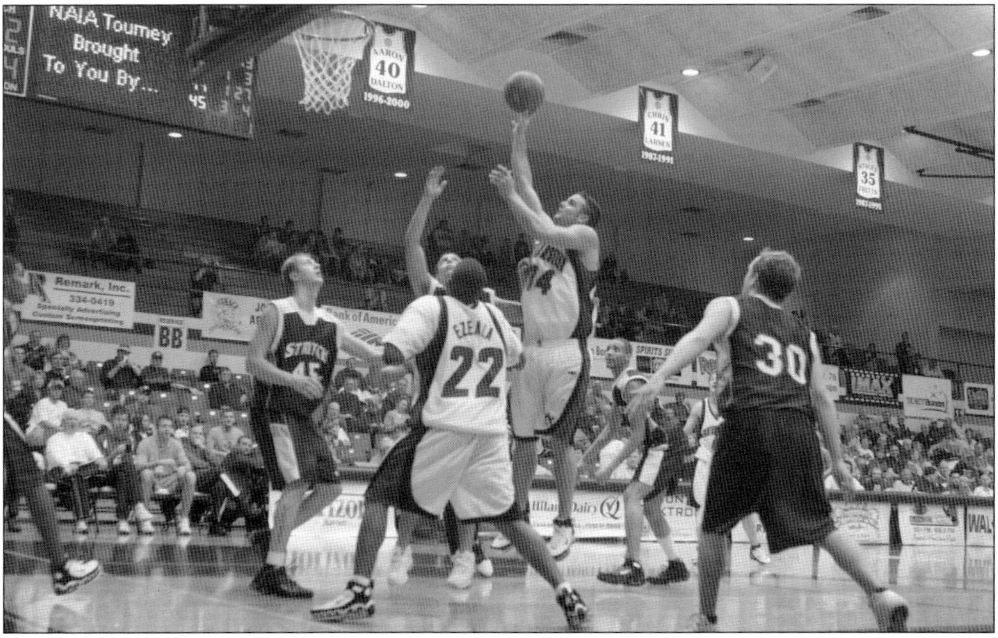

In the spring of 1998, the Builder men's basketball team finished as champions of the KCAC and journeyed to Idaho for the NAIA Division II national basketball tournament. It had been 43 years since the Builders last went to nationals. Although they lost in the first round, they came home with an All-American, Donald Carter, and an All-American Honorable Mention, Kyle Wollenberg. Carter was also named KCAC Player of the Year.

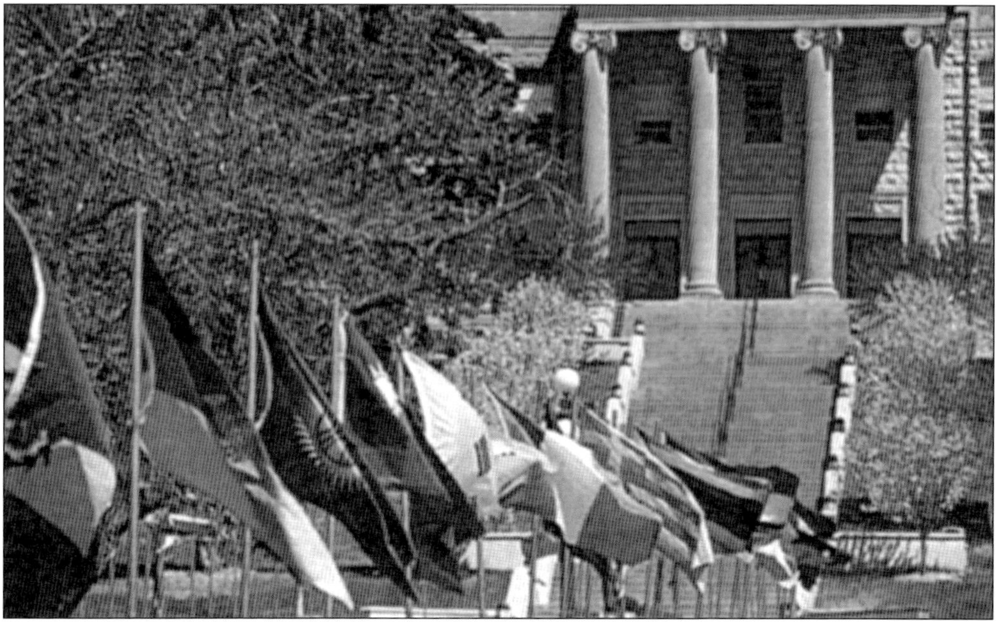

"Builders Around the World," a brightly colored collection of flags representing Southwestern students and faculty from other countries, flies from tall poles along Kirk Drive on special days at SC. The collection includes 34 flags from nations, as well as the UN flag, the US Foreign Service flag, and the Ambassador's Flag, which was presented by Dr. Loy Henderson (class of 1915), a former ambassador to India and career diplomat.

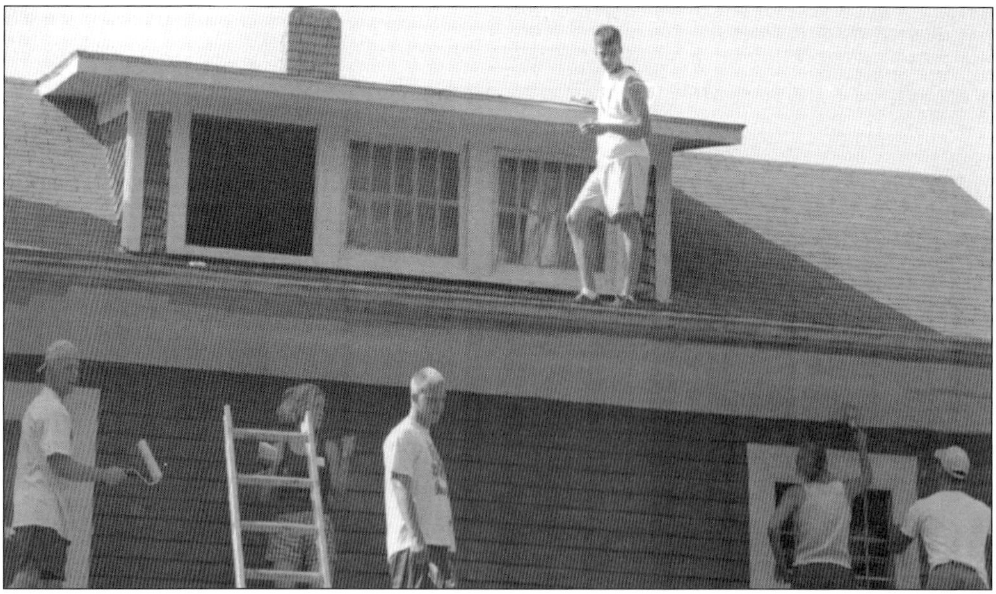

Freshman Work Day, which began in 1992, provides a rich learning experience for freshmen and exchange students, not only for the help they offered the needy in the Winfield community, but also in getting to know and work with one another. Typical projects include building a barn, scraping, staining, cleaning and painting houses, mowing lawns, and working in gardens. This social consciousness reflects a strong tradition dating back to the college's Methodist origins. (Photograph by Julie Morgan.)

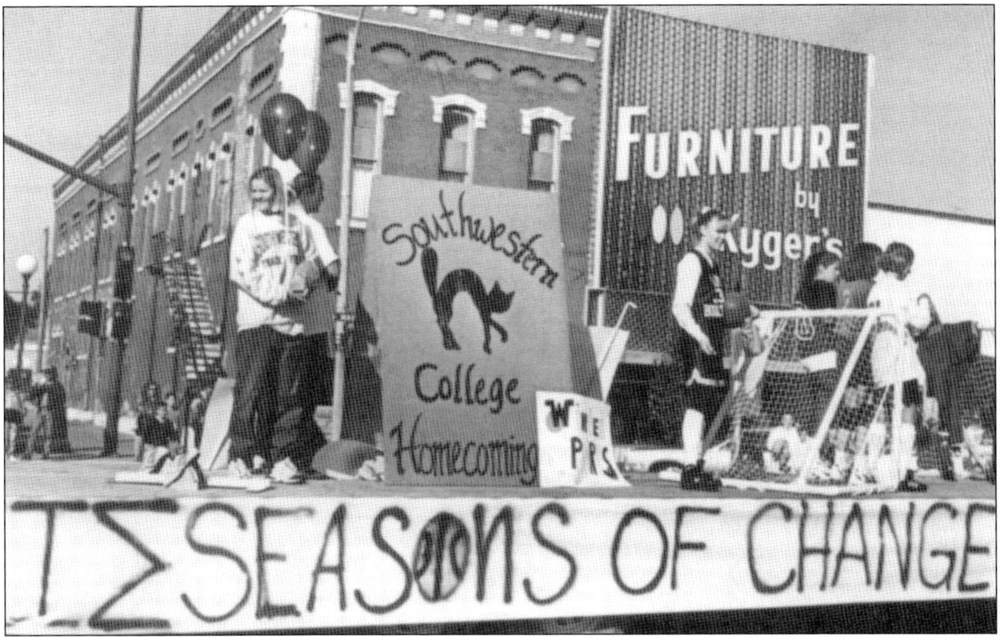

Southwestern students continue the tradition of designing, building, and riding on a float for the homecoming parade, which travels down Main Street. The first "Home-coming Day" dates to November 11, 1923, when various houses on College Hill were decorated for the occasion and vied for a chance to win a $15 prize for the best house, given by the Rooters Club. The theme for this 1998 float was "Seasons of Change."

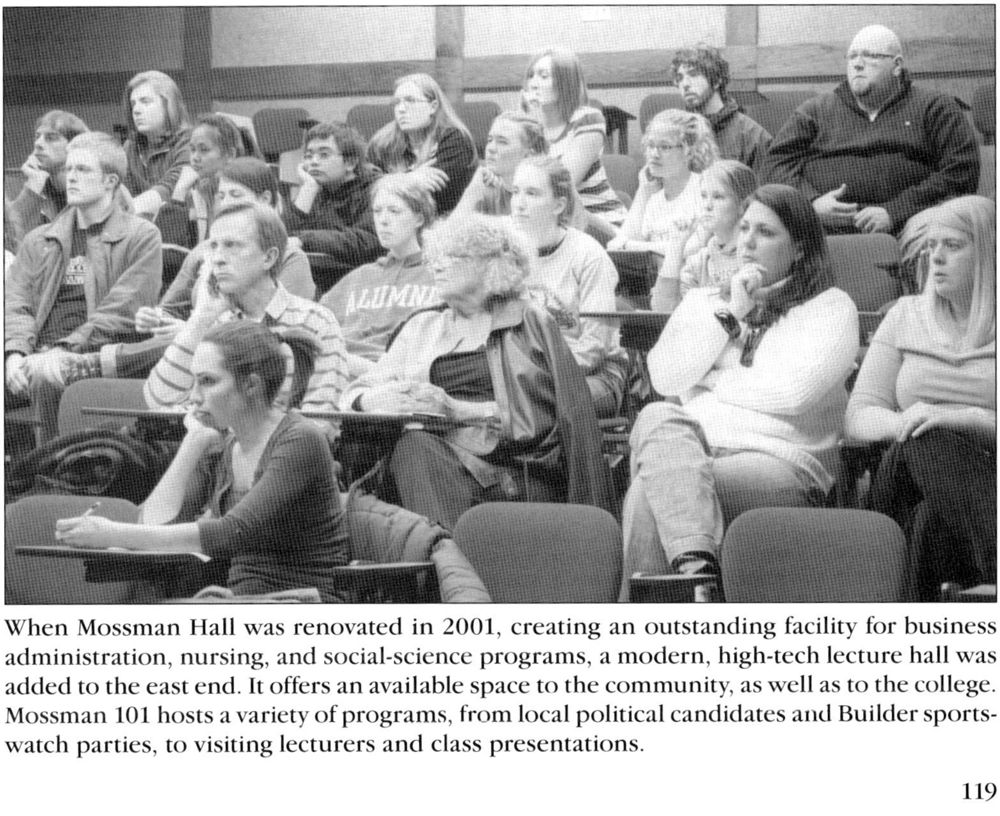

When Mossman Hall was renovated in 2001, creating an outstanding facility for business administration, nursing, and social-science programs, a modern, high-tech lecture hall was added to the east end. It offers an available space to the community, as well as to the college. Mossman 101 hosts a variety of programs, from local political candidates and Builder sports-watch parties, to visiting lecturers and class presentations.

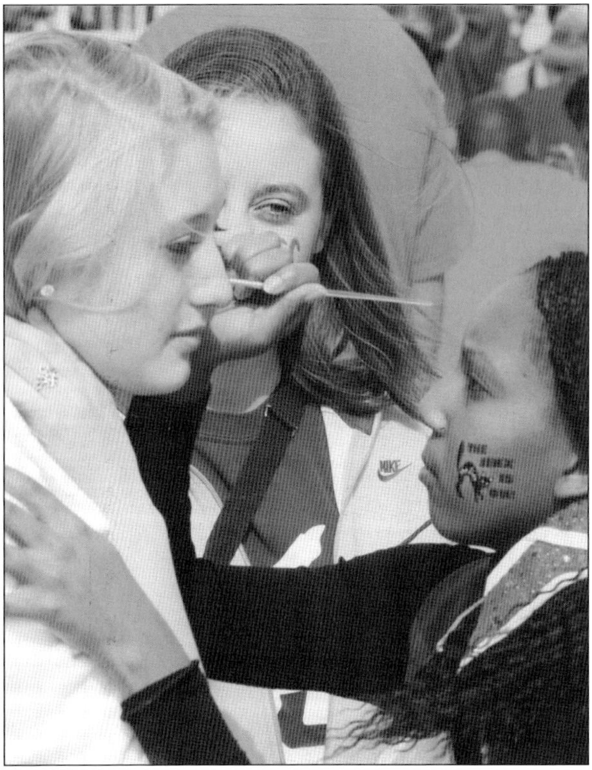

Maurica Cliett, nursing sophomore, paints the face of Kaci Hutchinson, biology freshman, as part of the tailgate festivities during family weekend on October 22, 2013. The cheerleaders painted fans' faces before the Builders played the University of Saint Mary. (Photograph by Richard Gould.)

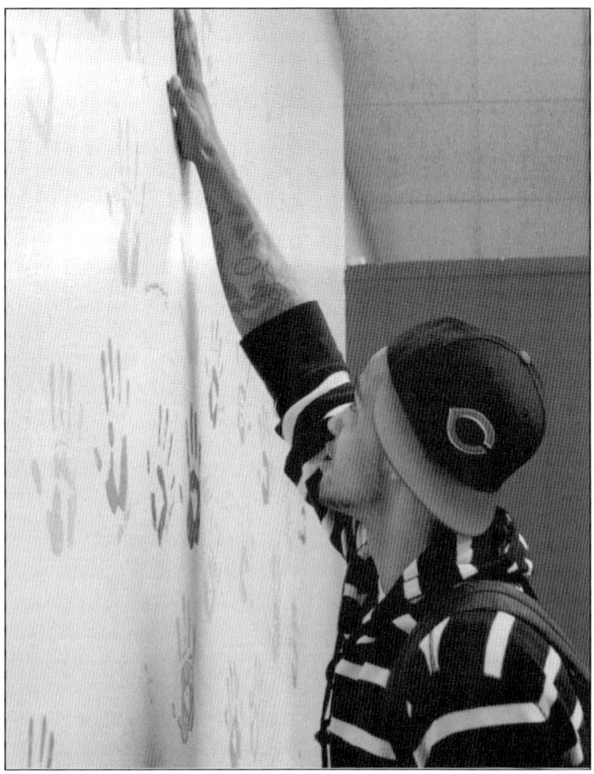

Chris Nelson, business management senior, puts his handprint on the "Unity Through Diversity" wall in the Campus Life office in 2012. This was the second year Student Foundation, or StuFu, gave students the opportunity to put their handprints on the wall to show unity. (Photograph by Clinton Dick.)

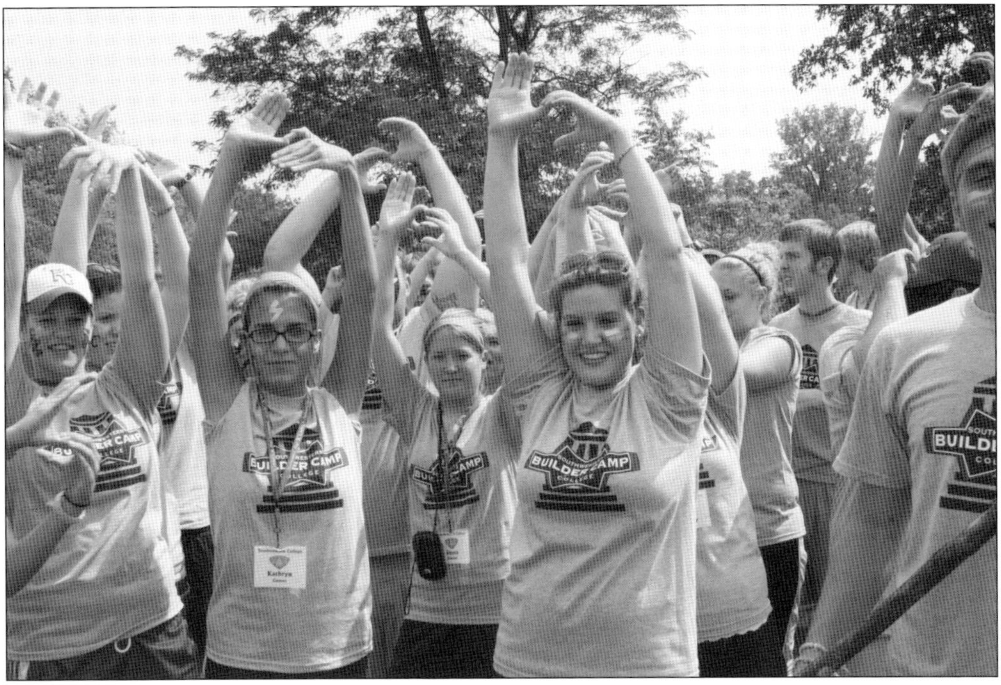

A new tradition for freshmen orientation began in fall 2006 with the start of Builder Camp, a three-day adventure for incoming freshmen. Sponsored by Student Life, Builder Camp highlights include a welcome by the president, a highly competitive tug-of-war, skits, workshops, team-building exercises, a 9 Lives improv performance, tetherball, volleyball, ultimate Frisbee, a zip line, laser tag, and lake activities. The camp leaves students exhausted before classes even begin.

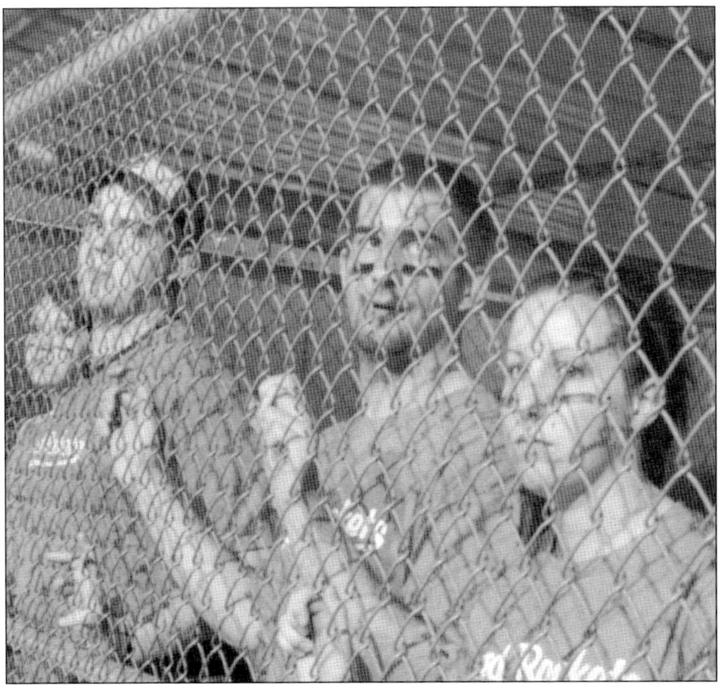

Fans at a recent Lady Builder softball game cheer on the team at the fence of the impressive Winfield facility, the Broadway Sports Complex. The first season of Southwestern College softball was spring 2004, when the Builders finished in second place at the KCAC conference tournament.

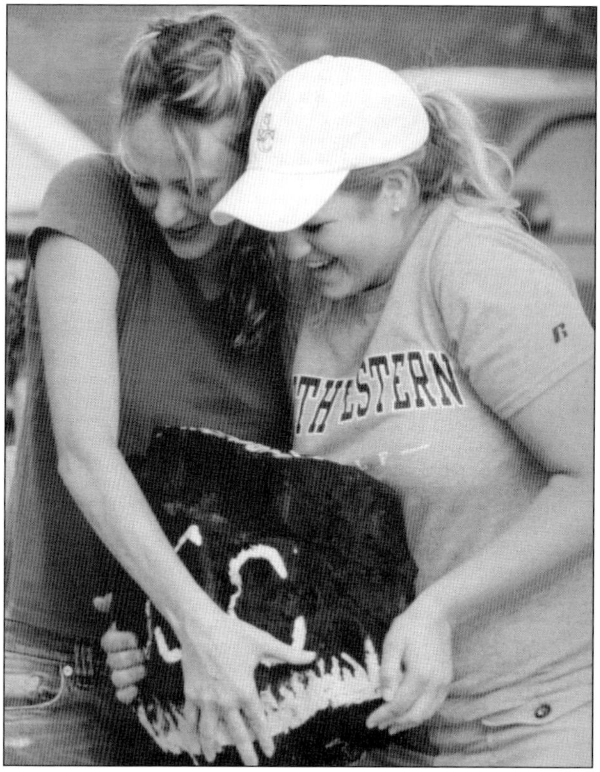

Amy Kellner (left) and Kaydee Johnson represent the 2009 women's golf team as they carry their rock to be placed on the mound. The Mound was transformed in October 2006, with a new retaining wall, alumni tributes in brick, and an adjoining plaza, making the area ideal for outdoor programs, such as the Order of the Mound and chapel. (Photograph by Diane Dixon.)

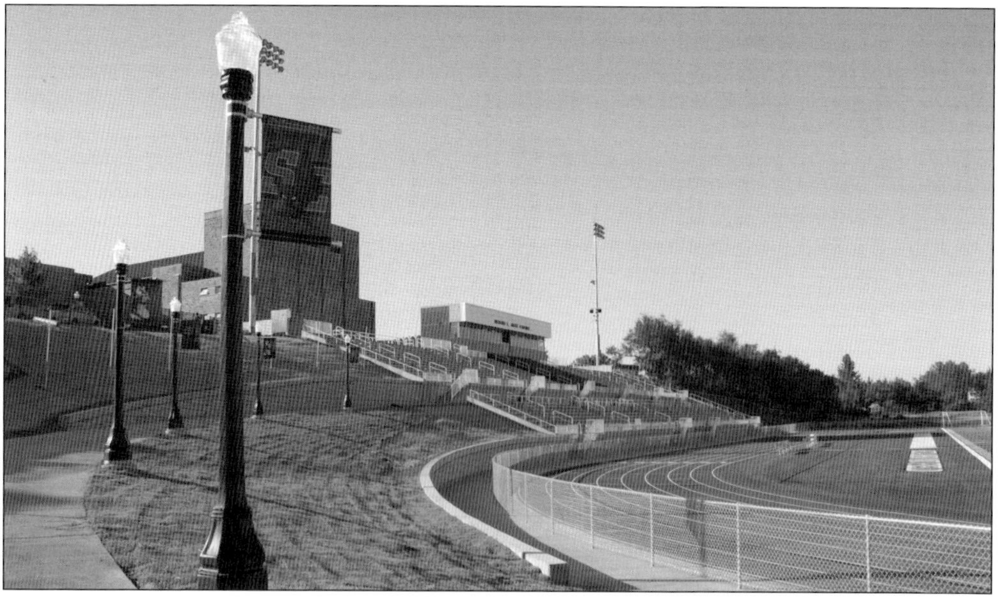

Builder sports enthusiasts were thrilled when the Richard L. Jantz Stadium was renovated, along with the new track, in 2004. It was named after SC's legendary track and cross-country coach, Jim Helmer (class of 1971), who was inducted into the NAIA Cross-Country Hall of Fame in 2001. In 2008–2009, both the men's and women's teams took first place in the KCAC championships, marking the 30th consecutive championships under Helmer. Few programs in America can match this success.

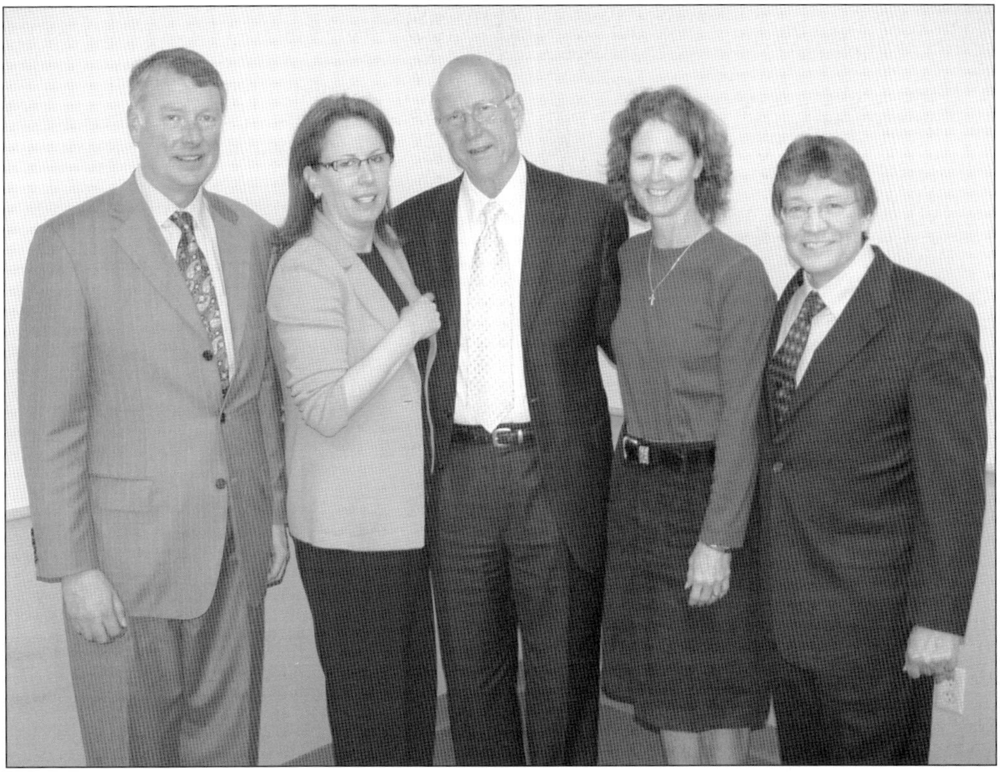

Kansas senator Pat Roberts (center) joins Jill and Tom Docking (left) and Bill and Judy Docking (right) after a recent Docking Lecture at Southwestern College. The Docking Lectures on Leadership and Public Affairs are underwritten by the Dockings and Union State Bank. The Docking family has played a prominent role in public service in Kansas for over half a century.

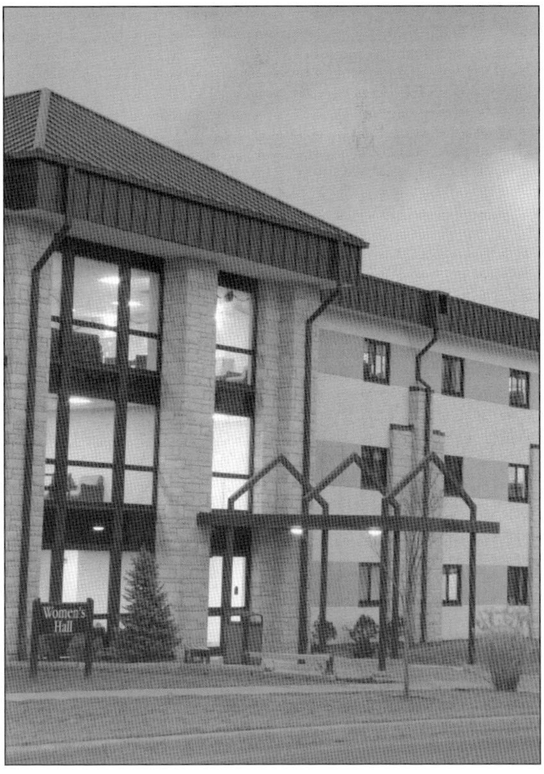

At the corner of Soward and Warren Streets sits beautiful Cole Hall, named after Ward M. Cole (class of 1930), a generous Wellington physician and active trustee from 1954 to 2000. Ward and his wife, Ruby, started a series of endowed scholarships and provided major funding for the 1998 elevator in the Christy Administration Building. In 2001, he was presented an honorary doctorate of medical science.

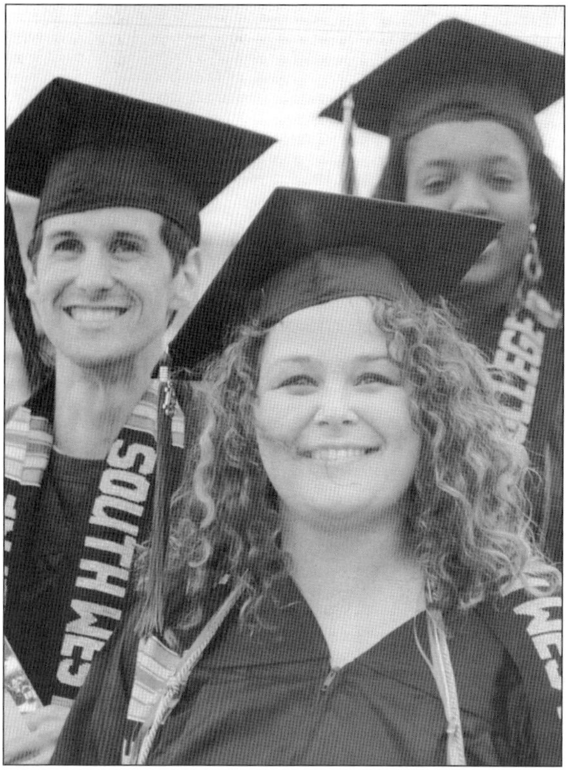

Shown here are, from left to right, Derreck Carter-House, biology senior; Danielle Morford, marine biology senior; and Mariam Mamah, biology senior. The students locate their families before the 2013 graduation ceremonies. Carter-House was one of two seniors who took home the prestigious Professor Fran Jabara Leadership Award, annually decided upon by faculty. (Photograph by Jonathan Woon.)

Southwestern faculty dressed in their academic regalia line the top steps of the 77 as they file into a recent honors convocation, held the afternoon before graduation. The recipients of the most-coveted honor of Masterbuilder are traditionally named during this special ceremony. The Masterbuilder distinction is given to six graduating seniors who best typify the Builder spirit. The faculty and student body select the recipients.

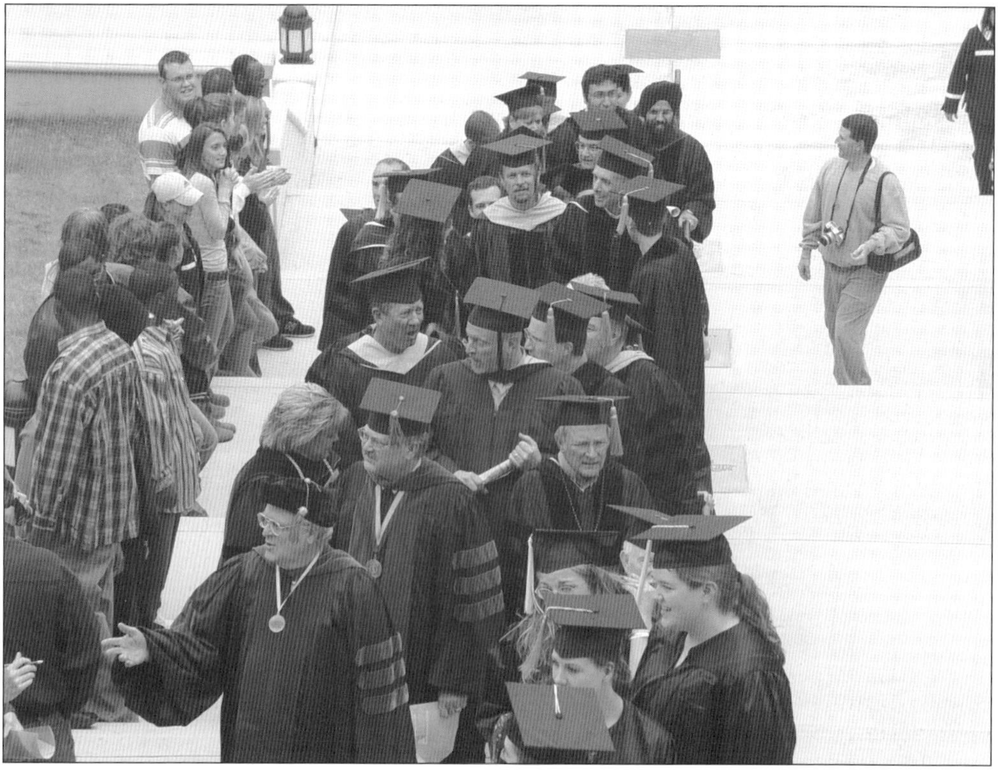

Band and orchestra students take a break from playing during the 2010 graduation ceremonies. The musicians performed far above the reserved seats because graduation was conducted inside Stewart Field House due to inclement weather. (Photograph by Hannah Podschun.)

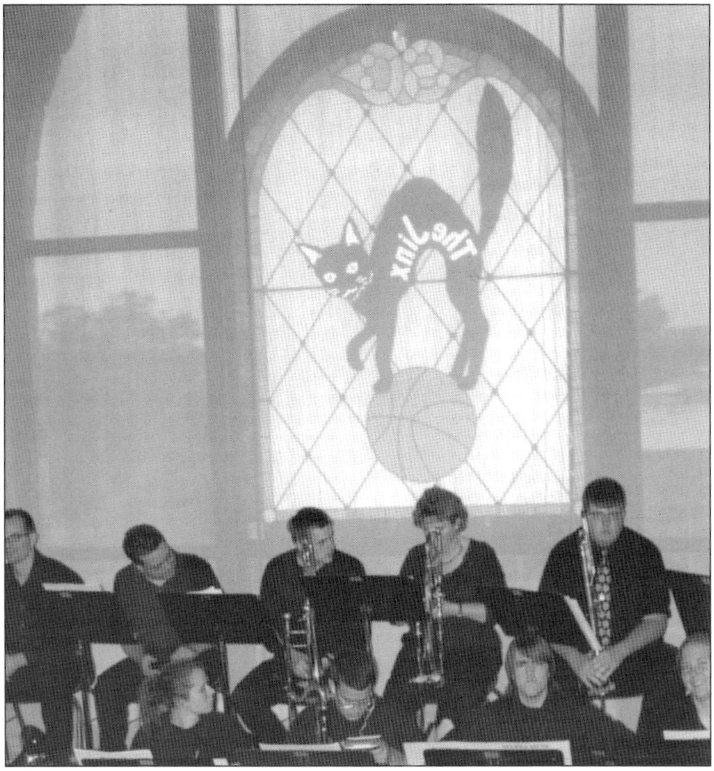

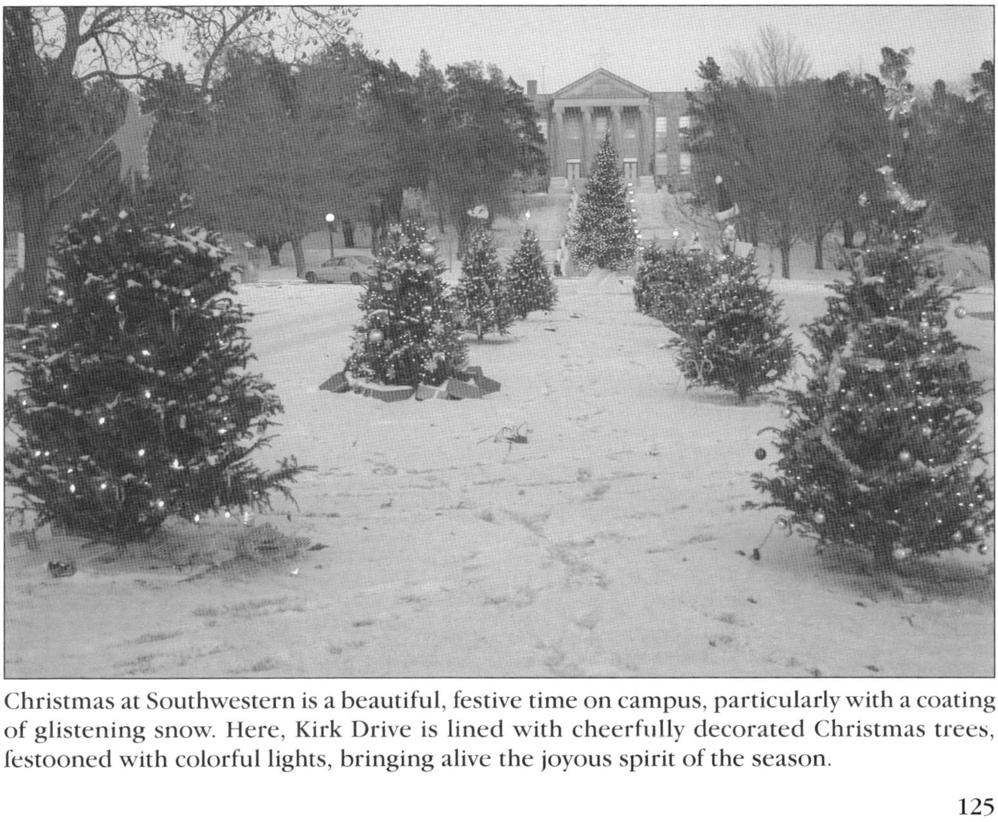

Christmas at Southwestern is a beautiful, festive time on campus, particularly with a coating of glistening snow. Here, Kirk Drive is lined with cheerfully decorated Christmas trees, festooned with colorful lights, bringing alive the joyous spirit of the season.

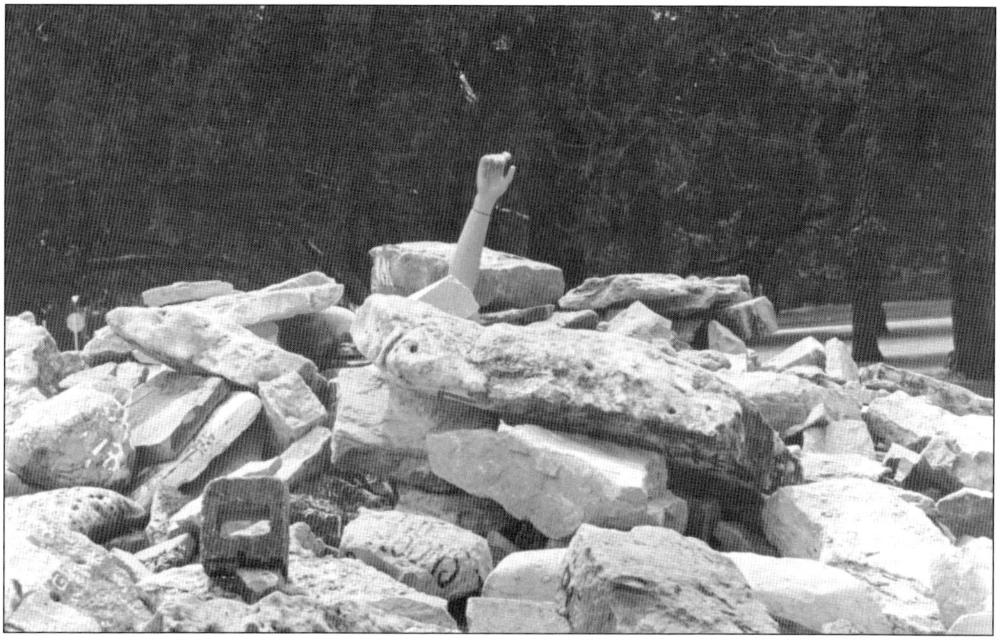

As published in the *Moundbuilder* in 2010, "We leave our family, our friends and the place we used to call home to move to a campus smaller than some high schools. We embark on a journey of change, inching closer to the real world with every moment that passes. People we meet become like family. Places we have never been become places we never want to leave. The best experiences of our lives become treasured memories that we never want to forget. We share four years of eating in the cafeteria together, working on class projects, pulling all-nighters and partying on the weekends. It's not until we graduate that we realize that our time as a Builder is only just beginning. Our lives are under construction."

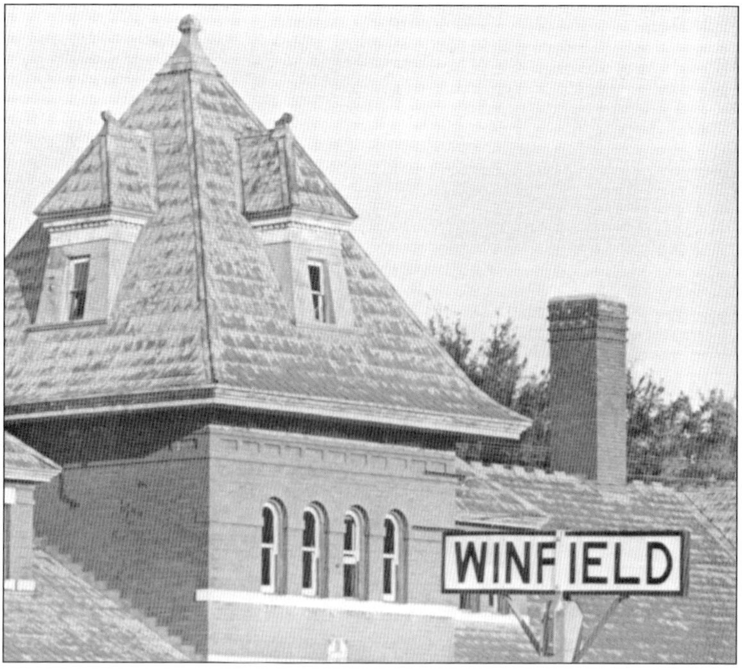

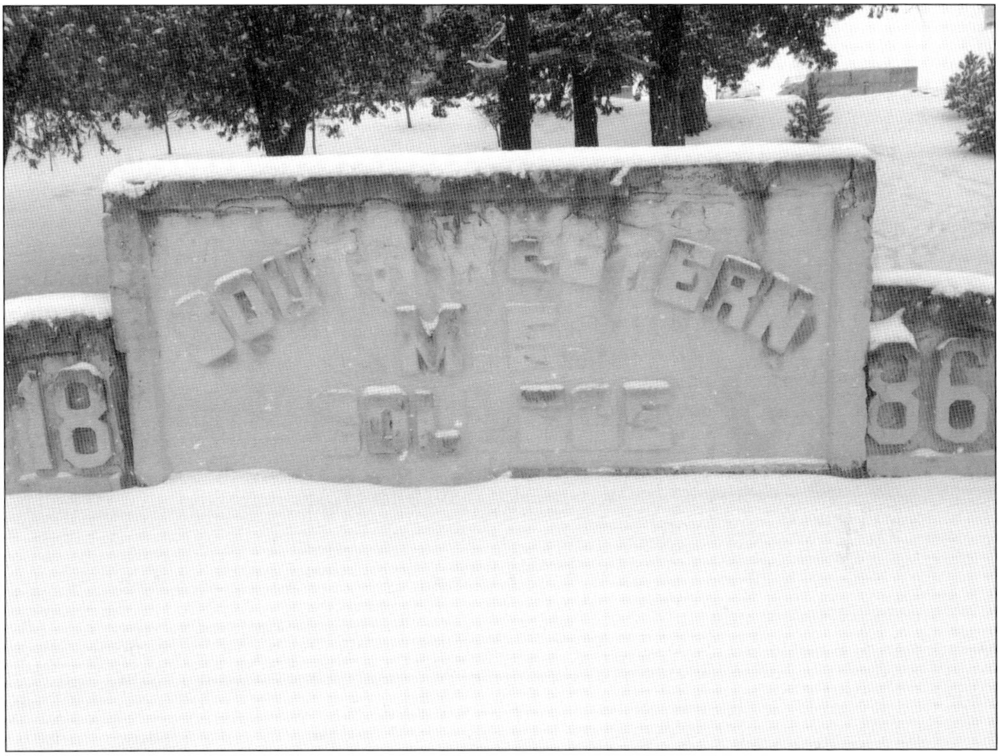

"Southwestern College consists of all who come into and go forth from her halls, who are touched by her influences, and who carry on her spirit. Wherever you go, Southwestern College goes with you, wherever you are at work, there Southwestern is at work," so said Pres. C. Orville Strohl.

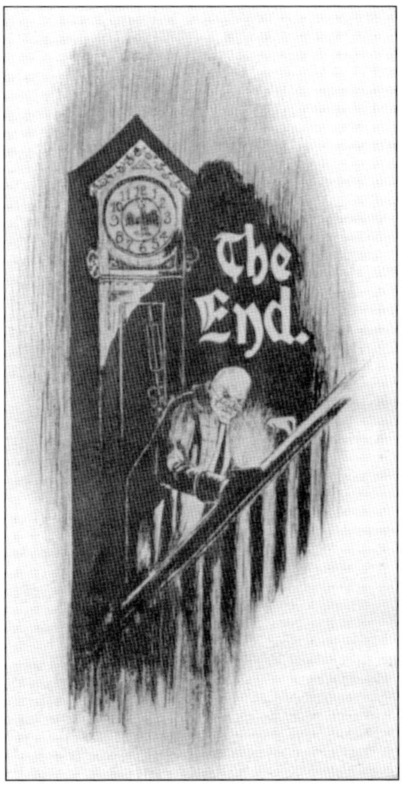